The Logic and Limits of Political Reform in China

JOSEPH FEWSMITH

Boston University

CAMBRIDGE
UNIVERSITY PRESS

CAMBRIDGE UNIVERSITY PRESS
Cambridge, New York, Melbourne, Madrid, Cape Town,
Singapore, São Paulo, Delhi, Mexico City

Cambridge University Press
32 Avenue of the Americas, New York, NY 10013-2473, USA

www.cambridge.org
Information on this title: www.cambridge.org/9781107612549

First published 2013

Printed in the United States of America

A catalog record for this publication is available from the British Library.

Library of Congress Cataloging in Publication Data

Fewsmith, Joseph, 1949–
The logic and limits of political reform in China / Joseph Fewsmith.
    p. cm.
Includes bibliographical references and index.
ISBN 978-1-107-03142-5 (hardback) – ISBN 978-1-107-61254-9 (paperback)
1. Political participation – China.   2. China – Politics and government.
3. Local government – China.   4. Democratization – China.   I. Title.
JQ1516.F49   2013
320.951–dc23   2012023175

ISBN 978-1-107-03142-5 Hardback
ISBN 978-1-107-61254-9 Paperback

The Logic and Limits of Political Reform in China

In the 1990s China embarked on a series of political reforms intended to increase, however modestly, political participation to reduce the abuse of power by local officials. Although there was initial progress, these reforms have largely stalled and, in many cases, gone backward. If there were sufficient incentives to inaugurate reform, why wasn't there enough momentum to continue and deepen them? This book approaches this question by looking at a number of promising reforms and understanding the incentives of officials at different levels and the way the Chinese Communist Party operates at the local level. The short answer is that the sort of reforms necessary to make local officials more responsible to the citizens they govern cut too deeply into the organizational structure of the party.

Joseph Fewsmith is Professor of International Relations and Political Science at Boston University. He is the author of *China Since Tiananmen: From Deng Xiaoping to Hu Jintao* (2008), which is the second edition of *China Since Tiananmen: The Politics of Transition* (2001); *Elite Politics in Contemporary China* (2001); *The Dilemmas of Reform in China: Political Conflict and Economic Debate* (1994); and *Party, State, and Local Elites in Republican China: Merchant Organizations and Politics in Shanghai, 1980–1930* (1985). He is the editor of *China Today, China Tomorrow* (2010) and co-editor, with Zheng Yongnian, of *China's Opening Society* (2008). He is very active in the China field, traveling to China frequently and presenting papers at professional conferences such as the Association for Asian Studies and the American Political Science Association. His articles have appeared in such journals as *The China Quarterly*, *Asian Survey*, *The Journal of Contemporary China*, *Modern China*, and *Comparative Studies in Society and History*. He is one of seven regular contributors to *China Leadership Monitor*, a quarterly Web publication analyzing current developments in China. He is also an associate of the John King Fairbank Center for East Asian Studies at Harvard University and of the Pardee Center for the Study of the Longer Range Future at Boston University.

Contents

Figures and Maps

Figures

Maps

Abbreviations

CCP	Chinese Communist Party
CDIC	Central Discipline Inspection Commission
CPPCC	Chinese People's Political Consultative Conference
CPSU	Communist Party of the Soviet Union
FIC	Federation of Industry and Commerce
HRS	Household Responsibility System
MCA	Ministry of Civil Affairs
MOFTEC	Ministry of Foreign Trade and Economic Cooperation
NGO	nongovernment organization
NPC	National People's Congress
PRC	People's Republic of China

Acknowledgments

This project started six years ago when I was a scholar at the Woodrow Wilson Center for International Studies in Washington, D.C., where I enjoyed the hospitality of Lee Hamilton and Robert Hathaway and learned from my colleagues. At the time, I thought it probable that political reform in China would follow, albeit with a lag, the course of economic reform – gradual moves that would, over time, increase political participation and create institutions that would constrain the behavior of local officials. Greater liberalization of the system seemed a real possibility, and the various experiments unfolding in political reform suggested that the central government supported such reforms and that there were real interests at the local level for doing so. So I began to search out examples of what appeared to be the most promising examples of reform. The *China Leadership Monitor*, an online journal that I have been fortunate enough to be involved with since its inception, provided a terrific platform for trying out my ideas. The Smith Richardson Foundation has generously supported the *China Leadership Monitor* over the years, and I am happy to acknowledge their support.

Procrastination is rarely seen as a virtue, but, in the case of this project, watching the evolution of Chinese reform over the past six years has not only led me to a deeper appreciation of the dynamics of reform but also forced me to pay closer attention to the sustainability of reform efforts at the local level. That is to say, although the creation of new and effective institutions seemed possible when I started this project, time has suggested that reforms that seemed likely to lead to new institutions and more predictable government have withered as time has passed. Innovation is one thing; institutionalization another.

In trying to understand the dynamics of reform, why institutions are created, and how they are sustained, if they are, I have put myself in debt to many people, many of whom may have views different from those I have come to hold. In all cases, however, they have been generous in sharing their insights. So it is with great gratitude that I thank Cai Dingjian (whose passing in 2010 caused much sadness), Chen Sheng-yong, Chen Yimin, Gregory Chin, Clifford Edmunds, Fang Ning, Feng Yue, Bernie Frolic, Han Fuguo, Gao Xiang, Gao Xinjun, Guo Dan, Guo Xiaoming, He Junzhi, He Zengke, Hu Wei, Jia Xijin, Jiang Hua, Jiang Zhaohua, Jing Yuejin, Lai Hairong, Lang Youxing, Charlotte Lee, Cheng Li, Li Fan, Liu Yawei, Ma Jun, Alice L. Miller, Carl Minzner, Mo Yifei, Niu Meili, Jean Oi, Pan Wei, Elizabeth J. Perry, Qin Hui, Shi Weimin, Bernard Silberman, Tang Tsou, Wang Changjiang, Wang Guoqin, Wang Jian, Wang Jingyao, Wang Xiaodong, Wang Zhenyao, Robert P. Weller, Yang Fan, Yang Xuedong, Yu Jianrong, Yu Jianxing, Yu Keping, Yu Xunda, Xiang Jiquan, Xiao Gongqin, Xu Xianglin, Xu Yong, Zhang Xueming, Zhao Wenmian, Zheng Yongnian, Zhou Meiyan, Zhou Yi, and many others.

The ideas presented in this book were developed not only through observation, reading, and discussion but also by presenting my views at talks at Middlebury College, Benedictine College, Kings College, the China Law Center at Yale University, the Harvard Yenching Institute at Harvard University, the Fairbank Center at Harvard University, and Stanford University. I appreciate the opportunity to exchange ideas with those who attended and challenged me to think more deeply.

Finally, I want to thank Nancy Hearst of the H. C. Fung Library at Harvard University for her careful editing, making my prose smoother than it is naturally, cutting out redundancies and inconsistencies, and ensuring accuracy. Lewis Bateman, Mark Fox, Stephanie Sakson, and Shaun Vigil at Cambridge University Press have made the publication a smooth and enjoyable process. I am deeply grateful to all those who have helped me better understand the reform process in China and those who have made my presentation of my findings more understandable, but, alas, the errors that remain are my responsibility alone.

J. F.

Introduction

The story of China's rise over the last three decades is largely a political story, one that seemed highly unlikely when it started. A century of political decline, internecine conflict, and revolution hardly seemed like a propitious foundation for economic development. But the death of Mao Zedong in 1976 and the rise of Deng Xiaoping at the Third Plenary Session of the Eleventh Central Committee in 1978 gave the Chinese Communist Party (CCP) a new lease on life. Its leaders were well aware that its legitimacy was weak. People talked of the "three crises" – spiritual (*jingshen weiji*), belief (*xinyang weiji*), and culture (*wenhua weiji*).[1] Not only was the charismatic leader dead, but the leader who tried to routinize charisma, Hua Guofeng, was repudiated by the Dengist coalition.[2] Raising the banner of "practice," Deng Xiaoping turned to performance legitimacy to restore the CCP's reputation.

In 1978, promises of economic development were difficult to believe. Per capita urban income was 316 yuan, and in the rural areas one-quarter of the population lived on incomes of less than

---

[1] The best depiction of the atmosphere in the early 1980s remains Chen Fong-jing and Jin Guantao, *From Youthful Manuscripts to River Elegy*, pp. 13–88.

[2] I have pursued this thought in Fewsmith, "Political Creativity and Political Reform in China?" pp. 227–246. See also Tang Tsou, "Reflections on the Formation and Foundations of the Communist Party-State in China," p. 295.

50 yuan per year.[3] The situation was so bad that the party's senior economic specialist, Chen Yun, warned that if something were not done, peasants in the countryside would flock into the cities to demand food. Desperation and weak legitimacy led the CCP to embark on a course of economic reform, starting with the household responsibility system (HRS) in the countryside.[4]

The key to economic development was political stability, and the key to political stability was strong and stable relations at the top of the system and regularization of the party system below. Senior political leaders, such as Deng Xiaoping and Chen Yun, strongly believed that radical activists needed to be weeded out, inner-party norms restored, and discipline imposed. In 1978, about half of the 35 million members of the CCP had been admitted during the Cultural Revolution.[5] Many of them had advanced their careers through "beating, smashing, and looting," or otherwise supporting the violence of the Cultural Revolution, and they saw the abandonment of radical Maoism as a threat to their careers. However, the revolutionary veterans who returned to power following the death of Mao Zedong saw the reassertion of party norms – understandings of "normal" inner-party life that had been asserted in the past but frequently overridden by an imperious Mao and then rejected altogether during the Cultural Revolution – as essential, both for legitimizing their return to power and for creating the conditions for economic reform.

Reestablishing inner-party norms and implementing Dengist visions of economic reform were not easy tasks for a deeply factionalized CCP. At the Third Plenary Session of the Eleventh Central Committee in December 1978 the party restored the Central Discipline Inspection Commission (CDIC), which was headed by senior Politburo member Chen Yun.[6] Reasserting party norms

---

3 Wu Xiang, "Yangguan dao yu dumu qiao."
4 Chen Yun, "Jianchi an bili yuanze tiaozheng guomin jingji," pp. 226–231.
5 Bruce Dickson, "Conflict and Non-compliance in Chinese Politics," pp. 172–173.
6 Graham Young, "Control and Style," pp. 24–52; and Lawrence R. Sullivan, "The Role of the Control Organs in the Chinese Communist Party, 1977–83," pp. 597–617.

and discipline was a difficult and often thankless task, but the CDIC produced the "Several Principles on Political Life in the Party" (*Guanyu dangnei zhengzhi shenghuo de ruogan zhunze*), which were adopted by the party in 1980. Party members were urged to struggle against the factionalism and anarchism promoted by followers of Lin Biao and the Gang of Four and to promote tolerance within the party, objectives not easily reconciled. Individual party members were allowed to retain their own views and to express those views within the party, as long as they carried out decisions of the party. Different viewpoints should be expressed within the party and decision making should be collective. But discipline must be maintained, and leading cadres should not be afraid of criticizing views that contravened the party's general line or individuals who engaged in factional behavior.[7]

An important part of the rationalization of inner-party life was the institution of a retirement system. The revolutionary veterans who returned to power with the Dengist coalition following Mao's death had neither the physical vigor nor the intellectual background to carry out economic reform. Chen Yun began pushing the issue of retirement in 1981, and in 1982 the Central Committee issued regulations specifying age-based retirement.[8] Veteran cadres were gradually retired in favor of "more revolutionary, younger, better educated, and more professionally competent" leaders.[9]

In seeking such leaders, the party turned naturally to engineers. Engineers tended to be less ideological and thus to have engaged in fewer political struggles during the Cultural Revolution. They were well educated and had a desire to get things done. Many of the best had been educated at Tsinghua University, where President Jiang Nanxiang had stressed that students should be "both red and expert" (*you zhuan you hong*). Not having the extensive networks or revolutionary experiences of

---

[7] "Guanyu dangnei zhengzhi shenghuo de ruogan zhunze."

[8] Chen Yun, "Tiba peiyang zhongqingnian ganbu shi dangwu zhi ji," pp. 262–266; and Melanie Manion, *Retirement of Revolutionaries in China*, p. 65.

[9] Hong Yung Lee, *From Revolutionary Cadres to Party Technocrats in Socialist China*.

their forebears, such technocrats were more content with steady promotions through bureaucratic careers. Membership on the Central Committee gradually came to reflect political positions attained through step-by-step rise rather than ideological views or simply personal networks with top leaders (though such ties remain important).[10]

Part of normalizing party life was to hold party congresses, those gatherings of party delegates to select, or at least ratify, the selection of a new Central Committee, at regular intervals, as called for by the party charter. Historically, the party had not done a good job of carrying out this provision of its rules. For instance, the Seventh Party Congress was held in 1945, the Eighth in 1956, the Ninth in 1969, the Tenth in 1973, and the Eleventh in 1977. The dates of these congresses marked important turning points in the party's political evolution rather than regularly scheduled events. The Twelfth Party Congress, however, was held on schedule in 1982, and the CCP has maintained this quinquennial schedule ever since, despite periods of tension within the party including the events surrounding the Tiananmen crackdown and the ouster of then-party general secretary Zhao Ziyang.

These and other measures mark real steps toward the routinization of political life and are particularly noteworthy for coming so soon after the enormous upheavals engineered by Mao. If the normalization of party procedures that occurred after Mao's death is impressive, it is also true that the relative stability that appeared on the surface rested on an informal but important balance of power among the top political leaders. In general, Deng Xiaoping did draw on people from across the political spectrum, avoiding the appearance of factionalism, except when it came to control of the military, which he kept firmly in the hands of his colleagues from the Second Field Army.[11] Nevertheless, tensions arose as leaders disagreed

---

[10] Cheng Li, *China's Leaders*.
[11] Alice L. Miller, "Institutionalization and Changing Dynamics of Chinese Leadership Politics," pp. 61–79.

over cultural, ideological, economic, and political issues. The new institutional arrangements were not strong enough to contain the political pressures, which were pushed over the edge in 1989 by issues of corruption, inflation, succession, ideology, and popular protest.

Perhaps unexpectedly, the political meltdown that resulted in the crushing of popular protest, the ouster of Zhao Ziyang, the promotion of Jiang Zemin, and – more than two years later – Deng's famous "Southern Journey" that reinvigorated reform brought about a new informal balance of power, confirmed at the Fourteenth Party Congress in September 1992, that seemed to reinforce ongoing processes of institutionalization. The new, post-Tiananmen equilibrium was stabilized by the fortuitous order in which senior leaders passed from the scene – the leftist leader and former president Li Xiannian dying in 1992, Chen Yun in 1995, and Deng Xiaoping in 1997.[12] Although the leadership since then has not been entirely bound by institutional arrangements, understandings of the "rules of the game" have constrained competition among the political elite and raised the costs of violating the unwritten rules, as Bo Xilai, Chongqing party secretary, discovered in 2012. China has thus enjoyed two decades of "normal," or mostly normal, politics at the top.[13]

Relative stability at the top of the system seemed to provide conditions for the normalization of relations between the CCP and society, tensions that, ironically, had been exacerbated, or at least reshaped, by the breakup of the communes and the relative depoliticization of everyday life as the party had pulled back, creating a "zone of indifference" between itself and the private realm.[14] Indeed, in the wake of Tiananmen, when political reform was no longer possible at the elite level, reformers increasingly focused their attention to the local levels where there were

---

[12] On Li Xiannian's political attitudes, see Zhao Ziyang, *Prisoner of the State*, p. 244.

[13] Joseph Fewsmith, *China since Tiananmen*. For interpretations of the fall of Bo, see Joseph Fewsmith, "Bo Xilai and Reform," and Alice Miller, "The Bo Xilai Affair in Central Leadership Politics."

[14] On the zone of indifference, see Tang Tsou, "Introduction," p. xxiv.

increasing problems but some political room to begin at least to address them.[15]

As new interests and groups emerged, they began to challenge the all-encompassing interests of the party. For those who study nongovernment organizations (NGOs),[16] the emergence of civil society,[17] and the impact of new technologies such as the Internet and social media,[18] the filling of this space between the party-state and the private realm with new groups suggests a turn toward democracy, sooner or later. There is no question that NGOs and other interests are crowding into this space in a way that is unprecedented in post-1949 China,[19] but the key question is whether these new societal interests can translate their energies into meaningful political reform. To do so means changing the rules of the game – that is, the rules by which political actors are chosen and the behaviors in which they can engage – and there is very little evidence to date that this is the case. Indeed, one of the main points that emerges from the research undertaken for this book is that there has been little change in the way in which local cadres are selected and promoted or in the development of institutions that might meaningfully constrain their behavior.

Chinese society is contentious and growing more so all the time. In 1993, there were some 8,700 "mass incidents," and

---

[15] Of course, there were those who had been thinking about local reform before Tiananmen; after all, the Organic Law of Village Committees was first enacted, on a trial basis, in 1988. However, one impact of Tiananmen was to force reform-minded intellectuals to increasingly focus their attention on local levels.

[16] Yili Lu, *Non-Governmental Organizations in China*; Jonathan Schwartz and Shawn Shieh (Eds.), *State and Society Responses to Social Welfare Needs in China*; and Robert Weller (Ed.), *Civil Life, Globalization, and Political Change in Asia*.

[17] Timothy Brook and B. Michael Frolic (Eds.), *Civil Society in China*.

[18] Guobin Yang, *The Power of the Internet in China*; Susan Shirk (Ed.), *Changing Media, Changing China*; and Yongnian Zheng, *Technological Empowerment*.

[19] The understanding of social organization in China is contested. See William T. Rowe, *Commerce and Society in a Chinese City*, and Frederic Wakeman, Jr., "The Civil Society and Public Sphere Debate."

by 2010 this number had increased to some 180,000 – roughly 500 incidents every day.[20] In most instances, according to party sources, these incidents are caused by the abuse of power.[21]

The development of conflicts between local cadres and local people is very much a principal–agent problem. Cadres in China exist within a five-tier system, extending from the central government through the provincial, municipal (or prefectural), county, and township levels. Villages, which are below townships, are not formally a part of the state administrative system, but the party extends its control through party branches to this most basic level. By invoking party discipline and setting out clear criteria, the central government can exert control over issues that it cares about, from birth control to severe acute respiratory syndrome (SARS) prevention. However, the five-tier system also allows much room for slippage. As discussed in Chapter 1, local cadres are evaluated primarily on their ability to develop the economy, with little attention paid to the means; abuse of power and social conflict are frequent consequences.

It is not in the interest of the central authorities (the principal) to have local agents abuse their power; the problem is how to monitor the behavior of its agents. This is difficult to do within the context of an authoritarian regime. Basically, the central government can adopt top-down measures, such as changing the incentives facing local cadres or better monitoring of their behavior, or it can adopt bottom-up measures, such as giving the media greater room to report misbehavior or increasing political participation in an effort to make illicit behavior, such as bribery, more difficult and, perhaps, to make cadres more responsive to their constituencies. In practice, the state tries to do both. Top-down measures are frequently ineffective, forcing the state to explore political reform, which, so far, has taken place largely under the rubric "inner-party democracy" (*dangnei minzhu*).

---

[20] The 180,000 figure comes from Sun Liping, "Shehui zhixu shi dangxia de yanjun tiaozhan."

[21] Zhonggong zhongyang zuzhibu ketizu (Ed.), *Zhongguo diaocha baogao 2000–2001*, p. 84.

This book focuses on these experiments with political reform and increasing political participation – a goal that the CCP has repeatedly endorsed – because such efforts raise the question of institution building, and only new institutions can potentially constrain the behavior of local cadres in a meaningful way.

This focus on institutions not only tells us much about what is and what is not changing in China, but also raises important theoretical issues. There is a vast literature on institutions, but relatively little on how institutions are created.[22] This is a critical question. Whether one is thinking in terms of long-term economic development or political change, institutions are central, especially when one is looking at a relatively uninstitutionalized environment, such as China. Perhaps an examination of China can tell us something about the forces that generate or inhibit institutions in general.

Douglass North defines institutions as the "rules of the game in society" or, in more academic terms, the "humanely devised constraints that shape human interaction." In thinking about constraints, North refers to incentive structures that reward certain behaviors and sanction other behaviors over time. Institutions can develop along different paths, some generating long-term economic growth and others not. Because of accumulated costs (path dependence), it is not easy to switch from one institutional arrangement to another.[23]

Most authors, however, use the term "institution" to mean something more concrete. Whereas North sees parliaments, political parties, and courts as organizations operating within an institutional setting (and affecting the course of development of that institutional framework over time), other authors use the term "institution" to mean what North calls "organizations." Because the focus of this book is considerably narrower than North's interest in the *longue durée*, it will follow the more popular usage.

---

[22] David Kreps, *A Course in Microeconomic Theory*, p. 530, cited in Paul Pierson, *Politics in Time*, p. 103.

[23] Douglass C. North, *Institutions, Institutional Change and Economic Performance*, p. 3.

The problem of institutional creation is often glossed over, assuming institutions arise either because they are needed or because exchange and cooperation bring them into being. However, functionalist explanations can hardly account for the failure of economically rational institutions to appear in many parts of the world or for the creation of bureaucracies in top-down fashion in order, in part, to drive economic development. Similarly, the assumption that institutions arise cooperatively as means of reducing transaction costs and uncertainty underestimates the degree to which institutions represent power arrangements as well as the ways in which power can prevent their emergence.[24]

Some authors have taken a historical approach, arguing that institutions are created over long periods of time to meet evolving domestic political needs.[25] Charles Tilly sees international conflict as the most important factor in creating institutions, coining his famous summation, "States make war, and war makes states."[26]

Such explanations make sense in the European context, particularly when viewed over a long period of history, but they often do not explain institutionalization in other contexts or in shorter time frames. Bernard Silberman argues that bureaucratic professionalism in the nineteenth century was a product of the uncertainty and need for legitimacy surrounding new regimes following revolutionary moments. Which type of bureaucracy emerges depends on the degree of uncertainty accompanying the birth of the new regime.[27]

In recent years there has been a surge of interest in the creation and role of institutions in authoritarian regimes. Dan Slater, picking up on Tilly's suggestion that conflict forges state institutions,

---

[24] For a critique of funtionalist explanations, see Bernard S. Silberman, *Cages of Reason*, pp. 26–31; for a critique of cooperative explanations, see Terry M. Moe, "Power and Political Institutions."

[25] Thomas Ertman, *Birth of the Leviathan*.

[26] Douglass C. North, *Institutions, Institutional Change, and Economic Performance*; and Douglass C. North, "Institutions."

[27] Bernard S. Silberman, *Cages of Reason*.

looks at the role of domestic conflict in bringing about different forms of authoritarian states in Southeast Asia.[28]

Jennifer Gandhi is more interested in how institutions are used by authoritarian regimes to enhance their legitimacy and extend their rule. Her argument assumes that all institutions, whether single parties, legislatures, or other means to channel opinions between state and society, represent "concessions" that society and potential opponents of the government extract from the state.[29] This observation certainly does not apply to pre-reform China, when the party and other institutions were used to impose radical societal change and to purge society of those deemed a threat to the new regime. However, it applies more readily – at least up to a point – to post-Mao China, when the party moved, in Kenneth Jowitt's terms, from an "exclusionary" orientation, in which the party tries to maintain its separation from society as it tries to impose its structure on the society it is remolding, to an "inclusionary" strategy, in which the party begins to co-opt elements of society. This inclusionary strategy recognizes, however implicitly, the legitimacy of society as separate from the state, thus raising the question of boundaries.[30]

One can think of boundaries between state and society as "hard" or "soft." Hard boundaries require the rule of law and an independent judiciary (for adjudicating boundary disputes, among other things). The existence of hard boundaries implies drawing a clear line between public and private. Where the line is drawn is hotly contested in all modern societies, but, as Judith Shklar points out, what is important "is not so much where the line is drawn, as that it be drawn."[31] Drawing a line between public and private is a matter of institutionalization, of creating boundaries between where the state stops and where society starts, and the rules by which relations between the two are governed.

---

[28] Dan Slater, *Ordering Power.*
[29] Jennifer Gandhi, *Political Institutions under Dictatorship.*
[30] Kenneth Jowitt, *New World Disorder*, pp. 88–120.
[31] Judith N. Shklar, "The Liberalism of Fear," p. 24.

It has often been noted that the distinction between public and private is less clear in Asia than it is in the West; citizens in Asia accept intrusions in their "private" lives that would not be tolerated in the West. As Benjamin Read has shown in his careful study of neighborhood organizations in Beijing and Taipei, most people accept a considerable overlapping of the public and private at the grassroots level. However, Read makes it very clear that there are major differences between the neighborhood associations in authoritarian Beijing and those in democratic Taipei. In Beijing, citizens may accept intrusions into their lives, but neighborhood associations are very much a part of the control system. In Taipei, there is also an acceptance of public and private being unusually close by Western standards, but local wardens (*lizhang*) are elected through increasingly competitive elections, and cooperation with local police is voluntary. Taipei's neighborhood associations are embedded in an effective legal framework; Beijing's are not.[32] So even in Taipei, where public and private seem to be conflated at the local level, the distinction between public and private in the political structure is real and important. The boundary between state and society is much harder in Taipei, whereas it is difficult to define such a boundary in Beijing. Institutionalization of societal interests remains extremely weak.

Authoritarian regimes by definition resist rule of law and an independent judiciary. However, one can imagine soft boundaries emerging in authoritarian systems as societal organizations emerge and as regimes give greater space to society.[33] Such soft boundaries may – or may not – indicate the possibility of democratic transition as societal organizations grow within the authoritarian system.[34] However, even the creation of soft boundaries

[32] Benjamin Read, *Roots of the State.*

[33] Edwin A. Winckler, "Institutionalization and Participation on Taiwan."

[34] The argument here is not that these organizations force regime transition; changes in regime type almost always come from divisions within the regime. See Guillermo O'Donnell and Philippe C. Schmitter, *Transitions from Authoritarian Rule,* esp. p. 19. But the development of societal organizations can raise questions among the elite about the tenability of strategies of repression, and such societal organizations appear vital to the emergence of civil society and

implies constraint of state action, a hardening of the line between state and society, and an increasing institutionalization of the relations between the two. Institutionalization of state–society relations, whether soft or hard, "brings society in" but also binds the party-state – and that has been staunchly resisted to date.

There are two main types of state–society friction that have developed in recent years. On the one hand, there are many areas of China where impoverished peasants have clashed with local cadres over taxes and land requisitions.[35] Such conflicts of interest seem to be the main source of the recent mass incidents. On the other hand, along the prosperous east coast a growing entrepreneurial class, particularly those who are party members, has increasingly argued that its views need to be taken into account. Taking entrepreneurial views into account does not necessarily mean the better provision of public goods – on the contrary, collusion between entrepreneurs and party officials can lead to the further distortion of public policy – but it can also lead to modestly more open governance. Progress in this regard is fragile and does not appear to be leading to democratization, but there is perhaps a greater degree of openness.

These two different types of conflict are exemplified by the two provinces examined most closely here. On the one hand, Sichuan province, in China's southwest, outside the capital of Chengdu, is generally poor and backward. It is has undertaken experiments in "inner-party democracy" since the early 1990s,

democratic consolidation following regime transition. See Robert P. Weller, *Alternative Civilities*, and Robert P. Weller (Ed.), *Civil Life, Globalization, and Political Change in Asia.*

[35] As the recent case of land seizures in Wukan village in Guangdong province illustrates, conflict over official rapaciousness is not limited to the poor hinterland; indeed, the rising price of land along the prosperous east coast has led to numerous conflicts. Such conflicts, however, have usually been dealt with through some combination of money (additional compensation) and coercion, rather than political reform. Interior provinces, lacking such resources, have responded either with coercion or, in some cases, limited political reform. On the conflict in Wukan village, see Sally Wang, "Tension after Village Leader Dies in Custody"; and Edward Wong and Michael Wines, "Provincial Officials Meet Leader of Protesters Who Took Over Chinese Village."

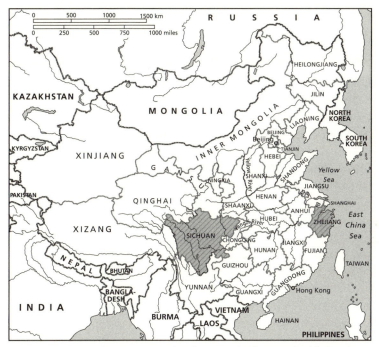

MAP 1. China, with provinces of Sichuan and Zhejiang highlighted

in part because the province suffered considerable societal tensions, but such conflicts were generally mild enough to be dealt with through modest reforms. Local authorities do not experiment with political reform in places where heightened tensions are such that the experiments might spin out of control. In Sichuan, as in almost everywhere in China, experiments with inner-party democracy have been guided by the Organization Department of the CCP at various levels, and it is apparent that the Central Organization Department in Beijing encouraged such efforts, at least into the first decade of the twenty-first century. To a certain extent, undertaking political reform appears to have been a Sichuan provincial strategy to distinguish the province in Beijing's eyes; because the province was too poor to impress central authorities through economic growth, political reform became an alternate strategy.

In contrast, Zhejiang, on China's east coast, is one of China's most prosperous areas and certainly its most entrepreneurial. Unlike Guangdong in the southeast, which pioneered the processing industry by depending on strong local government and foreign investment (mostly from Hong Kong) in its early years, Zhejiang developed a private economy, particularly along its poor southeast coast. This was home to the "Wenzhou model," which was based on the private economy. Wenzhou also pioneered the growth of trade associations and chambers of commerce – organizations suppressed by the socialist transformation in 1956 and not resuscitated until the 1980s.[36] The implications of these business associations for "civil society" are explored in Chapter 4. In addition, in Wenling, north of Wenzhou, there have been experiments in "participatory budgeting" and in expanding the role of the local people's congress. Thus, Zhejiang has become a laboratory for "deliberative democracy,"[37] or perhaps better termed "consultative authoritarianism." This experiment is analyzed in Chapter 5.

Both of these experiments – inner-party democracy and societal (or at least elite) demands for greater accountability – suggest a logic by which new, formal institutions might be created and by which the Chinese political system might gradually evolve into a more pluralistic, law-constrained, and democratic (at least in some sense of the word) society. It is an evolutionary course supported both by many intellectuals and at least parts of the Chinese government. Yu Keping, China's best-known advocate of this sort of gradual change in the political system, has long advocated "incremental democracy" (*zengliang minzhu*).[38] Yu's hope is to add increments of democracy to the Chinese system bit by bit, believing that, over time, this will change people's consciousness and ways of doing things. New, formal institutions will emerge gradually. The China Center for Government

---

[36] Han Fuguo, *Minying jingji zhidu bianqian de gongshanglian.*
[37] Ethan J. Lieb and Baogang He (Eds.), *The Search for Deliberative Democracy in China.*
[38] Yu Keping, *Zengliang minzhu yu shanzhi zhuanbian zhong de Zhongguo zhengzhi*; and Keping Yu, *Democracy Is a Good Thing.*

Innovations, which Yu started at Peking University in Beijing, and the China Center for Comparative Politics and Economics, which he started at the Central Compilation and Translation Bureau, have given biannual awards since 2000 to those local governments judged to have made the greatest innovations in local governance. These awards are highly valued, and the competitions have received hundreds of applications.

For any sort of incremental democracy or institutional innovation to occur, however, there must be people at the local level who are willing to take some risks. At first, this seems counterintuitive. China's party system is quite conservative; after all, those who do not make mistakes can expect long, if sometimes unexciting, careers, whereas those who make mistakes can incur high risks. Yet it is evident that there is a steady stream of officials willing to innovate.

This pattern of behavior suggests that there are incentives for such innovation, and if there are incentives to innovate, it suggests that innovation will both continue and deepen over time, if only because of path dependency and increasing returns from institutional innovation. In other words, the existence of incentives to innovate suggests that there is fertile ground for the development of formal institutions and that strategies for incremental democratization might indeed be successful. Unfortunately, this is not what we observe in reality. Though conditions might change in the future, the various innovations that we have seen so far have failed to lead to the sort of formal institutions that can be self-sustaining. Thus, if there are incentives for innovation, we have to ask why there are also limits to these innovations.

The search for limits leads one quickly back to the CCP itself. There are reasons – to be explored in the following pages – for the party, at both the highest and most local levels – to seek innovation; unfortunately, there are also reasons, mostly organizational, for the party to limit the scope of innovation. In the face of societal and political pressures to create formal institutions, the party has proven capable of resisting pressures to allow self-sustaining innovation. Whereas pressures for formal institutions work to define the lines between public and private, as Shklar suggests are needed, the party works to blur those lines.

This then is the story of the logic that drives the CCP to innovate, but also the story of the party's resistance to innovation. At the moment, it seems that those forces seeking to blur the lines and to prevent institutional checks on the party have emerged as the more powerful. This conclusion is the same as saying that the CCP recognizes clearly that its own structure is a source of many of the problems it faces – from corruption to the abuse of power, mass incidents, increasing public distrust, and so forth – but that it prefers to continue to blur the lines rather than to permit the emergence of formal institutions that will constrain party power. And this is the problem that the people of China now face.

This study is based on careful observation of important reform experiments undertaken since the late 1990s. Most of the cases discussed in the pages that follow received recognition by the China Center for Government Innovations and the China Center for Comparative Politics and Economics. In other words, these instances of reform have been recognized as among the most successful in China. The question, however, is not just one of innovation but rather one of institutionalization. Can these reforms that started as success stories be sustained? Can they be deepened over time? Can they fulfill their early promise as steps toward more accountable government? In order to answer such questions, this study exploits a wide range of written materials, numerous discussions with scholars and officials in China, and repeated visits to localities throughout China.

In the course of exploring these issues, this study has tried to understand why power is abused at the local level (Chapter 1), the impact of top-down versus bottom-up reforms (Chapter 2), the motivations for carrying out local reform, particularly inner-party democracy, as well as the limits of such reforms (Chapter 3), the prospect that economic reform will generate civil society (Chapter 4), and the degree to which some sort of "deliberative democracy" might affect governance (Chapter 5). In each instance, the focus is on the institutionalization of the reforms – can they be sustained over time, and will they mean-ingfully constrain the behavior of local officials?

Although China has tried and is continuing to experiment with many types of political innovation, so far the results have been disappointing. Given the increase in societal tensions over the past decade or more, the failure to implement reforms that have a meaningful impact on local governance comes with a huge cost in terms of public cynicism, the draining of government legitimacy, and greater social tensions. We explore these costs in the Conclusion.

I

The Problem of Governance in China

On June 22, 2008, a sixteen-year-old girl by the name of Li Shufen went out in the evening with three young men, all of whom were reportedly well-connected politically in Weng'an county of Guizhou province. Late that night, officials came to her house to tell her parents that their daughter had committed suicide. Li Shufen's father, doubting the officials' explanation, requested an autopsy. Soon there were rumors that the girl had been raped and murdered, so her family kept her corpse on ice, demanding an adequate explanation. Following a second autopsy on June 28, the local Public Security Bureau notified the family that "since the cause of death has been ascertained [i.e., drowning], the preservation of her body is no longer necessary" and it demanded that the body be interred that day or the police would handle the matter themselves.[1]

Rather than calm the situation, the notification angered residents, who continued to suspect foul play. There were many reasons why the people of Weng'an distrusted officials. Weng'an is a poor county in the poor province of Guizhou, not far from the prefectural city of Zunyi, where the Chinese Communist Party (CCP) had paused along the Long March in January 1935 to

[1] This account of the background to the Weng'an incident is drawn from Ding Buzhi, "Weng'an, 'bu an' de xiancheng," and Wang Weibo, "Fengbao yanzhong de Weng'an guanyuan." It largely follows my article, "An 'Anger-Venting' Mass Incident Catches the Attention of China's Leadership."

convene a meeting that would lead to Mao Zedong becoming preeminent leader. In 2008, Weng'an county was still overwhelmingly agricultural, with 90 percent of the population engaged in farming. There were, however, other resources in the area, including the potential for hydropower and the development of phosphorous and coal resources. When the Goupitan Hydropower Station was built in 2004, more than 4,000 peasants were relocated, but others refused to be moved, complaining bitterly about the low compensation that they were offered. When county party secretary Wang Qi went to Jiangjiehe village, where most of the peasants to be relocated lived, residents blocked the road and would not allow Wang and his entourage to leave unless they were offered higher compensation. Soon the police showed up and over thirty villagers were injured in the ensuing conflict. In 2007, after again demanding that all residents relocate, the government moved in with bulldozers and leveled houses and fruit trees. Fields were sprayed with herbicides to prevent the crops from ripening. Some 1,000 villagers were thus forcibly relocated to Seven-Star village in the country seat, where they continued to believe that their compensation was too low.[2]

Like many areas with mines, there was collusion between party officials and mine owners, as well as much criminal activity. Organized crime was apparently prevalent in Weng'an, with the Yushan (Jade Mountain) gang, formed in 1998, being the largest and most important. It was reported to have fifty big and small chieftains. According to *Southern Weekend*, gang members occupy the "top of the pyramid" in the mining sector. "Some mines could hardly proceed with their business operations if they don't accept the gang's terms," according to one local resident.[3] As reporting on the Weng'an incident revealed, much of the reason the Yushan gang could not be rooted out was because of its corrupt relations with the local police.[4]

---

[2] Ding Buzhi, "Weng'an, 'bu an' de xiancheng."

[3] Ibid.

[4] One of the factors that exacerbated the Weng'an incident was that the victim's uncle had quarreled with a public security official, who subsequently ordered Yushan gang members to harshly beat the uncle. See Lin Weiping, "Shehui xiefen shijian de jili yu gong'an zhifa weidu," p. 20.

As this description suggests, social tensions had built up in Weng'an over a number of years. Residents did not believe that Li Shufen's death had been a suicide. After the Public Security Bureau demanded the cremation of Li's body, anger boiled over. Two of Li Shufen's middle-school classmates held up a white banner declaring "Seeking Redress for Injustice Done to the Masses" and they began a march along the road that runs through the county seat. Where the road passed through Seven-Star village, apparently many discontented peasants who had been moved there when the Goupitan dam was built joined the protest.[5]

By the time the marchers reached the county party and government headquarters, their numbers had swelled to more than 10,000. But no one from the county government building came out to receive them. The crowd went on to the Public Security Bureau offices, 100 meters down the road. Xiao Song, the county deputy public security head who was in charge of letters and visits, arrived at the Public Security Bureau about an hour after the crowd had converged. The situation quickly became heated. Xiao told the crowd to select five representatives, as they were supposed to do according to the Regulations on Letters and Visits. A young man rushed forward and shouted at Xiao, "Your mother's ass!" A county official told the crowd not to use dirty language with the county head, to which the crowd, rising to the challenge, responded angrily, "Dickhead county head!" Police soon appeared and they and the crowd began shoving one another. Thereafter, the crowd broke into the public security building and began smashing things and throwing bricks at the police. The crowd became more incensed when they realized that they were being videotaped. The confrontation soon became violent and the crowd torched forty-seven offices in the county Public Security Bureau and 104 offices in the county government building. It also destroyed at least ten police cars.[6]

---

[5] Ibid.; and Luo Changping, "Weng'an '6.28' shijian liubian."

[6] Wang Weibo, "Fengbao yanzhong de Weng'an guanyuan." Liu Zifu presents the public security people as being far more restrained, but he describes many details of the incident. See *Xin qunti shijian guan – Guizhou Weng'an '6.28' shijian de qishi*. Liu reports that twenty-two police cars were destroyed (p. 16).

FIGURE 1. Public Security building in Weng'an

The Weng'an incident is one of many recent "anger-venting incidents" (*xiefen shijian*), as political scientist Yu Jianrong has called them. Similar to other such incidents, those swelling the crowds and burning the public buildings were not directly related to Li Shufen, whose death had initially touched off the anger. Indeed, at the time of the incident, Li's immediate family was out of town. The anger that boiled over that day had long been in the making, and the death of Li Shufen was simply the catalyst that touched off the violence.

The Weng'an incident does not typify governance in China, but it does underscore some features of governance in contemporary China that are universally present, if not so extreme as in Weng'an. Most obviously, the cadres in Weng'an were under pressure from higher levels to promote the rapid growth of the local economy, and development of hydropower and mineral resources was an obvious way to accomplish that goal. In general, cadres in China face two basic demands: economic growth and social stability.[7] Within this framework they also face a number of other demands: to deliver taxes (even though agricultural taxes and miscellaneous fees were abolished in 2006) and to provide welfare, education, family planning, and so forth. This vertical structure, which sets targets for lower-level cadres, is what social scientist Rong Jingben and his colleagues call a "high pressure" system.[8] Lower-level cadres are evaluated for purposes of year-end bonuses and possible promotions through the cadre evaluation system (*ganbu kaohe zhidu*). Because the rewards and sanctions of this system are ample, cadres are highly responsive to it.[9]

---

[7] A recent article comments that "economic targets carry a decisive weight in the political evaluation targets." See Chen Jiaxi, "Siying qiye dangjian de kunnan yu fangxiang." This statement is consistent with the cadre evaluation forms that I have seen and with statements by local cadres. Understanding that emphasizing economic development might distort the implementation of policy, the party has experimented with introducing other criteria, especially the notion of a "green GDP" and a measure of people's satisfaction. See Zhuang Guobo, *Lingdao ganbu zhengji pingjia de lilun yu shijian*, pp. 48–64. Although such criteria may have attenuated the fixation on economic development, it appears that economic criteria still remain dominant.

[8] Rong Jingben et al., *Cong yalixing tizhi xiang minzhu hezuo tizhi de zhuanbian.*

[9] In speaking of the responsiveness of cadres to the cadre evaluation system, one has to keep in mind the different levels of the political system. The cadre evaluation system does not allow Beijing to enforce all but the most basic demands (such as the emphasis on GDP growth and family planning). The cadre evaluation system is implemented level by level, and each level interprets high-level demands in ways that are favorable to it. At the local level, cadres

The high demands on local officials do not go unrewarded. There seems to be a tacit understanding that local officials can pursue their private interests – often through corruption – as long as they accomplish the goals set for them by the higher levels. It is difficult to know, given its hidden nature, if corruption is more or less widespread in wealthy or poor areas (one assumes the sums involved are greater in the more developed areas), but it seems more noticeable in poor areas and thus breeds more hostility (even though there are more petitions to higher levels from Zhejiang, a wealthy province, than any other province).[10]

Given the demands of the higher levels for rapid economic development and the cadres' own desires to siphon off some of the returns on that growth, it is sometimes difficult to achieve the second goal, the maintenance of social stability. The higher levels have not been too picky about the methods employed to maintain social stability. In Weng'an it was apparent that the local public security forces were quick to use force to suppress discontent, often in conjunction with local gangs. Although news reports on Weng'an did not mention organized crime running illegal businesses, in many parts of the country public security forces collude with organized crime to run gambling houses and to engage in other illegal activities.[11]

In general, some combination of resignation, intimidation, and the simple desire to pursue one's own livelihood keeps citizens and officials from clashing, but on occasion, as in Weng'an, tensions will boil over. When they do, it is usually because local officials have gone too far in terms of abusing their power.[12]

In short, the center faces a classic principal–agent problem. Beijing delegates power downward through the party. This is a

seek to expand local revenue. Their efforts to do so are evaluated by the next higher level, which also has an interest in higher revenue.

[10] Chen Xiwen, "Dangqian de nongcun jingji fazhan xingshi yu renwu," pp. 7–11.

[11] This has been particularly obvious in Chongqing, where the party secretary, Bo Xilai, launched a major campaign to root out organized crime. See Joseph Fewsmith, "Bo Xilai Takes on Organized Crime."

[12] See Zhonggong zhongyang zuzhibu ketizu (Ed.), *Zhongguo diaocha baogao 2000–2001.*

system that served the CCP well during the revolution; cadres at higher levels were hardly in a position to exert close supervision over subordinates, who were often hundreds of miles away. Therefore, it was necessary to delegate authority and then to hold the party official at the next lowest level responsible for the results. In turn, the latter official sought significant freedom to choose his subordinates and to manage affairs in ways he (in China, most all local party secretaries are men) saw fit.

This structure meant that the promotion system was highly personalistic, with one level selecting officials at the next lower level. It also meant that promotion decisions were made by a small group of people. Although it would appear that opening up decision making would generate better personnel choices, stricter adherence to procedures, and less abuse of power, secrecy has served the interests of the party well. If, for instance, the names of candidates for promotion were known in advance, it would inevitably stimulate the formation of local factions that would then promote one or another candidate, making local governance more difficult. Hence, there has been a strong tendency to keep personnel decisions in the hands of the party secretary; a county leader can use secrecy either to break up or to promote local interests of various sorts, but either way such secrecy helps to maintain control in his own hands.[13]

This practice of highly concentrated authority exercised with a minimum of consultation has long been legitimized by the principle of the "party controlling the cadres" (*dang guan ganbu*), which might be said to be the central principle guiding the organization and practice of the CCP. It is a principle that places control firmly in the hands of leaders at higher levels. For a lower-level cadre to receive his bonus and to have a chance at promotion, the most important thing to do is to please the party secretary at the next higher level.[14]

---

[13] Xu Xianglin, "Dang guan ganbu tizhi xia de jiceng minzhushi gaige," pp. 106–112.

[14] Zhuang Guobo, *Lingdao ganbu zhengji pingjia de lilun yu shijian*; Maria Edin, "State Capacity and Local Agent Control in China," pp. 35–52; and

The centrality of county party secretaries is documented in Zhou Qingzhi's recent study of an unnamed county in northwest China.[15] The core of the local power structure is the personnel system, and the local party secretary has nearly total control over the selection of both county-level cadres and township party secretaries and deputy secretaries. When there is a need to promote a cadre, the county party secretary "sets the tone" for the characteristics they should be looking for, and then the local Organization Bureau will nominate someone in accordance with this tone. The deputy party secretary with responsibility for that sector will approve the decision (or not), and the party secretary's conference will make the final decision. In this particular county, the conference consists of the party secretary and the three deputy party secretaries. Once they have decided, the nomination is put to the standing committee of the local people's congress for formal appointment. It is, however, the decision of the party secretary's conference that has substantive meaning.[16]

This system of nearly total control over appointments of lower-level cadres is in the interests of the CCP. It is central to the party's efforts to mobilize the political system on behalf of economic development; organizational incentives (bonuses, promotions) line up well with personal incentives (including possibilities for corruption) to promote growth. But because power is so concentrated and opaque and because it revolves almost entirely around GDP growth, it is a system that can be easily abused. There are frequent externalities such as the building of wasteful "image projects," environmental degradation, low-quality education, poor health care, and the accumulation of local debt. Prior to 2006, abuse frequently took the form of overtaxing the peasants, generating "rightful resistance."[17] Since the abolition of agricultural taxes and miscellaneous fees in 2006, land has become the primary point of contention. The temptation to take

Susan H. Whiting, "The Cadre Evaluation System at the Grass Roots," pp. 101–119.

[15] Zhou Qingzhi, *Zhongguo xianji xingzheng jiegou jiqi yunxing*, p. 109.

[16] Ibid.

[17] Kevin J. O'Brien and Lianjiang Li, *Rightful Resistance in Rural China*.

over land can be great. In 2005, for example, only one-third of the 163,000 hectares of state-owned land was sold through "bidding, auctions, and listings" – in other words at market prices. The other two-thirds was sold through nonmarket means; the price difference between land sold openly and nontransparent deals was four to five times, or about five million yuan per hectare.[18] A more recent survey covering seventeen provinces concluded that since the late 1980s, 43 percent of peasants have had their land procured at least once, and in 17.8 percent of cases land was procured coercively. Overall, 12.7 percent of peasants received no compensation at all. Since 1999, 64.7 percent of peasants received one-off payments averaging 18,739 yuan (a bit under $3,000), and the selling price of procured land averaged 778,000 yuan per mu (1 mu equals one-sixth of an acre) – nearly forty times the price paid for it.[19]

In wealthier areas, where investment funds are plentiful, the demands for economic development can often be pursued without coming into direct conflict with local citizens, though there have been some notable exceptions. But demands for economic development in poorer areas often pit local cadres directly against the people whom they are governing, either through excessive taxation or, in recent years, by seizing land without providing adequate compensation. When officials in Weng'an moved villagers out of Jiangjiehe village so that they could construct the Goupitan dam, they were simply following the logic of this system.

"Mass incidents" of various sorts have become a major and continuing problem in China. As is well known, their number rose from 8,700 in 1993 to 87,000 in 2005, when the government stopped releasing systematic data.[20] According to *Outlook Weekly*, there were 90,000 cases of "mass incidents"

---

[18] Fang Ning, "Yong minzhu he fazhi de banfa chuli maodun," and Gao Peiyong, "Jian quan fenpei jizhi diaocheng liyi geju."

[19] Sun Chunfang, "Renmin daxue wancheng 17 sheng nongcun tudi diaocha"; Ye Jianping, Feng Lei, Jiang Yan, Luo Yi Pu Luo Si Te Man, and Zhu Keliang, "2008 nian nongcun tudi shiyongquan diaocha yanjiu."

[20] C. Fred Bergsten et al., *China: The Balance Sheet.*

in 2006, and the trend was rising.[21] The 2009 *Blue Book on Chinese Society* reports that there were "more than" 80,000 mass incidents in 2007.[22] In 2008, there were major mass incidents, involving thousands of people in Weng'an (Guizhou), Fuyu (Shaanxi), Huizhou (Guangdong), and Menglian (Yunnan), among others.[23] By 2010, there were some 180,000 mass incidents, seventy-two of which were said to have had widespread influence.[24]

Such incidents are a direct reflection of the structure of CCP power. As Carl Minzner has put it: "Chinese central authorities do not want local township officials colluding to falsify tax records or engaging in ill-conceived development projects. Nor do they want rural residents burning down local government buildings. Nonetheless, these are direct results of the cadre evaluation systems that Chinese authorities use to govern their local agents."[25]

Mass incidents do not appear to be a direct threat to the continued rule of the CCP,[26] but they do undermine legitimacy in a general way because they reflect poorly on governance and the image of the party. Corruption shares roots with social protest. Just as the hierarchical structure of the political system, with its personalization of power and demands for economic growth,

---

[21] "'Dianxing quntixing shijian' de jinghao."

[22] Ru Xin, Lu Xueyi, and Li Peili (Eds.), *2009 nian Zhongguo shehui xingshi fenxi yu yuce*, p. 10.

[23] One should not take numbers of mass incidents too literally, much less conclude that such incidents in 2007 were fewer than in 2006 just because they were reported to be "more than 80,000," which is fewer than the 90,000 reported for 2006. Without better data, the most we can say is that mass incidents have risen throughout the past decade or more and this trend seems to be continuing. See Zhongguo shehui kexueyuan, 'shehui xingshi fenxi yu yuci' ketizu,' "Liwan kuanglan," p. 10.

[24] Sun Liping, "Shehui shixu shi dangxia de yanjun tiaozhan." On the difficulty of interpreting numbers of mass incidents, see Carl Minzner's blog at http://sinolaw.typepad.com/chinese_law_and_politics_/2007/03/are_mass_incide .html, accessed December 1, 2011. For an early analysis of their impact, see Murray Scot Tanner, "China Rethinks Unrest."

[25] Carl F. Minzner, "Riots and Cover-Ups," p. 59.

[26] Martin King Whyte, *Myth of the Social Volcano.*

often pits the interests of local officials against those of the common people, generating protest, it also provides opportunities and even pressures to pursue corruption. Although the party has railed against corruption and has taken a variety of measures to try to stem it, the problem continues to worsen.[27]

Even though corruption is sometimes blamed on the introduction of reform and market forces, the problem has been with the People's Republic of China (PRC) from its beginnings. As early as 1951, Mao Zedong launched the "three-anti" campaign to fight against corruption, waste, and bureaucracy. Two high-level officials in Tianjin, Liu Qingshan and Zhang Zishan, were executed to show the determination of the party.[28] But when Liu Shaoqi's wife, Wang Guangmei, investigated conditions in Taoyuan production brigade in 1963–1964, she reported that 85 percent of brigade cadres were corrupt.[29]

Nevertheless, the forms of corruption continue to evolve. When the "two-track" price system was introduced in the mid-1980s, cadres found that they could arbitrage the difference between in-plan prices and market prices to their personal advantage. It was precisely this form of corruption that so offended students in the spring of 1989 who protested against, among other things, "official profiteering" (*guandao*). This corruption tended to be individual and for personal consumption and pleasure.

As economic reform deepened and the differences between plan and market diminished, there was less of an opening for this sort of corruption. But the growing wealth of the country meant that there were more opportunities to profit from abuses of power, either from the various sorts of approval that were needed by economic actors or from opportunities for investment. This meant that holding office could be profitable, and many people were willing to pay to hold office. The result was that the buying and selling of office (*maiguan maiguan*) became more prevalent, with some officials simply selling offices openly – a given office

---

[27] Author's interviews.
[28] Xiaobo Lü, *Cadres and Corruption*, p. 58.
[29] Harry Harding, *Organizing China*, p. 207.

was "listed" at a specified price. The selling of office, as Zhai Guang puts it, "went from retail to wholesale." For instance, the party secretary of Shaanxi's Yang county transferred over 400 cadres at one time, apparently in exchange for bribes. Similarly, the party secretary of Fujian's Zhenghe county transferred 545 cadres in ten separate batches. So many transfers within such a short period of time reflects the increase in abuse of power and corruption.[30] Similarly, Li Shuchun, the party secretary of Jiangsu's Xiangshui county, transferred 102 cadres in the two hours before he was reassigned, and Wang Hulin, the party secretary of Shanxi's Changzhi county, transferred 432 cadres as he was being transferred to a new post. Indeed, the power to use people was the "mother of corruption."[31]

In recent years, the party has imposed a number of regulations in its efforts to stop such behavior, as will be discussed below, but local authorities always possess more information than high-level authorities about local circumstances. Thus, even though the regulations are intended to increase higher-level control over cadre promotions, localities can use the advantages of information asymmetries to negate the intent of the regulations.[32] How this can be done is explained by one cadre who had been convicted of selling offices (it is not explained how he was exposed, but the odds of being caught appear to be quite low). For him, the imposition of formal procedures presented no obstacle to blatantly illegal activity. As he puts it:

Every time prior to the verification of cadres, I would hold a secretaries' office meeting to set a "tone." I would use the age, work experience, educational background, experience, and rank of those who had given me gifts to set a standard and demarcate a scope. I absolutely would not name anyone's name, but would let the Organization Bureau go "find people" within the "scope" that I had demarcated. After they had found them, we could proceed according to the procedures. On the surface,

---

[30] Zhai Guang, "Tuoshi maiguan maiguan jiaoyi," pp. 53–55.
[31] He Zengke, "Chuangxin tizhi cong yuantou shang yufang he zhili fubai," pp. 368–369.
[32] Guo Peng, "Asymmetrical Information, Suboptimal Strategies, and Institutional Performance."

the rationale was clear and the procedures lawful, but in reality, this was using individuals to draw lines and using individuals to define the scope. I used this method to reward all those who had given me gifts.[33]

The goal of this and other forms of corruption has evolved from personal consumption to capital accumulation. Cadres often use ill-gotten gains to invest in enterprises in expectations of ever-larger gains. As one corrupt official puts it, "Make lots of money and you can become a high-ranking official. And once you are a high-ranking official, you stand to make even more money."[34] This tendency is particularly conspicuous in the coal industry where officials either are given or demand company shares in exchange for protection (which is needed because the mines frequently violate safety regulations).[35] In 2002, Zhang Baoming, head of the State Administration of Work Safety, blamed official corruption and protection networks for most of the previous year's one million industrial accidents and more than 130,000 deaths.[36]

In short, as political reform lagged behind economic reform, there was a tendency for corruption to be ever more closely tied to the abuse of power and to networks of local officials, and to become more deeply embedded. Indeed, it was difficult to escape from these networks and pressures even if one wanted. When Li Changping was appointed party secretary of Qipan township in Hubei's Jianli county, he gathered some old classmates together to listen to their advice on how to be a good official. One classmate said that several party secretaries he knew had sincerely wanted to be good officials but within a few months of assuming office, they all became what the peasants called "idiotic, mediocre, and corrupt officials." To consolidate their power, the classmate continued, the party secretaries had to

---

[33] Wen Shengtang, "2003 nian de fanfubai douzheng," p. 162.
[34] Shi Xin, "'guangchang heishi' xianxiang saomiao," pp. 26–28.
[35] See, e.g., Wang Xiangwei, "Official's Half-Billion Yuan Stash Just Drop in Bucket," p. 5.
[36] "Safety Chief Praises Media Watchdogs."

protect the interests of cadres at the same level and the interests of the leaders at higher levels "at the expense of the people."[37]

The pursuit of the interests of local cadres drove the relentless expansion of local government as well as the institutionalized deceit of higher levels. As Li Changping writes in a letter to Premier Zhu Rongji that later became famous, "Any newly appointed leader unable to withstand internal and external pressures, needs to abuse his authority by putting some people on the government payroll." This "need" led to the continuous expansion of the size and expense of local government. Li reports that in 1990 there were 120 cadres in Qipan township; in 2000, when he addressed his letter to the premier, there were 340. In 1995, Li writes, 70 percent of towns and townships had savings, but by 2000 some 90 percent had deficits of at least 4 million yuan.[38] These deficits were in the interests of local cadres who saw making high-interest loans to towns and townships as a source of additional income.[39] Moreover, local authorities knowingly passed erroneous figures up to higher levels. In 1999, Li writes, Jianli county's revenue was less than 180 million yuan, but it reported revenue in excess of 220 million yuan. Similarly, in 1999 the per capita income of peasants in the county *declined* by 800 yuan (a huge decline), but the official report declared that incomes had *increased* by 200 yuan.[40]

Li's description of conditions in Hubei is borne out by a study undertaken by the Central Party School during the same period. Using Hunan province as an example, it was reported that the average indebtedness of towns or townships there was 2–3 million yuan; village-level collectives had average debts of 100,000 yuan. Nationwide, there were some 38 million cadres, a ratio of one cadre for every thirty citizens (this figure would grow to about 50 million by 2008).[41] There were more than 600,000 cadres in *excess* of the authorized number (*bianzhi*) at the county

[37] Li Changping, *Wo xiang zongli shuo shihua*, pp. 11–12.
[38] Ibid., p. 5.
[39] Ibid., p. 20.
[40] Ibid., p. 4.
[41] Wang Xiaoqi, *China's Civil Service Reform*, p. 24.

level and above, and more than 2 million excess cadres at the town and township levels.[42]

In his path-breaking study of peasant resistance in Hunan, political scientist Yu Jianrong confirms the picture presented in these studies and concludes that the basic causes of cadre–peasant conflict are structural. The cadre selection system makes lower-level cadres "absolutely obedient" to higher levels, whether or not what is being asked of them conforms with national policies; the frequent transfers of cadres from outside the area reward short-term behavior; and the web of interests in local areas makes it extremely difficult for problems to be exposed and rooted out.[43]

Differences in geography, economic structure, wealth, and historical development patterns make it extremely difficult to generalize about China, but there is a great deal of consensus that local government expanded rapidly in the 1990s, that the indebtedness of local governments grew dramatically, and that relations with peasants in many parts of the country deteriorated, sometimes to a dangerous extent. For instance, Zhao Shukai, a researcher at the State Council Development Research Center, estimates that the number of employees in township governments approximately tripled between the mid-1980s and the mid-1990s. Despite repeated pressure from the central government, township governments would not reduce their payrolls, frequently resorting to various deceptions to hide the numbers of employees. Even when the township governments could not pay their employees on time or had to go into debt to pay them, or both, they would not reduce the size of their payrolls. Obviously, there were benefits to employees in terms of job security and extra-bureaucratic opportunities, so they remained on the payrolls even if their salaries were not disbursed regularly. Township party secretaries also found it easier to keep such people on the payrolls than to deal with disgruntled laid-off cadres.[44]

---

[42] Zhonggong zhongyang zuzhibu ketizu (Ed.), *Zhongguo diaocha baogao 2000–2001*, p. 85.

[43] Yu Jianrong, "Nongmin you zuzhi kangzheng jiqi zhengzhi fengxian," p. 12.

[44] Zhao Shukai, "Xiangcun zhili," pp. 1–8. See also Jean C. Oi and Zhao Shukai, "Fiscal Crisis in China's Townships," pp. 75–96.

According to a survey conducted by the Ministry of Agriculture, as of 1998 town and township governments had a total indebtedness of over 177 billion yuan, or an average of 4 million yuan per town or township – precisely what Li Changping had estimated in his letter to the premier. In addition, village debts reached 418 billion yuan. A survey done seven years later found township debts averaging over 10 million yuan.[45]

As fiscal woes mounted at the township level, cadres increasingly became responsible for collecting their own salaries. As Zhao Shukai writes:

In many places, ensuring income not only is the responsibility of township and town leaders, but also the assignment for virtually all township and town personnel. We have found from our investigations that one common way employed by township and town leaders is to give township and town cadres the assignment of collecting taxes and fees in each and every village, and their collection performance is directly linked with these cadres' wages. Those who fail to fulfill their assignments not only receive no wages, but also have to raise money to be delivered to the upper departments.[46]

The combination of hierarchical control, personalization of power, frequent transfers, and dense social networks (among local elites), as Yu Jianrong suggests, places local government in conflict with local citizens. Such conflict lies behind the tens of thousands of mass incidents in China today, including the Weng'an riot described above.

As will be discussed, the CCP has tried to restrain the behavior of local agents through a number of mechanisms, but to date it has refused to allow the institutionalization of mechanisms that could restrain the exercise of party power. Thus, when confronted with a continuation of mass incidents, which are an inevitable result of the power structure, and the possibility of checking the party's power through the creation of formal institutions, the party has consistently opted to maintain its hierarchical and, in local terms, arbitrary power. Thus, the conflicts

[45] Yang Minghong, "Quxiao nongyeshuihou de Zhongguo xiangcun zhili jiegou," p. 156.
[46] Zhao Shukai, "Xiangcun zhili," p. 3.

we see in contemporary China are rooted in a failure to build the local state in ways that are responsive both to vertical control and to serving the constituents.

Representation

China's hierarchical cadre system has been challenged by the dynamics of reform. On the one hand, the end of the Cultural Revolution and the collapse of Maoist ideological authority opened up new questions of legitimacy that continue to plague the system. On the other hand, the breakup of the commune system and implementation of the Household Responsibility System (HRS) in agriculture (whereby peasants farmed a contracted piece of land that was owned by the collective) exposed new tensions. Previously, taxation had been hidden. Village cadres collected grain, sold it at the local grain station, and gave peasants whatever cash was left over after various costs were deducted. However, with implementation of the HRS, under which peasants took responsibility for marketing their own grain, taxes had to be collected from individual households. In this way, the costs of village government, previously hidden, became very visible, and peasants resisted paying the taxes to cadres. Peasants felt that cadres did not earn their salaries. At the same time, townships pressed village cadres to pass on their tax revenues so that the townships could pursue their own economic construction plans. Conflict was inevitable.[47]

As local conflicts increased, higher-level officials vigorously debated what to do. With the support of the Ministry of Civil Affairs (MCA) and the head of the National People's Congress (NPC) Peng Zhen, the NPC approved the Organic Law of the Villagers Committees on a trial basis in 1987. Peng Zhen was a conservative official, but he was convinced that village self-management would reduce tensions in the countryside and strengthen CCP leadership.[48] The Tiananmen demonstrations

---

[47] Tyrene White, "Village Elections."
[48] Ibid.

and suppression the following year ushered in a dramatically more conservative political atmosphere, under which the notions of village autonomy and elections were challenged. Peng Zhen and vice chairman of the Central Advisory Commission Bo Yibo, however, continued to support village elections, and, under the management of the MCA, elections of varying quality spread throughout the country.

Under the Organic Law, villagers were supposed to choose their village heads, but the elections did not solve the problem of representation; in some ways they exacerbated it. Electing village heads (*cunzhang*) only highlighted the difference between their popular mandate and the absence of a similar mandate for the village party secretary (and party branch).[49] The party branch could argue that its authority was based on implementing the "unified" leadership of the party and that party leadership was supreme, but village heads could argue that villages were self-governing and that their authority came from the people of the village. Who elected the party secretaries?

This question was posed in acute fashion in 1991 in Daiyudian village in Hequ county, Shanxi province, when villagers drew up a complaint against the local party secretary, listing twenty-three charges including embezzlement. In the midst of end-of-term elections, the county party Organization Bureau knew it had to develop a different method for selection of party secretary or face a major crisis. It decided to allow villagers to express, by secret ballot, their preferences for party secretary. When one person, who fortunately turned out to be the party's favorite, emerged as the most popular choice, the village party committee voted for that candidate. This system, known as the "two-ballot system," spread through much of Shanxi province and into Inner Mongolia and parts of Henan province, though in much attenuated form.[50]

---

[49] Technically, party secretaries and branch members are elected by the party members in the village, but in reality the party leadership is chosen by the township party committee and ratified by the village party organization.

[50] Lianjiang Li, "The Two Ballot System in Shanxi Province," pp. 103–118.

The conflict between party secretaries and village heads, however, grew sharper after the Organic Law was revised and promulgated in 1998. The revised version of the law went further than the earlier draft in that it required elections and specified that the village committees would have authority over public expenditures. The new regulations not only clashed with long-standing practices in the countryside, they also clashed with the "CCP Regulations on the Organization of Grassroots Work in Rural Areas" (*Zhongguo gongchandang nongcun jiceng zuzhi gongzuo tiaoli*), also promulgated in 1998. The latter regulations emphasized the authority of the party secretaries, thus setting the stage for conflict.

One such conflict arose in eastern Shandong province when fifty-seven village heads resigned collectively. Although they had been elected by their respective villages, the party secretaries had refused to turn over to them the official seals, without which they could not conduct official business, including authorization of public expenditures.[51]

This conflict took a more tragic turn in Paihui village in Wu'an city, under Handan municipality in southern Hebei province. Discontent was widespread in the area, with conflict focusing rural finance.[52] Over half of the petitions received at Wu'an's Office of Letters and Visits accused village cadres of financial malfeasance or unfair management of public affairs. When village elections were held in 2000 over half of the village cadres lost their posts. Of the 1,900 newly elected village committee members, more than 1,000 were under the age of thirty-five, signaling a rejection of the old leadership and the rise of a new generation. Moreover, 480 of the newly elected village committee members (nearly 25 percent) were not members of the CCP.[53]

In Paihui village, in an effort to increase collective income, the party secretary ordered the sale of idle materials at the village steel

---

[51] Lu Tang and Du Bin, "'Shandong Qixia 57 ming cunguan jiti cizhi shijian' zhenxiang."

[52] This case is discussed in Joseph Fewsmith, "Institutional Innovation at the Grassroots Level."

[53] He Zengke, "Nongcun zhili zhuanxing yu zhidu chuangxin."

factory. Tragically, in the process of dismantling the material, there was an accident in which one person was killed and another injured. The village secretary sold the scrap material for 50,000 yuan, but paid 100,000 yuan in compensation for the death and injury. Of course, he wanted the village to make up for the extra 50,000 yuan. But he had not consulted the village committee before deciding on dismantling and selling the scrap material, so the village committee argued that he had been acting on his own and the loss was not the responsibility of the village.[54]

The conflict in Paihui village is not an isolated instance; on the contrary, more than 10 percent of the villages within the jurisdiction of Wu'an city were judged to be "chaotic" (*luancun*) or "difficult" (*nancun*) villages.[55] Accordingly, the Wu'an party leadership sent people to study conditions in twenty-three villages where relations between the party committee and the village committee were tense. The study group quickly concluded:

After the appearance of direct elections for village committees, viewed from the perspective of deep levels, it was a problem of the old village leadership system, work regulations, and decision-making style coming into conflict with ruling the country according to law, the acceleration of democratic construction, and the unprecedented development of democratic consciousness among the masses under the new circumstances. The fact that the functions of the village committee and the party branch were not clear, their relations were not smooth, the work lacked democracy, there is little transparency in handling things, and the supervision of the masses lacked force, etc., is directly relevant, but the most basic reason for the tense relations is that the operational mechanism for work in the countryside was seriously backward and is not appropriate for the party's leadership methods in villages and the style of a ruling party.[56]

In response to these problems and with a powerful push from the top, the Organization Bureau of Wu'an city promulgated a document calling for trial implementation of "one mechanism and

---

[54] Ibid., p. 6.
[55] Ibid., p. 4.
[56] Jing Yuejin, *Dangdai Zhongguo nongcun "liangwei guanxi" de weiguan jiexi yu hongguan youshi*, p. 141.

three transformations" (*yizhi sanhua*). The "one mechanism" affirmed the leading role of the party committee in accordance with the Regulations on the Organization of Grassroots Work in the Rural Areas, but the "three transformations" – standardization of the work of the party branch, legalization of village self-government, and adoption of procedures for democratic supervision – allowed for the establishment of a "joint conference of the village party branch and the village committee" (*cun dangzhibu yu cun weiyuanhui lianxi huiyi*). This new mechanism meant that important decisions, such as public expenditures, were to be made by the party committee and the village committee together.[57] At the same time, Handan municipality implemented what was then called the "village accounting agency system" (*nongcun kuaiji weituo daili zhi*), under which village accounts were kept at the township level, thereby making the misuse of funds at the village level much more difficult.[58] This system has since been popularized throughout the country as the system of "village accounts managed by the township" (*cuncai xiangguan*), a system that may reduce corruption at the village level but also hollows out the substantive responsibilities of village officials.

Institutional Innovation Does Not Mean Institutionalization

The case of Wu'an, like that of Daiyudian village in Hequ county, suggests that social crisis can generate institutional responses and that such responses, in turn, might provide a way out of the principal–agent problems created by the vertical structure of the party and the personalization of political power that it has perpetuated. Institutional innovation at the local level, in other

---

[57] He Zengke, "Nongcun zhili zhuanxing yu zhidu chuangxin," p. 17; and Jing Yuejin, *Dangdai Zhongguo nongcun "liangwei guanxi" de weiguan jiexi yu hongguan youshi*, p. 142.

[58] Jing Yuejin, *Dangdai Zhongguo nongcun "liangwei guanxi" de weiguan jiexi yu hongguan youshi*, pp. 148–150; and He Zengke, "Nongcun zhili zhuanxing yu zhidu chuangxin," p. 13.

words, might act as a check on the abuse of power and thus be a means of alleviating the tensions between cadres and masses.

Institutionalization, however, differs from institutional innovation. There is a lot of institutional innovation in China, but very little institutionalization of those efforts. Institutionalization depends on many factors, including local balances of power. For instance, the sort of conflicts that arose in Daiyudian and Wu'an reflect competition between local party secretaries and local village heads. The degree of competition between party secretaries and village heads depends, among other things, on their personalities and backgrounds. An older, experienced, and respected party secretary will not have difficulty dominating a younger and less-experienced village head, whereas a strong-willed, capable village head can challenge a party secretary, especially if the latter is considered corrupt or abusive.

To a certain extent, such conflicts can be mitigated by marginal institutional changes and informal arrangements rather than by more meaningful institutional changes. For instance, the "two-ballot" system has been institutionalized in many places as the "two recommendations, one selection" (*liangtui yixuan*) system. Under this system, villagers vote on the members of the party committee, providing an indication of individual popularity and possibly serving to keep an extremely unpopular person from becoming a local party secretary. Then the party members vote on the candidates, but most important, it is the party committee that makes the final decision. The party committee may or may not follow the results of the popular vote. Conflict with the village head can also be avoided by having the party secretary run as village head, a system known as carrying both posts on one shoulder pole (*yijiantiao*). This system, which has been adopted in about half of China's villages, ensures a minimum of popularity of the village party secretary but reflects a distrust of institutional arrangements that check power. Finally, conflict can be minimized by informal understandings, particularly by acknowledging that a village chief will become party secretary in due course after the party secretary retires. Few people are inclined to jeopardize their future power by challenging a party secretary in the short run. Of course, the entire conflict can be rendered meaningless by denying resources to the village, just what occurred after the abolition of agricultural taxes and miscellaneous fees in agricultural areas. Posts without power are not worth fighting over.

Conclusion

Since the beginning of the reform era, China has faced at least two fundamental problems in achieving good governance. On the one hand, China's party system still operates in a hierarchical system, a legacy of the party's revolutionary era. Although this system can be effectively mobilized to attain such diverse goals as birth control, disease prevention, and economic development, it is undermined by the principal–agent problems that afflict most hierarchical systems. Local cadres (agents) must respond to those at higher levels in the system, but because goals are often specified in crude terms – economic development – local agents are given a great deal of latitude in choosing the means and personnel for achieving these targets. Demands from the top tend to set the interests, both personal and professional, of local cadres against those whom they are governing, thereby generating conflict.

On the other hand, the breakup of the communes and the implementation of the HRS decreased peasant dependence on the political system, raising questions about the role of the party at the grassroots level and whom the party represented. These questions were particularly sharp at the village level because constitutionally the village was self-governing. Just as party and state offices were created at the township level when the communes were disbanded (even though the distinction between party and state meant little in practice), village committees were set up alongside party branches at the village level. As village elections spread, the relationship between the two became a point of contention. Although the two-ballot system and the "one mechanism and three transformations" system tried to subject the party to checks and balances, they could never be popularized or institutionalized without revoking the provision that the party secretary had ultimate authority, which was central to the Regulations on the Organization of Grassroots Work in Rural Areas. Of course, these regulations simply reflect the hierarchical nature of the cadre system. Hence, the problem could not be resolved at the village level.

How could political reform proceed? The focus inevitably shifted to the township level, a level close enough to popular pressures that there was a need to respond, yet still a part of the five-tiered party-state system and thus a part of the cadre system. Experiments could be conducted at this level without the danger, from the party's point of view, that they would "run out of control"; if successful, they could be popularized. Some experiments were encouraged by higher-level authorities; many were initiated at the township level but with the support of county authorities; and some were forced on the localities by local events. In a country as diverse as China, it was inevitable that reform experiences ran along a wide spectrum; they could be bottom-up experiments that increased popular participation and limited cadre initiative, or they could be top-down reforms in the local political economy. The next chapter will illustrate these two extremes.

2

Bottom-Up Reform versus Top-Down Development

On June 14, 1999, some 200–300 peasants surrounded the leadership compound in Maliu township, in impoverished Kai county, a remote, mountainous area up the Yangtze River from Chongqing in southwest China. The anger of the peasants had boiled over when they heard that cadres planned to renovate their office compound. Tensions had already been running high as cadres had been trying to squeeze extra funds from the peasants, and the thought that this revenue would be used to improve the lives of the cadres was simply too much. The peasants blocked the entrance to the township offices so there was no way for the cadres to leave the building. The local cadres' first instinct was to respond forcefully: arrest the leaders and suppress the outburst. But there were no police stationed in Maliu township; they would have to come from the county seat, 66 kilometers away. More importantly, any police action to suppress the peasants would have to be approved by the Political and Legal Affairs Office of the Kai County Chinese Communist Party (CCP) Committee. Fortuitously, the head of the office was a former teacher in Maliu township, and many of the people involved in the protest were his former students. He knew they were not bad people, so he demanded that local leaders find a way to resolve the incident peacefully. He was backed by the party

MAP 2. Chongqing municipality, indicating location of Maliu township

organization of Chongqing municipality, particularly its Organization Bureau.[1]

Maliu township is a fairly typical mountain settlement. The population is highly dependent on agriculture, with 97 percent of the residents relying on agriculture as their main source of income. Spread over 94 square kilometers, Maliu township's 7,241 households live in twenty-four administrative villages and one street committee. Agriculture is difficult and unrewarding, so more than 6,000 of the township's 27,112 people had left to make their fortunes elsewhere. Of those remaining, more than

[1] Gao Xinjun, "Weiji guanli he houxuanju zhili de chenggong fanli."

7,000, or about one-quarter of the population, were impoverished. Their annual incomes averaged about 1,021 yuan, less than half the average income in the township.[2]

The party organization in Maliu township was weak. There were only 616 party members, a little more than 2 percent of the local population, or somewhat less than one-half the national figure. They were organized in twenty-four village party branches, three school party branches, two branches for retirees, and one branch for administrative organs, making a total of thirty party branches. Only thirty members of these party branches were female – on average one female in each party branch. Only four were college-educated, and only fifteen were graduates of vocational institutes (*daxue zhuanke*); 510 had middle-school educations or less.[3]

For poor, rural areas like Maliu township, the 1994 tax reform, which shifted revenue from the localities to the center, was disastrous. Even in 2001, when the situation had improved somewhat, Maliu township had revenue of only 600,000 yuan – but expenses of 3 million yuan. Despite revenue transfers from the county, Maliu township had debts of 1.2 million yuan (at year-end 2003).[4] In the late 1990s, as revenue declined, cadres tried to think of other ways to extract funds from peasants. Given the pressures to raise more funds, cadres decided to forcibly extract fines from peasants. In the latter half of 1997, there was a month-long "four clean-ups" (*si qingli*) movement during which cadres attempted to collect fines that had been levied but not collected over the previous decade for violations of policies on childbearing, forestry, housing construction, and burials. Cadres were allowed to retain 3–5 percent of the fines that they were able to collect. This campaign raised one million yuan for the township. In one village of only 1,838 people, cadres extracted 60,000 yuan, or over 38 yuan per capita.[5]

[2] Basic information can be found on Kai county's Web site, http://kx.cq.gov.cn.
[3] Gao Xinjun, "Weiji guanli he houxuanju zhili de chenggong fanli."
[4] Ibid.
[5] Ibid.

As a result, relations between cadres and peasants were extremely tense. Cadres going into the villages were cursed and sometimes beaten. Peasants began sending petitions to the county, municipality (Chongqing), and even to Beijing. Many were willing to attend "peasant hero" meetings (meetings organized by outspoken peasants who would rally opinion against party policy, particularly on tax issues), but they would refuse to attend meetings called by cadres. Cadres lost their ability to undertake public works. In 1997 officials drew up plans to pave the roads throughout the township, but work began in only one village. There were efforts to begin building a bridge across the river (*shuanghekou*; see below) that divided the township, but the peasants, fearing corruption, refused to support the project. In 1998, the township was able to complete only 60 percent of its revenue tasks, with six villages collecting less than 20 percent of their revenue goals. Peasants were aware of the central regulations on revenue collection but believed that local cadres were violating these rules, so on market days (Tuesdays, Thursdays, and Saturdays) they would denounce the actions of local cadres through loudspeakers. In short, by the late 1990s Maliu township was known as a "troublemaker" township (*naoshi xiang*). In this, it was not atypical of other poor townships in the area where relations between cadres and residents were deteriorating.[6]

Plans to renovate the leadership compound, however, pushed peasant tolerance past the breaking point. Denied permission to respond forcefully, the party committee had to come up with a different approach. A new party secretary, Li Hongbin, had been appointed to Maliu township only a few months earlier, and he appears to have been an exceptionally capable and open-minded official. In thinking about how to respond to the incident at the township offices and the crisis in governance more generally, he seems to have drawn on the CCP's tradition of following the mass line, albeit with some important innovations. The first thing he did was to organize cadres to go into the villages and listen to the complaints. Each member of the party committee

[6] Li Hongbin, "Zai shi lingdao lai Maliu diaoyan zuotanhui shangde huibao."

was required to establish regular contact with twenty households in eight small groups in four villages. They were also required to hold "leadership reception days," on the first, eleventh, and twenty-first days of each month, as well as to hold special forums for retired cadres on the seventh day of each month.[7] This could not have been easy, given the extremely tense relations between cadres and peasants at the time; indeed, many cadres did not like this requirement and it took many of them a year or more to change their attitudes (if they ever fully did so). But the solution gave the peasants a channel for venting their emotions, forced the cadres to listen to complaints, gave the leadership a better understanding of the situation, and – one must assume – gave Li Hongbin the leverage he needed to change cadre behavior and to reach a solution.

Out of this effort came new, or revived, rules governing cadre behavior. Cadres were no longer allowed to play cards, gamble, eat, or drink for free. Lower levels were not allowed to spend money when receiving leaders from higher levels. The township set an example by auctioning off automobiles it did not need, and it also sold off a retail outlet that it ran. Efforts were made to make village finances open and accountable. Each village established a finance committee (*licai xiaozu*) and rules were established for the disbursement of funds: the village accountant would write the check, the party secretary would approve it, and the village head would dispense the funds. Li Hongbin established the principle that "cadres manage affairs, not money" (*ganbu guanshi bu guanqian*) in order to alleviate peasants' suspicions (apparently well-founded) of corruption.[8]

However, more was needed to establish the trust needed to undertake public works. Maliu township was certainly in need of new schools, roads, and other public works, but peasants rightly feared that public works projects would be opportunities for cadres to extract private benefits and that such projects

---

[7] Ibid.
[8] Gao Xinjun, "Weiji guanli he houxuanju zhili de chenggong fanli."

might never be completed. Li Hongbin decided to focus on the long-planned bridge over *shuanghekou* ("two rivers junction," named for the two rivers that converge at that point), which divided the bulk of the township from four small villages that lie up in the mountains across the rivers. The rivers not only cut off the villages from the market, but they were also dangerous, as peasants would periodically slip, particularly during flood seasons, and be swept away by the currents. There was a clear need for a bridge, but how could a bridge be built when there was so little trust? The local political leadership decided to use this project to rebuild public confidence.

The party committee raised 30,000 yuan in contributions from party and government cadres (the idea of cadres taking the lead in contributing funds is commonly used to defuse tensions with the masses) and another 7,500 yuan from the public. The four villages most affected by the project established a "Small Group for the Construction of the Two Rivers Junction Bridge" (Shuanghekou daqiao lingdao xiaozu). This committee then found technicians who drew up plans and estimated the cost at 240,500 yuan. With the 3,700 people of the four villages contributing, the burden came to 65 yuan per person, a substantial amount. The party committee then sought other technicians who found ways to reduce the cost to only 129,500 yuan, or 35 yuan per person.[9]

But the peasants were still unhappy, fearing corruption. So the party committee decided to expand the leadership groups so that each of the four villages would have a noncadre representative and, more important, that the noncadre member of the groups would manage all funds. One was named the accountant, one the purser, one the overseer (*baoguan*), and one was in charge of quality control. This was a way of implementing the principle that the cadres would manage the work and the peasants would manage the money. At the same time, the party committee asked

---

[9] Li Hongbin, "Maliuxiang dangwei tuixing 'babu gongzuofa' qingkuang jieshao."

FIGURE 2. Bridge across Shuanghekou

that the villages discuss the plans and vote on them. The result was that 95 percent of the villagers approved the plans.[10]

When the work was completed four months later, there was actually money left over. After much discussion, the party committee made the unprecedented decision to return the leftover funds to the peasants: 9.4 yuan per person. This step apparently carried great weight with the peasants, leading them to believe that the leadership really did have a change of heart.[11]

The Eight-Step Work Method

On the basis of this and similar experiences, the local party committee put forth the "eight-step work method" (*babu gongzuofa*), which was finalized in 2003. The eight steps were as follows:[12]

---

[10] Gao Xinjun, "Weiji guanli he houxuanju zhili de chenggong fanli."
[11] Ibid.
[12] Li Hongbin, "Maliuxiang dangwei tuixing 'babu gongzuofa' qingkuang jieshao."

1. Investigate the views of the people and understand what they want. Consensus on potential projects should be above 60 percent.
2. Hold a meeting of cadres and peasant representatives to decide on a preliminary plan.
3. Propagandize to achieve unified thinking.
4. Hold democratic discussions to finalize plans. Hold repeated meetings of cadres and village representatives to revise the preliminary plan. A construction leadership small group should be chosen at a meeting, and noncadre masses should make up more than half the membership. Similarly, a financial management committee composed of the masses should be established so the masses control the funds and the cadres manage only the work.
5. Households should approve the projects – 85 percent should agree or the projects should be deferred.
6. Divide work responsibilities among households.
7. Village small groups should organize the work.
8. Announce completion of the work – and have the villagers' financial management committee audit the accounts.

This procedure obviously builds on the "mass line" of the party, both legitimating the innovation and reflecting the path dependence of leadership methods. But it also introduces an important element of democratic decision making and procedure. Public works projects must be openly discussed and approved by villagers; there must be high transparency; and there must be extensive villager participation in all phases of the work and supervision. Indeed, one could rightfully object that the requirement for an 85 percent "super-majority" violates normal understandings of democracy, as a relatively small minority can hold up or block the implementation of important public works.

Whatever objection one might make to the eight-step work method on theoretical grounds, it seems to have worked in Maliu township. From 2000 to 2006, there were no petitions forwarded to higher authorities, suggesting that relations between cadres and masses really had improved. Moreover, by following more democratic procedures, a number of public works projects were completed. Some 327 kilometers of road were built, eight bridges were constructed, and running water was extended to 6,250 households, providing every household in the township with running water.[13]

A Shifting Balance of Power

Perhaps the most radical innovation in Maliu township was not the widespread involvement of villagers in deciding and supervising public works projects but rather the severing of the connection between cadres and material benefits when undertaking public works. For instance, in 1995 the villagers in Xingping village were clamoring for roads to be built. The cadres agreed, but demanded 200 yuan from each person. The village generated over 300,000 yuan, but built only 4.8 kilometers of roads. Later, after implementation of the eight-step work method, the peasants put in only 40 yuan per person but a longer length of road was completed at a considerable cost savings. Under the eight-step work method, the cadres could not benefit from public works.[14]

The story behind this innovation, however, is the changed bargaining power between villagers and cadres. The township was bereft of funds, so the cadres pressed the villagers – with the result that the villagers resisted, petitioning and engaging in collective violence such as detaining cadres in their township offices. Basic social order was breaking down – and higher-level authorities at the county level would not countenance large-scale repression. The result was that Maliu township had to adopt radical methods, forcing cadres to involve villagers in the decision-making process – and to accept a loss of income by abstaining from corruption. The lesson is that only a serious social crisis could generate the will to seek a radical solution that was institutionally innovative.

[13] Gao Xinjun, "Weiji guanli he houxuanju zhili de chenggong fanli."
[14] Ibid.

As one might guess, the eight-step work method, though praised by the Chongqing authorities, did not spread. In 2003 Huang Zhendong, party secretary of Chongqing, went to Maliu township to praise the method as a model for reform, but other places, many of which suffered the same sort of tense relations between cadres and masses, made few efforts to copy it. What made the model in Maliu township unique – incorporating peasant supervision of funds – was precisely why it did not appeal to other areas. In the absence of a crisis and without forceful leadership, there was simply not enough pressure to make other areas adopt the system of "cadres managing affairs, not money."

Not only was the model of Maliu township difficult to extend elsewhere, but it also proved difficult to sustain in Maliu itself. Li Hongbin was eventually transferred out of the township. By all accounts, his successor was a capable and decent individual, but he took perhaps a more legalistic approach to his position, trying to stop violations of the regulations rather than focusing on building a democratic atmosphere. The main problem, however, was structural, not personality (though the ability of the "number one" person to influence policy should not be underestimated).

As central policies to abolish agricultural taxes and miscellaneous fees were implemented, the income of the township fell drastically. By 2007, Maliu township had revenue of only 2,000 yuan (!) – and that small amount of revenue was later canceled completely. Expenses in excess of 3 million yuan had to be covered entirely by the county, which began receiving greater transfer payments from the provincial and central levels. The eight-step work method was not entirely abandoned – there were still projects being built on the basis of village consultation (*yishi yiyi*), but for most things the township was entirely dependent on the county. And that inevitably meant that township cadres were more sensitive to county authorities than they were to residents. The fiscal bond that had driven cadres and peasants together was broken, as was the democratic participation that had come into being.[15]

---

[15] Gao Xinjun, "Difang zhengfu chuangxin yuanhe nan chixu."

Qiu He: Development by Iron Fist

The experience of Maliu township suggests the possibility of significant political change *if* there is a sustained change in the balance of power between local cadres and society. In contrast, Qiu
He's approach to reform in northern Jiangsu province marked
a very different, top-down approach, one focused very specifically on economic development rather than on new institutional
arrangements that might regularize state–society relations.[16]

Qiu He was born into a poor family in Binhai county in northern Jiangsu in 1957. He studied at Nanjing Agricultural Institute,
graduating in 1982, and became a researcher in the provincial
agricultural academy and secretary of the academy's Communist
Youth League branch. By late 1984 he was already deputy party
secretary of the party office at the academy. After a period at the
Jiangsu party school, Qiu became deputy director of the plant
protection institute. In 1990, he was appointed deputy director of the planning section of the provincial science commission
and concurrently deputy director of its agricultural section. In
1995, he went to the University of Maryland for eight months
of training,[17] and in 1996 he became a member of the planning
group for the establishment of Suqian city, a newly established
city that was created by carving out four counties from Huaiyin
city in northern Jiangsu. By the end of the year, Qiu was named a
vice mayor of Suqian, a member of the city standing committee,
and concurrently party secretary of Shuyang county, one of the
four counties under the new city.[18]

In striking contrast to the part of Jiangsu that lies south of
the Yangtze River (Sunan), those parts lying north of the river,
particularly in the areas that lie near the borders of Anhui and
Shandong provinces, are extremely poor. The four counties of
Suyu, Shuyang, Sihong, and Siyang were combined to form the

---

[16] This section expands on Joseph Fewsmith, "Promotion of Qiu He Raises
Questions about Direction of Reform."
[17] Liu Binglu, "Qiu He Suqian shinian zhilu," p. 9.
[18] Ibid. and "Zhengyi renwu dangxuan fushengzhang, Qiu He shengqian ju tupo
yiyi?"

prefectural-level city of Suqian, which became the poorest of Jiangsu's cities. Furthermore, Shuyang county was the poorest county not only in Suqian but in all of Jiangsu. It had been one of China's revolutionary base areas, and in 1996 its per capita income was only one-third the provincial average.[19] With fiscal revenues of 120 million yuan at the time, it had annual expenditures of 260 million yuan and debts of 32.6 million.[20] It was an area where "illegal religious organizations" flourished,[21] where citizens regularly petitioned government, and, as we will see, where organized crime was a daily part of life and government.

Shuyang had a reputation as a place that "even the spirits could not make better."[22] It was also unbelievably filthy. On Qiu He's first night as party secretary, he walked through the county seat and stepped in human feces four times. The next day he ordered over 5,000 cadres onto the streets to clean up, and within two weeks there was a dramatic change in the physical appearance of the county.[23]

Corruption and crime were major problems in Shuyang. In 1996, there were 1,600 criminal cases, including 186 serious crimes such as murder, rape, and robbery. More than 270 people for whom arrest warrants were issued had fled, the most of any county in Jiangsu. The county's rate of resolving crimes was the lowest in the province, and many people suspected of crime were released on bail (a common way of protecting suspects from being sentenced).[24]

Shortly after arriving in Shuyang, Qiu He launched a "strike hard" campaign, but he soon discovered that any plans to arrest criminals were quickly leaked. At a meeting of 1,000 legal affairs cadres, he angrily declared, "The fundamental issue of law and order is that the criminals and police are all in one family!"

---

[19] Ibid.
[20] Zhang Li, "Zuifu zhengyi de shiwei shuji"; Bao Yonghui and Xu Shousong, *Zhengdao*, p. 13.
[21] Ibid.
[22] Ibid.
[23] Zhang Li, "Zuifu zhengyi de shiwei shuji."
[24] Bao Yonghui and Xu Shousong, *Zhengdao*, p. 42.

An embarrassed and angry police chief, Jiang Zhengcheng, caught up with Qiu He to say, "This is an insult to our Public Security Bureau. Take back that statement to avoid a [negative] influence." Qiu He responded coldly, "Are the police and criminals in one family? Let the facts speak for themselves."[25] One month later police chief Jiang Zhengcheng was transferred out of the county and all heads of Shuyang's forty-one police stations (*paichusuo*) were rotated. Within the year, 4,656 new and old cases had been resolved.[26]

Qiu He's predecessor, Huang Dengren, who had served in Shuyang for five years, had made a practice of selling offices. In 1997, one Yu Jingzhong, who had been transferred to Shuyang to lead antipoverty work, wrote a letter to provincial leaders revealing the overstaffing of local offices and other problems related to the rampant selling of offices. Yu's letter, however, had no effect on Huang Dengren, who was named a deputy party secretary of Suqian after the city was established.[27]

Hence Qiu He could not tackle the issue of corruption or establish his own authority unless he took on Huang and his network. But Huang and his close cronies apparently ran a tight operation, deciding all promotions and appointments. Their circle became known as the "second Organization Bureau" because it mirrored and effectively replaced the party's Organization Bureau.[28]

Qiu He organized an investigation group that took up residence in one of the local hotels where the members of the group could call people in for investigation. When the former head of public security, Jiang Zhengcheng, was isolated for questioning, he was able to persuade a housekeeper to take a note to a relative who subsequently bribed the head of the group that was questioning Jiang! When the trail of notes that flowed back and forth was finally discovered, Jiang's fate was sealed. And once

---

[25] Zhang Li, "Zuifu zhengyi de shiwei shuji," and Bao Yonghui and Xu Shousong, *Zhengdao*, p. 43.

[26] Ibid.

[27] Bao Yonghui and Xu Shousong, *Zhengdao*, p. 45.

[28] Ibid., p. 51.

Jiang's activities were discovered, Huang Dengren's network was revealed.[29]

Some 243 cadres were caught in this operation, including seven at the deputy department level (*fuchuji*). But Qiu He's tactics were draconian. One official told *Southern Weekend* that the exposure of corrupt officials reflected a political struggle among officials. The paper also noted that when focusing on law-and-order issues, the police stations were given quotas. "Isn't this like the struggle against rightists in those years?" joked one official. "Of course law and order are better, but it is certain that more than a few innocent people were nabbed."[30] The people of Shuyang, however, seemed to support Qiu He's efforts.

Urban Reconstruction

In 1996, when Qiu He arrived in Shuyang, there were few modern roads. A local saying maintained that "when the car starts to bounce, you have arrived in Shuyang." There was only one national road that went through the county and only four provincial roads. Altogether the county had only 56 kilometers of asphalt roads; of the 697 villages in Shuyang, 109 did not even have one.[31]

The road system was in such terrible shape in part because public finances were stressed and in debt. In 1997, however, the Asian financial crisis hit, driving prices down and forcing the government to use deficit spending to stimulate demand. In addition to funds that could be secured for the national and provincial roads, Qiu He mobilized labor and funds: peasants and workers were required to contribute eight days of unpaid labor (*nongmin yiwugong* and *laodong jileigong*) and the government deducted 10 percent of cadre wages and 5 percent of retired cadres' pensions. Such "contributions" continued for five years.[32]

---

[29] Ibid., pp. 50–60.
[30] Zhang Li, "Zuifu zhengyi de shiwei shuji."
[31] Bao Yonghui and Xu Shousong, *Zhengdao*, p. 62.
[32] Ibid., p. 65.

FIGURE 3. Broad streets in Suqian

In addition, peasants were assessed 300–400 yuan per year to pay for roads; those who resisted were either detained or beaten, sometimes to death.[33] In the first year alone, Shuyang built 152 kilometers of asphalt roads, and in 1997 and 1998 combined, it paved another 308 kilometers of oiled roads (*baiyoulu*).[34]

As such a frenzy of road building suggests, Qiu He was determined to remake Shuyang county. To do this required destroying old buildings and soliciting investments, both of which Qiu He did with a vengeance. Qiu forced people out of their homes, bulldozed them, and built new rows of two-story buildings, with shop space on the ground floor and the residences above. Locals quickly came up with a limerick: "Qiu He looks and buildings are bulldozed to Nanyangdang [one edge of the town]; Qiu He waves his hand and the buildings are knocked down to the Yi

---

33 Author's interviews.
34 Bao Yonghui and Xu Shousong, *Zhengdao*, p. 76.

River [the other edge of the town]. Don't cry if your house is destroyed, and don't laugh if it hasn't been bulldozed – Qiu He hasn't seen it yet!"[35]

In a famous story, as Qiu He was directing the demolition of houses one woman was attempting to retrieve a chest out from her house, but she could not get it through the door. The woman fainted as Qiu had the house demolished with the chest still in it.[36] The reason she was so emotionally wrought was that the government was not offering any extra compensation for her house, which had been recently constructed and she stood to lose a lot of money. For the next several years, she and her family had to live in a shack.[37] Peasants complained, sometimes even petitioning Beijing, but to no avail. Land values rose, easing some of their complaints, but critics argued that the higher property values hardly offset the cost of the houses that had been destroyed.[38] Qiu He defended his harsh development methods: "China has only fifty years to accomplish what the West did in 300 years. How can we do this? We can only compress time and develop."[39]

To solicit investments, Qiu made the attraction of capital the number-one political task of cadres. One-third of cadres were forced to leave their posts to seek out investments. Each was given a target according to rank, and failure to achieve the goal would result in being removed from office. Even teachers were sent off in search of investments, prompting them to go on strike. The controversy attracted the media, and CCTV's popular television show "Focus Interview" (*Jiaodian fangtan*) broadcast the first of its three reports on Qiu He, all negative, in 1998.[40]

---

[35] Lu Biao, "Zhengyi Qiu He."
[36] Zhang Li, "Zuifu zhengyi de shiwei shuji."
[37] Author's interview.
[38] Zhang Li, "Zuifu zhengyi de shiwei shuji"; author's interviews. Obviously, people's perspectives varied, depending on how new or old their previous houses were.
[39] Zhang Li, "Zuifu zhengyi de shiwei shuji."
[40] Ibid.

Suqian Party Secretary

In 2001 Qiu He was promoted to the position of party secretary of Suqian city. During the next four years,[41] he continued to pursue the same sort of urban construction and solicitation of investment that he had in Shuyang. Suqian, as noted above, had been created out of Huaiyin city, but when the area was divided up, Huaiyin retained the central city. Suqian's "central city" was geographically small and had a population of only 150,000, hardly large enough to become a center of economic growth. Determined to change this situation, Qiu He oversaw planning for a much-enlarged central city and demanded the construction of five major bridges across the Grand Canal that flowed nearby. Although Qiu He had squeezed money and labor out of the peasants in Shuyang, the scale of construction in Suqian provides evidence of considerable provincial support.[42] Qiu He also oversaw the selling-off of locally owned enterprises, a move that saved the city money and jump-started the market economy. By the end of 2006, there were only three city-owned enterprises left in Suqian.[43]

Most controversial, however, was not Qiu He's autocratic way of directing urban development but rather his decisions to privatize health care and kindergarten and high-school education. Despite the provincial support, the major issue still facing Suqian was the lack of sufficient funding. In 2000, city revenues totaled 680 million yuan. Assets of the various health-care facilities totaled 200 million yuan, but debts totaled nearly 100 million yuan. Wages could not be paid in full; for every 100 yuan owed, workers were paid 70 yuan. Equipment was old and outdated, and many of the staff were poorly trained.[44]

---

[41] In January 2006, Qiu He became vice governor of Jiangsu, and in January 2008 he became party secretary of Kunming city in Yunnan province.

[42] Bao Yonghui and Xu Shousong, *Zhengdao*, pp. 114–117.

[43] Ibid., p. 112.

[44] Ibid., pp. 143–144. The hospital has since been rebuilt and is now a beautiful, new facility.

Faced with this depressing situation, starting in 2000, Qiu He oversaw the auctioning-off of 134 of the 135 clinics and hospitals in the city, including those in the three counties and two districts under its jurisdiction. A major controversy arose when the city auctioned off the best hospital in the city, People's Hospital, which had been founded nearly a century earlier as a missionary hospital. When the auction took place on July 10, 2003, the workers and staff gathered outside to protest. Their fears were justified; their salaries inevitably would be cut in the reorganized hospital, even though the hospital's finances would recover and the hospital would indeed prosper. The hospital was purchased that day by the Jinling Pharmacy Group (Jinling yaoye jituan), based in Nanjing, for 70 million yuan.[45]

Suqian's health reform occurred right in the middle of on-going debates in China about how to reform the health-care system. Simply put, there were those who favored government-led approaches and those who favored market-based approaches. In late 2004, opposition to market-oriented approaches to health care started to appear in internal speeches, and Suqian was often cited as a negative example.[46] In August 2005, the State Council Development Research Center issued a report that concluded that market-oriented reforms "violated the basic laws governing the development of medicine and health care."[47] In June 2006, Professor Li Ling, deputy director of Peking University's China Economic Research Center, published a report on her visits to Suqian. A well-known supporter of government-led health reforms,[48] Li concluded not unexpectedly in her report that "at present, Suqian city's problem with expensive medical care has not been resolved, the burden the common people bear for health care has become worse, and potential future health-care problems lead one to be concerned."[49]

---

[45] Ibid., p. 150.
[46] Ibid., pp. 135–136.
[47] Guowuyuan fazhan zhongxin ketizu, "Guowuyuan yanjiu jigou dui Zhongguo yiliao gaige de pingjia yu jianyi."
[48] Zhou Qiren, "Suqian 'maiguangshi yigai.'"
[49] "Wei shenma Zhongguo yigai bu hui chenggong?"

However, evidence cited in Li Ling's report and in other sources suggests that Qiu He's market-oriented reforms were remarkably successful in at least some respects. As suggested by the worker protests mentioned above, the privatization of Suqian's health care widened incomes. Doctors' incomes rose from about 2,000 yuan per month to 3,000–4,000 yuan per month (more if they were shareholders in the hospitals). But nurses and staff saw their incomes fall by about one-half, from more than 1,000 yuan per month to 500–600 yuan per month. However, the common people benefited. The costs of seeing a doctor and buying drugs declined. The average cost of a hospital stay declined slightly, from 2,223 yuan in 2000 to 2,158 yuan in 2006 and the cost of stays in township clinics declined from 562 yuan to 545 yuan.[50] Equipment was upgraded and the number of medical procedures offered increased.[51] In addition, medical care in Suqian became highly competitive. By 2005, there were over 400 health-care facilities of various sorts and pharmacies had sprouted up all over the city. Service attitudes improved, and even Li Ling admitted that "the degree of satisfaction of the common people increased markedly."[52]

Medical care obviously became a highly profitable business in Suqian. Investment returns reached 50 percent, meaning the cost of purchasing a health-care facility could be recouped within only two years. Costs were obviously tightly controlled and staff wages declined, but the number of people visiting clinics and hospitals increased. The high profits appear to be the result of the increase in the number of medical procedures that were performed.[53]

Education

Education in Suqian was in as bad shape as just about everything else in the city. Suqian spent 40 percent of its budget on education, but enrollment was low. Only 55 percent of preschoolers

[50] Bao Yonghui and Xu Shousong, *Zhengdao*, p. 161.
[51] "Wei shenma Zhongguo yigai bu hui chenggong?"
[52] Ibid.
[53] Ibid.

attended one of the city's 415 kindergartens, and only 48 percent of middle-school graduates went on to high school.[54]

Reform started in 2002 when the Suqian government decided to privatize early childhood and high-school education (compulsory education, grades 1–9, is paid for by the central government). One of the first schools to be sold off was the Sihong county kindergarten, the only kindergarten in the county that was up to provincial standards. The county's plan was for the school administration to purchase half of the assets of the school and for the teachers to purchase the other half. The principal would become the largest shareholder, investing 380,000 yuan, and the teachers would each invest about 20,000 yuan. Teachers protested strongly, bombarding the national and provincial media with letters describing what was going on. CCTV's "Focus Interview," again visiting Suqian, reported that teachers had no money and the government refused to invest in the school, leaving the school entirely dependent on tuition. However, parents objected and started withdrawing their children, further tightening the funding situation.[55]

Even more serious problems were encountered when the city moved to sell off Maling high school, which had been founded as Zhongwu Academy in 1822. In this case, the principal invested 200,000 yuan, the assistant principal 100,000 yuan, and the director of instruction 50,000 yuan. One teacher exploded in anger: "Yesterday we were colleagues and today we are their workers (*dagongzi*)! Is this a joke? How can a school with a 180-year history as a public school be simply sold off when somebody calls for it to be sold off? After it is sold, what is the status of the teachers? Do you work if they tell you to work, and if they don't call you to work, do you become a 'social person' (*shehui ren*) [i.e., unemployed]? After so many years of blood and sweat, is it all lost in a minute?"[56]

Implementation was done crudely, leading to teacher strikes and investigations by higher levels (which ultimately backed

---

[54] Bao Yonghui and Xu Shousong, *Zhengdao*, p. 167.
[55] Ibid., p. 169.
[56] Ibid., p. 165.

the Suqian authorities), and the results remain controversial to this day.

Political Reform

Qiu He is primarily known for his autocratic style and radical moves to bulldoze unwanted housing, to improve the investment environment, to task subordinates with soliciting outside investment, and to reduce the financial burdens facing local government. He built his reputation as a one-man whirlwind who would do whatever it took to implement his vision of reform. Thus, it comes as some surprise that he is also known for implementing political reforms in Suqian, though the likelihood of these reforms leading to democratic institutionalization is exceedingly small.

Qiu He started with what is called "public showings" (*gongshi*): making a public announcement that a cadre is being considered for an appointment and giving anyone who might know anything negative about the candidate – such as corrupt behavior – a chance to speak up. When Qiu He was still in Shuyang county, one of the cadres whom he had just appointed was found to be involved in corrupt activities. So thereafter, when an appointment was about to be made, Qiu He began notifying people through circulars, radio and television broadcasts, and newspapers. People had ten days to report any problems. Depending on the severity of the problem, the candidate could either be called in for a talk or be passed over completely.[57]

When Qiu He moved to Suqian, he extended the political reforms, starting in Suyu county, which was later made into a district under Suqian. In 2003 a 28-year-old college graduate by the name of Li Aihua was elected party secretary through a "public recommendation, public selection" (*gongtui gongxuan*) procedure. Li emerged from a group of 223 candidates nominated by party members, local cadres, and representatives of the masses in a process known as a "sea recommendation" (*haitui*, after the

[57] Ibid., pp. 209–212.

"sea election," *haixuan*, adopted in villages). Although the initial nominating process appears democratic, subsequent rounds that winnowed the field of candidates were conducted by local cadres who, as elsewhere, seem to have voted as an "electoral commission" (see Chapter 3). Li Aihua was young but he was clearly on the "fast track" for promotion. After receiving a master's degree from Nanjing University in public administration, he became a "selected student" (*xuantiaosheng*) of the provincial party committee (a system whereby a number of just-graduated students are selected to be placed in various positions for training). The provincial Organization Department first assigned him to a township in Siping county and then to Suqian city where he worked in the Construction Bureau and Personnel Bureau, reaching the rank of deputy department head (*fuchuzhang*). His election may have accelerated a promotion that would be coming sooner or later, but it hardly went against party arrangements and may actually have facilitated Qiu He's efforts to replace inefficient cadres.

Political Support

In 2001, Wen Jiabao, who was still vice premier, visited Suqian and found the peasants there very unhappy. He told of one woman who, not recognizing the vice premier, spent a long time complaining about her burdens. "The matter has become an obsession on my mind," Wen later said. "Each time I go to Jiangsu, I always wonder about the current situation in Suqian. Are those peasants happy now?"[58]

Even Hu Jintao seemed to have some doubts. When the general secretary visited Suqian in 2006, he asked detailed questions about the public showings of cadres and the public recommendation, public selection system, but gave no indication of his attitude.[59] According to another account, however, Hu had said,

---

[58] Wu Qingcai, "Premier Wen Jiabao's Stories of Visiting the Countryside on Two Occasions."

[59] Liu Binglu, "Qiu He Suqian shinian zhi lu."

"To select one person is a mechanism, to choose a leading group (*lingdao banzi*) is a system (*zhidu*)."[60] This comment seems to suggest that Qiu He was not thinking in sufficiently systematic terms to satisfy the general secretary.

Qiu He's most immediate and important support came from Li Yuanchao, then party secretary of Jiangsu, who in 2007 was elevated to head the Central Organization Department in Beijing. Li visited Suqian many times, "fully affirming" Qiu's education and health-care reforms during a 2005 visit.[61] The controversy surrounding Qiu He and his forceful reform measures attracted a lot of high-level attention – fifteen officials from China's central ministries, the Central Discipline Inspection Commission (CDIC), and the Central Organization Department visited Suqian. Among these visitors was Li Jinhua, then the state auditor general, who declared that "facts prove that Suqian's way of thinking about development is correct; its reforms are very forceful and effective."[62]

Conclusion

Both Maliu township and Suqian city were poor and isolated, though being poor and isolated in the western reaches of Chongqing is of an order of magnitude different from being poor in northern Jiangsu. Regardless, the political stories of the two places are very different. Without resources and denied the right to use force, Maliu township developed an approach that was remarkably participatory and democratic. Building on the "mass line" tradition of the CCP, leaders in Maliu township worked to regain the trust of villagers. Projects had to be approved by an overwhelming majority of those who would contribute to and benefit from them. Critically, cadres were denied the ability to benefit from public-works projects. Alas, as transfer payments came into Kai county, leaders in Maliu township again heeded

---

[60] "Qiu He: Yige zhengyi guanyuan de chengming qianhou."
[61] Liu Binglu, "Qiu He Suqian shinian zhi lu."
[62] Ibid.

their administrative leaders more than the local population. The eight-step work method was not altogether forgotten, but it was practiced less frequently. Money – and power – came from above. Efforts to make local cadres more constituency-oriented and to institutionalize a new and more democratic relationship with residents deteriorated.

Qiu He arrived in Shuyang county at a time when the provincial government was determined to develop the perpetually poor parts of northern Jiangsu. Whatever efforts Qiu He made to wring savings out of the local government by divesting health care and noncompulsory education and to increase local income through forced contributions and investments, it is apparent that there was a major infusion of funds from the provincial level, as evidenced by the construction of broad, though underutilized, streets.

More impressive than the infusion of funds, however, was the political support Qiu He received from higher levels. When Li Changping went to Jianli county in Hubei (see Chapter 1), his classmates and friends had warned him that he would have to protect the interests of local cadres. Qiu He, with strong backing from above, broke the back of local networks by prosecuting his predecessor, Huang Dengren. It quickly became apparent that no one could defy Qiu He. There is no question that Shuyang county and Suqian city developed very quickly, but it is equally apparent that Qiu He's high-handed approach could hardly create institutions. As one local official put it, "Qiu He went to extremes in doing things. He did not care about procedures – only about outcomes."[63] As another commentator said, Qiu He was "autocratic" and exemplified "rule by man" instead of rule by law. Rather than discussing policies and building a consensus around them, Qiu simply "used his power (not authority) to compel people."[64] Some supporters defended such arbitrary ways as necessary. As one blogger noted, Qiu He had asked,

---

[63] Zhang Yulu, "Qiu He: Zai falü yu zhengce zhi jian 'wudao,'" pp. 40–41.
[64] Chen Jian, "Zhuozhe gaige guanghuan de zhuanzhi he renzhi geng zhide jingti."

"Can't one use rule by man to promote rule by law? Can't one use non-democratic means to promote democracy?" The problem, this blogger wrote, was that between rule by man and rule by law there existed a large "gray area." It was necessary to have strong cadres like Qiu He to cross this gray area.[65]

Although the late legal specialist Cai Dingjian from the Chinese University of Politics and Law rejected such arguments, he praised Qiu He as a good person who did much for the common people, but "the tragedy of strongman politics is that good officials always want to do everything themselves, to change the fate of the people, and to become the savior of the people, and they don't let people grasp their own fates." Although Cai supported Qiu's promotion of democratic elections and his strict management of officials, he argued that the test of a good official is the degree to which he or she can contribute to the creation of institutions. In the end, Cai wrote, Qiu He was an "autocratic official with unlimited power" who lacked a sense of law and human rights.[66] An official like this can use his power for good – or evil. Most importantly, when he leaves his post, nothing is left behind.[67]

Qiu He is one of a number of "officials with personality" (*gexing guanyuan*) who have emerged in recent years. Such people display a boldness not common in China's normally conservative, consensus-driven party bureaucracy. It appears that such people emerge, in part, out of a desire to distinguish themselves; whether the motive is idealism or a desire to accumulate "political accomplishments" so they can be promoted, or some combination of the two, these high-powered officials are often appreciated by superiors because the latter can take credit for their reforms. To emerge as an official with personality, however, usually requires substantial political backing, something Qiu He had in abundance. The problem, of course, was that Qiu He's reforms could be sustained only as long as he held his position. After he left, much of the old system was restored.[68]

[65] Guo Songmin, "Qiu He de 'huise didai zhili moshi.'"
[66] Cai Dingjian, "Women xuyao zenyang de gaigejia?"
[67] Ibid.
[68] Lu Biao, "Zhengyi Qiu He."

Maliu township and Suqian city lay at opposite ends of the spectrum of reform possibilities in China. The experience in Maliu township suggests a path to reform that will make cadres substantially more responsive to residents, whereas Qiu He's efforts in Shuyang county and Suqian city reflect the strengths of China's hierarchical cadre system. With sufficient support and a strong enough personality it was possible to force through enormous changes within a short period of time. But sustaining such efforts, much less making government more responsive to the people, was difficult precisely because the reform depended on the strong-willed individual. Qiu He was certainly effective in utilizing the power that China's political system could bring to bear, but he was not interested in building the sort of institutions that could constrain cadre behavior and thus could tackle the serious problems of governance such as those described in Chapter 1.

3

Inner-Party Democracy

As China began to emerge from the trauma of the 1989 Tiananmen events, its leadership began to cast about for new frameworks in which to think about political reform. After all, the problems that had generated vigorous debate on political reform and had led the Thirteenth Party Congress in 1987 to adopt proposals for removing party groups from State Council ministries and to establish a civil service were still there. "Democracy" was still a good word, and it would have a continuing impact on the way intellectuals and practitioners thought about political reform. Added to the discourse, however, were new concerns about institution building. Increasingly, people began to speak of the Chinese Communist Party (CCP) as a "ruling party" (*zhizheng dang*); the implication was that the time had come to do away with the sort of politics associated with the CCP when it was a revolutionary party (*geming dang*): secretive, personalistic, divided by political struggles, arbitrary, and often hostile to societal interests. It was time to subject the party to accountability, to normalize its relations with society, and to select its leaders at various levels in a more democratic way according to agreed-upon procedures. The party needed to rebuild its legitimacy through its own institutionalization.[1]

---

[1] Many of these ideas are embedded in Jiang Zemin's speech on the eightieth anniversary of the founding of the CCP. See "Jiang Zemin zai qingzhu jiandang bashi zhounian dahuishang de jianghua."

What such ideas meant in practice was open to debate and experimentation. Most people assumed that some sort of democracy – socialist democracy, whatever precisely that meant – would be a part of the formula. The Fourteenth Party Congress in 1992 declared that the development of socialist democracy would ensure that "institutions and laws will not change with changes in the leadership or changes in the views or focus of attention of any leader."[2] At the Fifteenth Party Congress, meeting five years later and only months after Deng Xiaoping's death, Jiang Zemin announced that "without democracy there would be no socialism or socialist modernization" and he called for "grassroots organs of power" to "establish a sound system of democratic elections." This call for democracy was closely linked to the efforts to create a more sound legal system and stronger institutions. The work report of the Fifteenth Party Congress stressed "governing the country through law" (*yifa zhiguo*).[3]

As the CCP sought to build institutions – and to distinguish "socialist democracy" from "Western democracy" – it drew on a long, if not very successful, tradition of "inner-party democracy" (*dangnei minzhu*). As early as the Sixth Plenary Session of the Sixth Central Committee, held in October 1938, Mao Zedong had stated, "Expanding inner-party democracy should be seen as a necessary step in consolidating and developing the party."[4] In 1942, at the start of the Rectification Campaign, Liu Shaoqi, then back in Yanan from a stint as political commissar of the New Fourth Army, issued a long exposition on inner-party democracy in his "Report on the Revision of the Party Charter" (*Guanyu xiugai de zhangcheng de baogao*). The party charter that passed at the Seventh Party Congress in 1945 included for the first

---

[2] Jiang Zemin, "Accelerating the Reform, the Opening to the Outside World and the Drive for Modernization, so as to Achieve Greater Successes in Building Socialism with Chinese Characteristics."

[3] Jiang Zemin, "Hold High the Great Banner of Deng Xiaoping Theory for an All-Round Advancement of the Cause of Building Socialism with Chinese Characteristics to the Twenty-First Century."

[4] Zhonggong zhongyang zuzhibu dangjian yanjiusuo ketizu (Ed.), *Xinshiqi dangjian gongzuo redian nandian wenti diaocha baogao (4)*, p. 80.

time regulations on party members' rights and obligations, giving legal guarantees to the exercise of democratic rights.[5] These early efforts to develop some sort of inner-party democracy were soon overwhelmed by Mao's political campaigns, but they did leave a repository of ideas that would be resurrected during the reform era.

With Mao's death, the CCP could begin to restore the norms it had once adopted, at least in principle. As noted in the Introduction to this volume, the party adopted the decision on "Several Principles on Political Life in the Party" (*Guanyu dangnei zhengzhi shenghuo de ruogan zhunze*) in 1980, calling for developing inner-party democracy by allowing different opinions within the party.[6] By the late 1980s, political reform, including inner-party democracy, had become a major topic within the party, and the Thirteenth Party Congress, for the first time in party history, had more candidates than seats for election to the Central Committee. This arrangement resulted in the failure of Deng Liqun, the head of the Propaganda Department, who had been slated to sit on the Politburo, to be elected. The resulting controversy ended up exacerbating tensions within the party rather than developing any sort of democratic atmosphere.

The use of military force to silence protests in the spring of 1989 and the ongoing tensions among the leadership meant that there could be no political reform at the elite level for the foreseeable future. However, the passage of the Organic Law of the Villagers Committees for Trial Implementation in 1987 and its subsequent reaffirmation at the National Conference on the Construction of Village-Level Organizations in August 1990 – after contentious debate following the Tiananmen crackdown – meant that political reform efforts could shift to the local levels. Armed with Central Party Document No. 19 of 1990, the Ministry of Civil Affairs vigorously promoted village elections.[7] Legislation

---

[5] Ibid.
[6] "Guanyu dangnei zhengzhi shenghuo de ruogan zhunze," p. 47, passim.
[7] Lianjiang Li and Kevin J. O'Brien, "The Struggle over Village Elections," pp. 131–133.

followed with the adoption of the Provisional Regulations Governing Grassroots CCP Organizing Elections in 1990, and their formalization in January 1994 as the Regulations Governing CCP Organization of Local Elections.[8]

Some local officials had undertaken efforts to reform government in the 1980s. In Inner Mongolia, Zhang Chu had slashed the size of government in Zhuozi county from fifty officials to only nine and had privatized local industry. Zhang was quickly attacked and subsequently transferred back to Beijing where he maintained a low profile. Of course, Zhuozi county quickly restored the *status quo ante*. Before he left Zhuozi county, however, Zhang attracted the attention of another reformer, Lü Rizhou, who in 1984 took thirty cadres with him to Zhouzi to learn from Zhang Chu. Returning to Shanxi's Yuanping county, which had been designated the only experimental county in the province, Lü Rizhou undertook economic reform, making his county the wealthiest in the area. But Lü too soon came under attack and was transferred out of the county.[9] So China's experience with local political reform in the 1980s was spotty and ineffectual.

Despite the CCP's long and rather unsuccessful history of implementing inner-party democracy, there is reason to believe that the combination of leadership transition and the collapse of the Communist Party of the Soviet Union (CPSU) brought about a new and perhaps more sustained effort to think about inner-party democracy and institution building as the need to regularize relations within the party and between the party and society increased. After the tensions associated with the Tiananmen crisis subsided – along with the passing of many senior leaders – and as Jiang Zemin slowly accumulated power, the stage was set for the transition of power. To the extent that any power transition can be pinpointed, Jiang can be said to have consolidated his

---

[8] The latter regulation is included in Zhongyang jiwei fagui shi, zhongyang zuzhibu bangongting (Eds.), *Zhongguo gongchandang dangnei fagui xuanbian (1978–1996)*, pp. 247–254.
[9] Luo Ke, "'Gaigepai guanyuan' de Zhongguo mingyun."

power at the Fourth Plenary Session of the Fourteenth Central Committee in September 1994, which formally announced that power in the party had been transferred from the "second generation" (the Deng Xiaoping generation) to the "third generation" (that of Jiang Zemin).[10]

Not long after this leadership transition, the CCP issued the "Interim Regulations on the Selection and Appointment of Leading Cadres of the Party and State" (*Dangzheng lingdao ganbu xuanba renyong gongzuo zanxing tiaoli*).[11] These regulations, whose formulation had been overseen by Zeng Qinghong, Jiang's close confidant and head of the Central Organization Department, tried to open up the decision-making process for selecting cadres by requiring that it include elements of democratic recommendation, inspection, preparation, discussion, and decision. The entire process was supposed to be guided by a promotion committee and was to include extensive consultation with a wide range of officials and colleagues at different levels. The intent was to constrain the ability of the "number-one leader" (*yibashou*) to single-handedly select cadres for promotion, thereby limiting the ability of local leaders to build factions, engage in corruption, and abuse authority – all of which exacerbate principal–agent control and social-order problems.

These regulations, which were rather modest in their enforcement provisions, went against the informal but deeply rooted practices of personnel management that had evolved over the years. As laid out in Chapter 1, the number-one leader, usually in consultation with a few of his close colleagues, monopolized the decision-making process. This practice of highly concentrated authority exercised with a minimum of consultation had long been legitimized by the principle of "the party controls the cadres" (*dang guan ganbu*), which might be said to be the central principle guiding the organization and practice of the CCP. It is a principle that places control firmly in the hands of leaders at

---

[10] Joseph Fewsmith, *China since Tiananmen*, pp. 168–171.
[11] "Dangzheng lingdao ganbu xuanba renyong gongzuo zanxing tiaoli," pp. 398–410.

higher levels. For a lower-level cadre to receive his bonus and to have a chance at promotion, the most important thing to do is to please the party secretary at the next higher level.[12]

The Development of Inner-Party Democracy

As noted in Chapter 1, the two most important tasks on which cadres are evaluated are economic development and social stability. Thus, it is not surprising that in the 1980s and 1990s cadres routinely collected more taxes than central policy required; without revenue, they could not pursue investment-led growth strategies. However, collecting taxes and fees is always coercive and sometimes violent, particularly as peasants became more cognizant of the disparity between central policies and local actions.[13] Areas such as Sichuan, poor and overpopulated, were ripe for social confrontation, and, indeed, a major riot broke out in Renshou county in 1993.[14] Tensions were notably high in Bazhong city, Nanbu county, and Suining city, for example. What these places in Sichuan had in common was that they were all poor, isolated, and highly in debt, and they had a significant level of social tension. They were, in short, good places to experiment with inner-party democracy.

Social tensions increased after the 1994 tax reform, which centralized revenues and left the localities, or at least those without significant industry or not near cities where residents could find work, bereft of local revenue. It is no coincidence that the number of mass incidents began increasing rapidly during this period. Many of these incidents were triggered by local cadres pressing impoverished peasants to pay more taxes, similar to what occurred in Maliu township.

---

[12] Maria Edin, "State Capacity and Local Agent Control in China," pp. 35–52; Susan Whiting, "The Cadre Evaluation System at the Grass Roots," pp. 101–119; and Zhuang Guobo, *Lingdao ganbu zhengji pingjia de lilun yu shijian.*

[13] Kevin O'Brien and Lianjiang Li, *Rightful Resistance in Rural China.*

[14] Joseph Fewsmith, "Notes on the First Session of the Eighth National People's Congress," pp. 81–86.

With tax reform, local revenue sources declined, but cadres still needed to develop their local economies. So they had to resort to increasing extra-budgetary funds. For instance, Nanbu county wanted funds to build a power plant to fuel its economic growth. The plant would cost some 650 million yuan, but the plant was not listed on the state economic development plan, so there was no hope of receiving funds from higher levels. At the time, however, there was growing peasant resistance in the area, with peasants petitioning complaints about local cadres to higher levels. On different occasions peasants would gather in front of the county party offices and demand that certain township cadres be removed from office. In 1996, the people's congresses of some townships in Nanbu refused to accept four out of the fourteen cadres recommended by the county party committee. As Lai Hairong comments, "This was unprecedented."[15]

The pressures to deal with peasant unhappiness fell upon the shoulders of local cadres. In too many cases, cadres resorted to coercion to maintain "social stability," putting public security personnel on the front lines – something that the Public Security Bureaus complained about on a regular basis.[16] But using force often exacerbated the situation, and peasants responded by petitioning higher-level authorities. Higher-level authorities, particularly in Beijing, took it as a negative sign when petitioners landed on their doorsteps, and that was not good for the careers of local cadres. Indeed, under the "single vote veto" (*yipiao fou-jue*) system, cadres in areas where peasants petitioned higher-level authorities (or violated other policies, such as family planning, which was subject to the same system) could not receive bonuses or be considered for promotion. So, similar to the cadres in Maliu township, they often had to find ways to restore some level of trust with the local population.

Nevertheless, we cannot explain the development of inner-party democracy as something forced upon the party by outside

---

[15] Lai Hairong, *Zhongguo nongcun zhengzhi tizhi gaige*, p. 86.

[16] See, e.g., Fu Guibao and Xu Chenglun, "Tuoshan chuzhi renmin neibu mao-dun yinfa de qunti shijianxing shijian," pp. 55–58; and Hu Zujun, "Guanyu gong'an jiguan yufang he chuzhi quntixing shijian de sikao," pp. 14–18.

pressure. Bottom-up pressure was real and without it inner-party democracy would not have developed. But Lai Hairong makes it clear in his recent study that local reforms were generally initiated by county party secretaries, and *not one* of the township elections he studied in Sichuan, the province that pioneered township elections, took place because of pressures from below. As he puts it, "All cases were initiated by the party committee."[17]

So inner-party democracy was as much, indeed more, of a top-down strategy to deal with party legitimacy and competence as it was something brought about by local discontent. The 1995 regulations on the appointment and promotion of cadres had already set out procedures to expand the number of people involved in selecting cadres for promotion. Inner-party democracy built upon these regulations.

The combination of bottom-up pressures and top-down efforts to improve local governance led to experiments with ten semi-competitive elections in Bazhong city in northern Sichuan in 1995–1996, an area infamous for its social tensions. China's first semi-competitive election for township head took place in December 1998 in Nancheng township in Qingshen county of central Sichuan when leaders of Meishan prefecture were persuaded by the provincial Organization Department to undertake the experiment. It was a tightly controlled election, with no public campaigning and with roving ballot boxes (that could easily be stuffed). It also remained secret until 2001 and thus had very little influence.[18]

Nancheng's election was clearly a top-down affair, so social tensions were not a factor in its implementation, but they were important in Suining city where there were disturbances in Xinqiao and Baoshi townships in 1996. Two years later cadres in these two townships were forced to step down because of financial malfeasance.[19] It was at that time, in 1998, that Zhang

[17] Lai Hairong, *Zhongguo nongcun zhengzhi tizhi gaige*, p. 84.
[18] Lianjiang Li, "The Politics of Introducing Direct Township Elections in China," pp. 709–710.
[19] There was also a township under Shizhong district's purview in which a disgruntled head of the armed police, fearing the local party secretary was

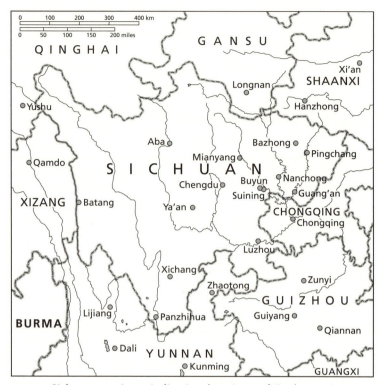

MAP 3. Sichuan province, indicating locations of Bazhong city, capital Chengdu, Pingchang county, Suining city, Buyun town, and Ya'an city

Jinming, from nearby Pengxi county, was appointed party secretary of Suining's Shizhong district. Zhang, who would soon become famous throughout the country for pioneering some of the boldest local reforms, was a forty-one-year-old woman with definite ideals. Fortunately for her, her ideas coincided with what the provincial Organization Department was thinking.

In the event, the chaos in Xinqiao and Baoshi forced her to think about democratic elections. As she explained: "Shortly after I became district party secretary, cadres in Xinqiao township

going to demote him, threw a hand grenade into the secretary's office. See Li Rong, "Zhang Jinming: Zhongguo jiceng minzhu shijian de tanluzhe."

collectively misused and stole the collective funds of the masses, and similarly cadres in Baoshi town misappropriated and stole public funds. The masses faced a crisis of trust in their cadres. It was just at this time that nine departments (*ju*) were selecting their deputy heads through open promotion, so we decided to select the town head of Baoshi through 'public recommendation and public selection' (*gongtui gongxuan*)."[20]

Thus in June 1998, the party committee of Shizhong district, which encompassed Xinqiao and Baoshi townships, set in motion a process that led to a more open election for township head. Anyone within the district who fit the criteria (including work experience and age) could register to run for office – sixty-nine people did so, of whom sixty-seven were deemed qualified (reflecting the Organization Bureau's decision to play as minimal a role as possible).[21] All candidates had to sit for a rigorous exam, a process that whittled the field down to six candidates. An "electoral group" (*gongxuantuan*) was set up to carry out a "democratic evaluation" (*minzhu ceping*), though this group was hardly democratic in its composition. It was made up of the three leading cadres (party secretary, village head, and accountant) of each village in Baoshi, department cadres in Baoshi township, leaders of Shizhong district, retired cadres, leading cadres of departments under Suining city, and delegates to the Baoshi People's Congress – in short, the local ruling elite. Nevertheless, the involvement of a group this large – over 200 people[22] – was a major departure from the practice of the party secretary simply conferring with a few close associates and deciding whom to appoint. In any event, this electoral group then interviewed the six remaining candidates and selected two of them to go on to the final round. The township people's congress then convened and voted, choosing a twenty-eight-year-old from the district Organization Bureau as the new town head.[23] The provincial

[20] Quoted in Lai Hairong, "Jingzhengxing xuanju zai Sichuansheng xiangzhen yi ji de fazhan," p. 66.
[21] Lianjiang Li, "The Politics of Introducing Direct Township Elections," p. 711.
[22] Lai Hairong, *Zhongguo nongcun zhengzhi tizhi gaige*, p. 62.
[23] Li Fan et al., *Chuangxin yu fazhan*, p. 116.

Organization Department was very happy with this successful experiment, and Zhang Jinming was invited to speak to a provincial meeting on organizational work.[24]

This election was quickly followed by another in Hengshan township, also in Shizhong district of Suining. The procedure was similar to that in Baoshi, but the electoral group was even larger – some 700 people. Again, an examination whittled down the original field of seventy-six to just six candidates, who were then interviewed by the electoral group. This time the electoral group chose just one candidate as the official candidate, and the people's congress then unanimously ratified its choice.[25]

Shortly thereafter, the first open party elections, what would soon be called "public recommendation and direct election" (*gongtui zhixuan*) took place in Lianhua and Dongchan townships. Under this system, all party members in a given location voted not only for the party committee, but also for party secretary.[26]

Sichuan had correctly judged the political atmosphere. The Third Plenary Session of the Fifteenth Central Committee, meeting in Beijing in October 1998, declared that in order to realize coordinated development of rural society and to preserve social stability, it was necessary to "strengthen the construction of rural grassroots democracy and the legal system." It went on to say that rural democracy was a "great creation" (*weida chuangzao*) of the Chinese peasants "under the leadership of the Chinese Communist Party."[27]

The Buyun Election

Feeling the wind at its back, the Suining city party committee reviewed its own experiences with limited electoral competition and decided to go further and implement direct elections. Having

---

[24] Lianjiang Li, "The Politics of Introducing Direct Township Elections," p. 711.
[25] Li Fan et al., *Chuangxin yu fazhan*, pp. 116–117.
[26] Ibid., p. 117.
[27] "Zhonggong zhongyang guanyu nongye he nongcun gongzuo ruogan zhongda wenti de jueding," 1.572.

made such a determination, the party committee looked for an appropriate place to hold this experiment. It had to be a place where the population was not too large, where the party organization did not have deep rifts, which did not have major problems with clan organizations and rivalries, and which was rather remote – because it would inevitably attract a lot of attention. After comparing the various townships under Shizhong district, the party committee settled on Buyun township, a remote area of only 16,000 people (4,000 of whom were working elsewhere and would not take part in the election) that was some thirty-five miles from the closest city.[28]

The Buyun election was different from previous elections in many ways. Prior to Buyun, all elections were indeed "inner party" – they were restricted to party members, and, in the case of "public recommendation and public selection," they were limited to party leaders in different posts. The Buyun election, as well as many to follow, would include nonparty people in the electoral process, though none so extensively as the election in Buyun. Nevertheless, Buyun and other areas that allowed nonparty people to take part are included in Chinese discussions of inner-party democracy because the process is quite clearly under the supervision of the CCP. Including elections that involve nonparty people under the rubric of "inner-party democracy" is quite consistent with usage of the term in official documents. For instance, Hu Jintao told delegates to the Seventeenth Party Congress, "We should spread the practice in which candidates for leading positions in grassroots party organizations are recommended by both party members and the public in an open manner...."[29]

In Buyun not only would all township residents be permitted to vote, but anyone twenty-five years or older, with a high-school education, who could collect thirty signatures on a

---

[28] Li Fan et al., *Chuangxin yu fazhan*, pp. 119–120. The story of the Buyun election has been told in several places. See Tony Saich and Xuedong Yang, "Innovation in China's Local Governance," pp. 185–208; and Lianjiang Li, "The Politics of Introducing Direct Township Elections," pp. 704–723.

[29] Hu Jintao, "Gaoju Zhongguo tese shehuizhuyi weida qizhi duoqu qianmian jianshe xiaokang shehui xin shengli er fendou."

nominating petition, could stand for election. The only restric-
tion was the posting of a twenty-yuan registration fee as a token
of seriousness.[30] Moreover, voters would be restricted to those in
Buyun; this requirement meant that it would be truly a local election. Cadres from higher levels would not be able to vote as they
were allowed in the more limited "public recommendation, public selection" model that had been adopted in Baoshi and other
townships. However, the greatest change was that it was decided
that the election would stand by itself, which is to say that the
people's congress would only ratify the election results, not vote
on the candidates. Whoever won the popular election would be
the winner.[31] This was obviously not "inner-party democracy"
but rather an open election for township head (the government
side of the leadership).

Candidates for election were nominated through two processes. On the one hand, the party organization nominated Tan
Xiaoqiu. Tan was a college-educated former soldier who had
served as deputy head of Buyun township before being transferred to Baima township (also under Shizhong district). The
party organization had already decided to transfer him back to
Buyun as township head before the idea of a direct election had
come up. Now that there would be an election, Tan would have
to face off against two candidates nominated through a public
process.

Altogether fifteen candidates registered as public candidates
in this election – four middle- and elementary-school teachers,
five township cadres, three entrepreneurs, two village cadres,
and one villager who had been working outside Buyun but who
returned to compete in the election. The job of winnowing this
field down to two formal candidates fell to the Conference of
Electoral Districts (Xuanqu lianxi huiyi), which was composed
of 163 people drawn from village cadres, regular villagers, the
presidium of the township people's congress, production team
leaders, and leaders from the township party and government.

---

[30] Li Fan et al., *Chuangxin yu fazhan*, p. 122.
[31] Ibid., p. 125.

Each of the fifteen candidates gave a twenty-minute talk and answered questions, and then the electoral conference voted. The two top vote-getters were Zhou Xingyi, a middle-school teacher in Buyun, and Cai Ronghui, the village head from Yandongzi village. The organizers had carefully decided to have two publicly chosen candidates so that the ensuing election would not appear to pit a party-backed candidate against a non-party-backed candidate.[32]

There were ten villages and one neighborhood committee in Buyun township; the three candidates spoke to campaign rallies in each of these areas, as well as on two occasions in public places in the center of the township. Each candidate had some advantages. Zhou was well-spoken and had received the most votes in the preliminary election, but he also had a tendency to exaggerate, so when people asked him specific questions he could not respond adequately and his popularity faded. Cai was from Buyun and had many years' experience as a village head, but he was not familiar with issues outside his village. Tan was not from Buyun, and so at first was regarded as an "outsider." But he was better educated, had seen more of China while serving in the army, and had served as a deputy township head in both Buyun and Baima. During the course of thirteen campaign rallies, Tan's strengths emerged as the other candidates' limitations became evident. When the voters went to the polls on December 31 – marking their ballots in secret in separate rooms – Tan emerged as the winner, with 3,130 votes, 50.19 percent of the votes cast.[33] There were, however, some voting irregularities that caused controversies and might have been enough to lift Tan above the 50 percent mark, ensuring that there would not have to be a runoff (which would have extended the election process).[34]

Despite the township's remoteness, Buyun's election quickly hit both the foreign and Chinese media, becoming a *cause célèbre*. Reformers hoped to build on it to promote democracy, whereas

---

[32] Ibid., pp. 132–134.
[33] Ibid., pp. 135–146.
[34] Lianjiang Li, "The Politics of Introducing Direct Township Elections," p. 716.

conservatives hoped to squelch it. Something of a compromise was reached. The *Legal Daily* denounced the Buyun election as illegal and in violation of the Constitution, but the commentary focused on the fact that direct elections bypassed the local people's congress, which by law should elect the township head, rather than rejecting the idea of inner-party (or even wider) elections altogether.[35] Suggesting deep ambivalence in Beijing, the authorities allowed the election results to stand (a decision no doubt made easier by the fact that the candidate favored by the party had won the election).[36]

Zhang Jinming also received critical support from the leadership of Sichuan province. A month after the election, and after the publication of the above-noted article in *Legal Daily*, a provincial department sent out a notice criticizing the Buyun election for violating the Constitution. Oddly, this notification had no signature or departmental heading. Shortly thereafter, however, someone on the Sichuan provincial party committee declared that the innovative spirit of the Buyun election was to be treasured, thereby saving Zhang's career and preserving the tolerant attitude toward local experimentation in the province.[37] There is no reason to doubt Zhang's idealist motives in launching the Buyun election, but it is also apparent that local issues could not be separated from higher-level issues. Zhang was not bucking the system but trying to innovate within a system that still was not sure which way it wanted to go.

By the time the three-year term limit for Buyun's township head was up, the atmosphere was quite different from what it had been in 1998. Zhang Jinming, who had promoted the election in 1998, was transferred to the position of deputy party secretary of Suining city in 2000, and her replacement was not enthusiastic about holding another election. Zhang, however, was still able to use her influence, and at the last minute Buyun

---

[35] Zha Qingjiu, "Minzhu buneng chaoyue falü."

[36] Vivian Pik-Kwan Chan, "Beijing Indicates Recognition of Landmark Township Election," p. 9.

[37] Li Rong, "Zhang Jinming: Zhongguo jiceng minzhu shijian de tanluzhe."

authorities decided to go ahead with another election. But the atmosphere was affected by the fact that Tan Xiaoqiu, who had decided to run for reelection, would be able to use the advantages of incumbency. These advantages were readily apparent when it was decided that the electoral conference would pick the two final candidates and not two candidates to pit against a party-backed candidate as in the previous election. The electoral conference was again composed of cadres from throughout the district, all of whom knew and many of whom worked for Tan. Thus it is not surprising that the electoral conference eliminated the person who appeared to pose the greatest competition to Tan. In his place they chose a cadre from the Land Management Bureau, which meant that he was Tan's direct subordinate. This situation was obviously awkward at best, and the candidate remained nearly silent during several campaign events, the number of which was cut in half due to lack of interest.[38] Nevertheless, Tan had offended some voters and the election still turned out to be close – Tan won by only a two-percentage-point margin.[39] Staying within the law, the local people's congress quickly held an official vote, which confirmed the results of the direct election, thus making the election legal.[40]

Ironically, it was after this election in 2003 that Buyun was recognized by the China Center for Government Innovations for its work on direct elections.[41] Perhaps even more ironically, shortly after the second Buyun election, Zhang Jinming was transferred out of Suining to Ya'an city, southwest of Chengdu (the capital of Sichuan), where she would head the Organization Bureau, a move that affirmed Zhang's work in Suining (after obvious controversy) and would pave the way for future reforms in Ya'an, but it also marked the end of reform in Buyun. Indeed, with Zhang's departure, reforms in Suining took a step backward. Whereas in 1998 three township party secretaries and two

---

[38] Lai Hairong, "Jingzhengxing xuanju zai Sichuan sheng xiangzhen yiji de fazhan," p. 60.
[39] Ann Florini, Hairong Lai, and Yeling Tan, *China Experiments*, ch. 3.
[40] Yi Hongwei, "Sichuan jiceng zhenggai ciqi bifu," p. 24.
[41] "Direct Election of the Township Leader."

township heads had been selected in Suining through the public recommendation and public election method (itself not very open), in 2001, apart from Buyun, the other townships selected only deputy heads through a competitive process.[42] The process in Suining endorsed a pattern that has largely been followed in Sichuan: Strong leaders promote reforms, but these reforms generally wither after these leaders move on.

Ya'an City

In 2001, before Zhang Jinming arrived in Ya'an, leading cadres had fared poorly in village and township elections. Under the leadership of the local Organization Bureau, Ya'an had adopted the public recommendation and public selection system to choose party leaders and "sea elections" (*haixuan*), a system of open nomination, to choose village heads. There are 1,110 villages under 174 townships in Ya'an, and in the 2001 election cycle, 64 leading township cadres, 181 village party secretaries, and 215 village heads lost their positions.[43] The younger cadres who took up leading positions in the villages and townships generally supported reform, so the atmosphere was favorable when Zhang Jinming was transferred to Ya'an.

Zhang Jinming's key reform in Ya'an was implementation of direct elections for party representatives. In recent years China has been promoting the standing representative system (*changrenzhi*) reform for representatives to party congresses. In the past, party congresses were convened every five years for the sole purpose of selecting the party committee at that level (at the quinquennial party congresses in Beijing, the party representatives select the Central Committee). Once the party congress ended, the representatives returned home and their status as representatives ended (of course, many of these representatives were

---

[42] Lai Hairong, "Jingzhengxing xuanju zai Sichuan sheng xiangzhen yiji de fazhan," p. 61.

[43] Xiang Guolan, "Tuijin dangnei minzhu de zhidu chuangxin," p. 176.

leading cadres in their localities and they retained those jobs). The idea of the standing representative system is that after the congress, representatives would retain their status, meet in formal session once a year to hear the party committee's work report, and serve as a liaison between ordinary party members and the party committee. Their status as representatives would be retained for their entire five-year term.

Zhang Jinming addressed the issue of how the representatives were to be selected. Traditionally, representatives had been appointed, either by higher-level leaders or by the leaders of various work units. That system obviously left ordinary party members out of consideration and kept the leadership isolated from both party members and the broader society. Starting in 2002, Zhang Jinming introduced direct elections for party representatives in two districts of Ya'an – the more urban Yucheng district and the more rural Rongjing county. According to the regulations, all those wanting to run as party representatives had to register in person; their names were listed on the ballot in stroke order; and voting was by secret ballot. Representatives were also from specific voting districts; if a representative could not fulfill his or her responsibilities for any reason, such as relocating from the area for work, the district, not a higher-level body, would select a replacement, thus reinforcing the idea that the representative represented a district.[44]

This experiment certainly attained one of its goals: the increased involvement of party members. In Yucheng district, 1,380 people – 12 percent of all party members in the district – competed for 325 positions. Of these candidates, 764 were self-nominated, 376 were nominated by others through petitions, and 240 were nominated by party units. In Rongjing county, 736 were nominated, constituting 13 percent of all party members in the county and over four times as many candidates as there were positions. Unlike in Yucheng district where all

---

[44] Sheng Ruowei, "Sichuan Ya'an shi dangdaihui changrenzhi shidian diaocha."

eighty-two electoral districts carried out direct elections, only four of the thirty-two electoral districts in Rongjing county held direct elections.[45]

One problem with the standing representative system as it was implemented in Ya'an and elsewhere is that the proportion of leading cadres among party representatives hovers around 60 to 70 percent. This, of course, ensures that the party representatives will not become too independent, but at the same time it undercuts the purpose of the system, namely to better supervise the exercise of authority. It also undermines the ability of the party representatives to develop expertise; by comparison, the people's congresses at various levels have greater, though still not great, specialization.

The standing representative system is intended to change the relationship between the standing committee, the whole committee, and the party representatives, giving the latter greater authority to supervise the former two. But how much authority? For instance, should party representatives have the authority to approve the appointment and removal of cadres? If they had this authority, the party representatives would become quite powerful, but ultimately the authority of any such body is limited by its position in the hierarchical party structure – all party members know that lower levels must submit to higher levels.[46] Perhaps the flaws in the system were simply too great; in any event, after Zhang Jinming was transferred out of Ya'an, the standing representative system was quietly abandoned.[47]

Zhang Jinming not only introduced a more democratic element in the selection of party representatives but also experimented with a "consultative" electoral mechanism for selection of township cadres. After Zhang was promoted to the position of deputy party secretary of Ya'an, she introduced elections in four small townships in 2006. Rather than allowing direct elections as she had in Buyun, Zhang organized advisory elections – the

---

[45] Xiang Guolan, "Tuijin dangnei minzhu de zhidu chuangxin," pp. 178–179.
[46] Li Ling, "Sichuan dang dahui changrenzhi shidian dianyan de sikao."
[47] Luo Ke, "'Gaigepai guanyuan' de Zhongguo mingyun."

voters cast ballots for all candidates standing for leading positions in these townships, but their votes were not decisive. On the contrary, this popularity contest was only one factor that the party organization took into consideration when appointing township leaders. As Thøgersen, Elklit, and Dong point out, the election results differed significantly from the positions assigned to the various cadres, though they did eliminate one incumbent deputy party secretary and two incumbent deputy mayors who did not make it to the top ten in their electoral contests.[48] Although this extension of the public recommendation and selection process was widely welcomed among reformers, conservatives criticized it for "weakening the leadership of the party." Sheng Huaren, then vice chairman of the National People's Congress (NPC) Standing Committee, complained in his comments in an article published in the party's theoretical journal, *Seeking Truth*: In the last two elections "individual localities" elected township heads directly, but this practice "did not conform to the provisions of the Constitution," and townships should avoid a "recurrence" of such practices.[49] It is no wonder that the number of experiments like that in Ya'an declined.

Li Zhongbin and Xindu

Xindu is a district on the outskirts of Chengdu, the provincial capital, and is unique for being the only district in Chengdu to experiment with electoral reform. Although many places in Sichuan have experimented with semi-competitive elections, they are almost all in poor and remote places: Suining, Nanpu, Ya'an, and Bazhong. Such places are more subject to the sort of social tensions that emerge when cadres attempt to extract wealth for economic development and, perhaps, personal betterment. Wealthier places, such as Chengdu, have more resources, so the

---

[48] Stig Thøgersen, Jorgen Elklit, and Dong Lisheng, "Consultative Elections of Chinese Township Leaders," pp. 67–89.

[49] Sheng Huaren, "Yifa zuohao xianxiang liangji renda huanjie xuanju gongzuo."

tensions between cadres and citizens usually are not quite so direct.

Xindu began its experiment with inner-party democracy in late 2003. The decision to undertake such an experiment came about when Li Zhongbin, the newly appointed party secretary of Xindu district, went to Beijing to meet Li Chuncheng, the Chengdu party secretary, who was then studying at the Central Party School. The two men decided that they should try out a new form of inner-party democracy, which they called "public recommendation and direct election" (*gongtui zhixuan*). The opportunity to do so came in the fall of 2003 when the party secretary of Mulan township was transferred to a new post, thereby leaving a vacancy.[50]

In the case of Xindu, a leading group to oversee the public recommendation and direct election in Mulan township was set up in November 2003. Li Zhongbin served as the head of this group, and the deputy party secretary and head of the Organization Bureau served as deputy heads. After many discussions, the Xindu district Organization Bureau decided on the "Implementing Methods for the Public Recommendation and Direct Election of the Mulan Township Party Secretary." According to these regulations there would be six steps, starting with publicizing the vacancy, going through the registration, inspection of candidates, understanding of local circumstances, convening of an open recommendation meeting, and direct election by party members. Altogether twenty people registered for the election, only eleven of whom were deemed qualified.

On December 4, a recommendation meeting was convened at the local middle school. The electoral conference in Xindu, like those in Suining, was composed of the leading party cadres of the district, village party secretaries and village heads, representatives of enterprises, township party delegates, delegates to the township people's congress, and members of the township Chinese People's Political Consultative Conference (CPPCC) and democratic parties (obviously, there was overlap among the leading

---

[50] Wang Yongbing, *Dangnei minzhu zhidu chuangxin yu lujing xuanze*, p. 54.

cadres in these various groups) – some 244 people in all. After listening to introductory speeches by the eleven candidates, the electoral conference voted, choosing Liu Gangyi and Li Yong as the two official candidates. On December 7 a meeting of all party members in the district was held; 639 people showed up for this vote. Liu Gangyi garnered 480 votes, and Li Yong received only 158 votes. Li Yong was the candidate favored by the district party committee, but Liu Gangyi, who had served as township head and deputy party secretary in Mulan township, was better known to local party members and thus won the election. No doubt, the fact that only one day was allowed for the candidates to understand local circumstances had favored the local candidate.[51] This experiment was subsequently expanded to all eleven townships in Xindu district.

One should not think of this as a free-ranging election. Not only was a leading group established to oversee it, but under this group there were several sections to oversee different aspects of the election: organization, supervision, propaganda, health, and meetings. Each section was headed by a responsible person and had a detailed work plan. Xindu was willing to innovate, but it was not willing to run the risk of the elections careening out of control. And they did not. After all, the election results suggest that the two people most favored by the local party organization became the finalists. So even though this experiment generated considerable competition – on average, each of the eleven townships holding elections had seven candidates – the results were well within the expectations of the local party committees. Thus, Xindu's innovation should be understood as a limited effort to promote well-vetted candidates rather than as a move toward popular democracy. But even this very limited opening favored local candidates over those promoted by the district party committee, suggesting that successful candidates would have to be more constituency-oriented than creatures of the supervising party organization. This trend is not necessarily

[51] Ibid., p. 54.

good, as it seems to solidify control by the local party elite over the local population.

A unique feature of the Xindu experiment is that the elected party secretary would then name members of his "cabinet," that is, other members of the party standing committee. The purpose of this innovation was that the party standing committee would be more "unified" and better able to fulfill the wishes of the party secretary – a measure that speaks to the reality of friction and conflict within local party standing committees. Of course, in giving the local party secretary such a free hand in selecting his associates, Xindu took on the single most troublesome aspect of the hierarchical control system – the over-concentration of authority in the hands of the local party secretary – and made it even worse. Indeed, if the case of Mulan township is any indication, inner-party democracy exacerbates principal–agent problems.[52]

Pingchang County

Pingchang is a large agricultural county tucked in the northeast corner of Sichuan province, one of three counties under the administration of Bazhong city. Poor and rugged, it was a part of the old Sichuan-Shaanxi revolutionary base area. As of 2005, it had a population of 970,000, 83 percent of whom were involved in agriculture. Nearly one-quarter of the population – some 192,318 people – lived below the poverty line of 930 yuan per year, and of these, 110,021 people lived below the absolute poverty line of 655 yuan per year.[53] The cost of medical care was one reason for the poverty. Over 40 percent of the poor had become impoverished because of medical costs.[54] In 2002, the county was listed as a key area for state antipoverty work.

Like many rural counties, Pingchang was administratively bloated and consequently it was constantly in debt. Originally the county had ten work committees (*gongwei*), thirteen offices

---

[52] Ibid., p. 57.
[53] Li Jiajie, "'Gongtui zhixuan' yu 'deng'e xuanju' bijiao,'" p. 107.
[54] Ibid., p. 109.

(*banshichu*), sixty-one towns and townships, and 504 villages. Many of these towns and townships were small and underpopulated, leading to inefficient government. Eight towns and townships were so small they did not even have periodic markets, a regular feature of rural life, and thirty-nine towns and townships had populations of under 15,000.[55]

Redistricting eliminated all ten work committees and thirteen offices. It reduced the number of towns and townships to twenty-seven, and the number of village party committees from 504 to 461. At the same time, the cutting of 362 organs eliminated 2,506 jobs, and the number of leadership posts in the towns and townships fell from 473 to 243. The total number of people working in the towns and townships fell from 1,111 to 880, a reduction of 21 percent, and the number of people working in service organizations fell from 1,951 to 987, a reduction of 49.4 percent. In addition, 231 people were "separated" (*fenliu*) from town and township government organs, and another 964 people were separated from service organizations. In addition, 2,760 temporary workers were laid off (*qingtui*). Altogether, government restructuring eliminated the jobs of 68 township leaders (*yibashou*), 232 deputy township leaders, and over 3,000 others.[56] One can imagine the resistance this effort encountered.

The number of people who worked in government and service organizations and as temporary workers reflected very real social pressures to provide jobs in a poor area. Bloated government, however, was expensive, as were the projects that were undertaken. As a result, local governments were in debt: The average debt of each town or township was over 90 million yuan, but some had accumulated debts of over 200 million yuan.[57] Many of these debts were owed to local residents; indeed, some 150,000 local residents were owed money by the local townships. Local cadres were actually assigned to try to find people who would

[55] Zhou Hongyun, "Sichuansheng Pingchangxian xiangzhen gaige qingkuang jiqi sikao," p. 4.
[56] Ibid.
[57] Ibid., p. 25.

lend money to the government. The poverty of the local governments and the likelihood that the debts would not be paid off
led to violent confrontations. Some offices of local towns and
townships were smashed, and local leaders had to fear for their
safety. However, debt-holders worried that if redistricting and
political reform were to be carried out, thereby eliminating some
towns and townships, the debts would be written off and never
repaid.[58]

A difficult situation was made intolerable when the state eliminated the agricultural tax and miscellaneous fees. A boon to
peasants, it hit townships across rural China hard. In Pingchang,
total town and township income fell from 140 million yuan to
only 30 million yuan, resulting in a severe fiscal crisis.[59]

The fiscal crisis was certainly the main reason that Pingchang
undertook extensive reforms, but there were other important reasons as well. With the introduction of village-level democracy,
village heads were elected by the people, giving them greater
standing with the villagers than the party secretaries who were
appointed. Moreover, with the marketization of the economy, the
local party organization could not do much to help the peasants
(recall that this is a poor rural county, so there are few collective
funds), and the peasants simply did not pay much attention to
the local cadres. To the extent that peasants and cadres inter-
acted, it was apparently an unpleasant interaction. No figures
are available about the number of rural protests or petitions in
this area, but there are many references to the tense relations
between cadres and peasants. Perhaps one-third of town and
township budgets were spent on entertainment costs,[60] something that would easily anger the local population.

The problem in Pingchang was not only one of governance
but also one of general paralysis of the local party organization.
There were 12,838 party members in the county who had no

[58] Li Jiajie, "'Gongtui zhixuan' yu 'deng'e xuanju' bijiao," p. 112.
[59] Zhou Hongyun, "Sichuansheng Pingchangxian xiangzhen gaige qingkuang
jiqi sikao," p. 25.
[60] Ibid.

party or government positions. For them, there was little point in becoming party members. As one old party member put it, "In the past, when we held the receipt for paying our party dues in our hands, we felt honored and proud. But now we feel it is a burden and a nuisance." So collecting party dues was a central problem.[61] In addition, the corruption of local party organizations alienated party members. It was critical, party secretary Liu Qianxiang thought, to reaffirm the position of party members in the party organization and to respect their decisions. Because the party system had always emphasized loyalty to superiors rather than to the people it was supposed to serve and because the economic reality was such that most peasants could ignore their party secretary, noncadre party members, along with nonparty people, criticized the way the party tried to exercise leadership and simply doubted the legitimacy of the party.[62] So the problem was not only a matter of improving relations between cadres and peasants but also a matter of rebuilding the legitimacy of the party among party members.

Bazhong municipality and Pingchang county each had a history of reform. As early as 1995–1996, there had been ten public recommendation, public selection elections in townships in Bazhong, making it the first place in China to experiment with inner-party democracy. In 2001 Lingshan township in Pingchang county carried out the country's first "public recommendation and direct election" for party secretary. The newsweekly *Oriental Outlook* called this "the first experiment with public recommendation and direct election in the history of the CCP."[63]

In July 2002, the Bazhong party committee transferred Liu Qianxiang to Pingchang county as party secretary. In October Liu decided that towns and townships in the county should continue the public recommendation and direct election system, and accordingly he decided that cadre positions should not

---

[61] Quoted in Liu Qianxiang, "Sichuansheng Pingchangxian gongtui zhixuan xiangzhen dangwei lingdao banzi chenshu baogao," p. 38.

[62] Ibid., p. 39.

[63] Zhou Hongyun, "Sichuansheng Pingchangxian xiangzhen gaige qingkuang jiqi sikao," p. 25.

be guaranteed – they should be promoted or demoted according to their capabilities (traditionally, cadres are almost never demoted). Readjusting administrative boundaries would test this determination.[64] The decision to implement inner-party democracy was closely related to the redistricting. With that many high-level jobs being lost, it was important to maintain the appearance of fairness. As Liu was thinking about these issues, he was encouraged by the declaration of the Sixteenth Party Congress in November that "inner-party democracy is the life of the party."[65]

Final encouragement came a year later, in December 2003, when Politburo member Zeng Qinghong and head of the Central Organization Department He Guoqiang listened to reports on the Lingshan experiment at a meeting in Chengdu. They "fully affirmed" this form of inner-party democracy and urged further explorations.[66] It was right after this meeting that Pingchang drew up a document on implementing public recommendation and public election to select leaders in one-third of the towns and townships in the county.[67]

Immediately following issuance of this document, candidates had fifteen days to register. The candidates had to have been CCP members for at least two years, to have worked for at least three years, and to be forty-five years of age or less. Candidates for township party secretary had to be at the deputy department rank (*fukeji*) (township party secretaries are department-level cadres). The county party committee reviewed the credentials of each candidate.[68]

First, there was a meeting of all party members in a given township. Nonparty members were allowed to participate in this process, again extending the definition of "inner-party

---

[64] Li Jiajie, "'Gongtui zhixuan' yu 'deng'e xuanju' bijiao," p. 113.

[65] Jiang Zemin, "Quanmian jianshe xiaokang shehui, kaichuang Zhongguo tese shehuizhuyi shiye xin jumian," p. 39.

[66] Liu Qianxiang, "Nongcun shehui zouxiang minzhu zhili de lujing xuanze," p. 45.

[67] "Zhonggong Pingchang xianwei guanyu zai xiangzhen huanjie zhong kaizhan gongtui zhixuan dangwei lingdao banzi shidian de shishi yijian," pp. 303–308. The decision was issued on December 25, 2003.

[68] Ibid., p. 306.

democracy," although their number could not exceed 30 percent of the participants. Altogether 726 nonparty members and 2,901 party members took part in these nine township meetings. At the meetings, the candidates each presented his or her views and responded to questions. Finalists were then chosen by secret ballot. Two candidates were chosen for the position of party secretary; one more candidate was chosen for the position of deputy party secretary than there were positions (the number of deputy party secretaries varies depending on the size of the township); and one more candidate was chosen than the number permitted for members of the party committee.[69]

Voting then took place in three rounds. A meeting of all party members (this time excluding nonparty members) voted first for the party secretary. The loser in this round of voting was then eligible to run for deputy party secretary, and the losers in this second round could then run for party committee. By voting from the top down, the Pingchang method avoided the "all or nothing" quality of the elections in Xindu. The separate elections for party secretary, deputy party secretaries, and party committee members also avoided the over-concentration of power that was inherent in the Xindu model.

The Pingchang reforms were widely regarded as very successful. They represented the most extensive experiment to date with the public recommendation and direct election system. In 2006, these reforms were recognized by the China Center for Government Innovations, which awarded Pingchang county one of its ten biannual awards for local innovation. The following year, the China Center for Comparative Politics and Economics published an important book touting the experiment,[70] and the experiment was reported extensively in the Chinese press.

Alas, the reforms did not last long. Although Liu Qianxiang faced real difficulties in Pingchang, he had his own ambitions a strong personality. The pressures on him were the same as they

---

[69] Liu Qianxiang, "Sichuansheng Pingchangxian gongtui zhixuan xiangzhen dangwei lingdao banzi chenshu baogao," p. 309.

[70] Wang Changjiang, Zhou Hongyun, and Wang Yongbing (Eds.), *Dangnei minzhu zhidu chuangxin.*

were on other party secretaries in Sichuan and elsewhere: Promote economic development and maintain social stability. Social stability had been a real problem at the time of the public recommendation and direct election of the Lingshan township party secretary in 2001. By 2004, the biggest problem in Pingchang was the fiscal crisis. As a result, there was no way to develop the local economy. Redistricting greatly reduced administrative expenses, and implementing political reform gave some assurance that those who took up the remaining posts had not been selected through personal favoritism. Unable to pursue economic development, Liu chose to make his mark by pursuing political reform, much like Zhang Jinming in Suining and Ya'an, which is not to say that his reforms had not been approved by higher levels – they had been. But it nevertheless took a strong person to force through these reforms in a top-down manner.

By 2006, however, the agricultural taxes and miscellaneous fees had been eliminated and cadres began to resent the political reforms. In 2005 Li Zhongbin, the party secretary who had led the reforms in Xindu, was transferred to Bazhong municipality. Although a strong reformer himself, he soon clashed with Liu Qianxiang. At the same time, cadres in Pingchang, many of whose jobs had been eliminated by the redistricting, began expressing resentment. The atmosphere also changed at the provincial level. In 2008, the provincial party committee endorsed the more conservative model of public recommendation, public selection (*gongtui gongxuan*) rather than Liu Qianxiang's model of public recommendation and direct election (*gongtui zhixuan*). Whereas Liu's reforms previously had been supported by higher levels, he was now accused of "weakening the leadership of the party" and asked to write a self-criticism. He refused. Thereafter, he was repeatedly investigated for corruption, but the investigations found nothing. Nevertheless, in April 2008 he was forced to leave Pingchang and take up another post.[71]

---

[71] Gao Xinjun, "Pingchangxian dangnei minzhu gaige zhi shang."

Almost immediately, the reforms Liu had put in place began to unravel. Although Liu's redistricting had reduced the number of towns and townships from sixty-one to twenty-seven, after his departure the number increased to forty-three.[72] As of 2012, Pingchang does not even carry out the system of public recommendation, public selection.[73] It is true that Liu Qianxiang had a very strong personality and he clashed with Li Zhongbin above him and the cadres below him, but the failure of reform in Pingchang county was not so much personal as it was structural. An effort to carry out such an extensive reform threatened too many cadres; without strong support from above (as Qiu He had in Shuyang and Suqian), local networks inevitably fought back.

Outside Sichuan

Sichuan province clearly led the implementation of inner-party democracy, in terms of both starting early and the number of experiments. By the 1998–1999 election cycle there were some 300 inner-party elections; by the 2003–2004 election cycle there were more than 2,000. Most of these were for lower-level offices, but in the 2003–2004 end-of-term elections, about one-third of Sichuan townships conducted inner-party elections for township party secretary.[74]

By the 2003–2004 election cycle, inner-party elections had spread to other provinces as well, indicating support for this idea from the Central Organization Department in Beijing. At the least, there were elections in Henan, Guangdong, Yunnan, and Jiangsu. But most of these elections were tightly controlled, reflecting organizational desires to curtail local networks, to rein in corruption, to pursue procedural legitimacy, and to involve more party members in decision making rather than representing a broader opening to societal interests or responding to any bottom-up pressures for democracy, however defined.

---

[72] Ibid.
[73] Author's interviews.
[74] Lai Hairong, *Zhongguo nongcun zhengzhi tizhi gaige*.

One exception was the broad experiment undertaken in Honghe Hani and Yi Autonomous Prefecture in Yunnan, which seemed for a while to breathe new life into inner-party democracy. More indicative of overall trends, however, was the tightly controlled process undertaken in Xuzhou in northern Jiangsu. This instance is particularly noteworthy because it was obviously backed by then provincial party secretary Li Yuanchao, who was subsequently promoted by Hu Jintao to head the party's powerful Central Organization Department in Beijing.

Honghe Hani and Yi Autonomous Prefecture

In November 2002 Luo Chongmin was transferred from his position as party secretary at Yunnan Nationalities University to become party secretary in Honghe prefecture, an impoverished minority area nestled next to Vietnam. Born in Wenjiang county, Yunnan province, Luo had spent most of his life working at the grassroots. A "sent-down youth," barefoot doctor, and worker, he did not complete middle school until he was thirty, but he was obviously a very bright, self-educated man. He received his doctorate when he was over forty, and along the way authored some eighteen books on economics and management.[75]

Unlike many of the elections in Sichuan where social tensions were an important background factor, Luo's desire to implement elections seems to have come from idealism rather than governance issues per se. Luo was inspired by the elections Zhang Jinming had overseen in Suining and was determined to carry out similar reforms. The Sixteenth Party Congress, which convened in November 2002, called for building "spiritual civilization" and expanding grassroots democracy. Luo took that recommendation seriously and launched the furthest-reaching township elections since those in Buyun.

After study, Luo decided to launch his reform in Shiping county, an impoverished area supported by transfer funds from

---

[75] Luo Ke, "'Gaigepai guanyuan' de Zhongguo mingyun," p. 84.

the state.[76] In February 2004, the Honghe Hani and Yi prefectural party committee approved a document calling for public recommendation and direct election of township heads in seven townships of Shiping.[77] Until that time, this election model had been used only in individual townships; thus, expanding it to townships throughout a prefecture represented a significant step forward. The prefecture set up a leadership small group consisting of leading cadres from the party committee, the people's congress, the CPPCC, the discipline inspection commission, and relevant departments. A deputy party secretary of the prefecture was appointed as head of the group. The prefecture also transferred several cadres who were familiar with grassroots work to guide and supervise the elections.[78]

Keeping in mind the legal provisions on the role of the people's congresses, Honghe prefecture called for each township to hold a meeting of its people's congress. The congress would pass resolutions endorsing the elections, select an election commission from its membership to take charge of the elections, and then recess until the final stage of the elections.[79] Each of the seventy villages in the various townships of Shiping county selected an electoral commission to recommend candidates.[80]

There was no lack of competition. Altogether there were seventy-seven preliminary candidates; after verifying their credentials, there remained sixty-six.[81] In one township there were as many as nineteen candidates, whereas the township with the fewest number of candidates had only seven.[82] By all accounts,

---

[76] Tian Shubin, Li Ziliang, and Wang Yan, "Shiwan baixing xuan 'xiangguan,'" pp. 16–20.

[77] There were nine towns and townships in Shiping county, but the heads of two of them had just been transferred in, so it was decided to conduct elections only in the seven remaining towns and townships. See ibid.

[78] Zhou Ping, "Yunnansheng Honghezhou daguimo de xiangzhen zhixuan yanjiu."

[79] Tan Zhongying and Zeng Xinyuan, "Xianji fanweinei zhixuan xiangzhenzhang yinchu de sikao," p. 67.

[80] Ibid.

[81] Ibid.

[82] Ibid., pp. 67–68.

higher levels did not "internally designate" (*neiding*) candidates for township head, but candidates were required to have a high-school degree and some economic and social administrative experience and to reside in the township where they were to stand for election. They had to be between twenty-five and forty-five years of age.[83] Each candidate gave a talk before a joint conference (*xiangzhen lianxi hui*) composed of voters' representatives, village party committees, and the presidium of the township people's congress; thereafter, the joint conference voted by secret ballot. The top two vote-getters became the formal candidates.[84]

Formal candidates went to each voting district, based in the villages, and gave talks. This was followed by the voting. There were 103,513 eligible voters throughout the county, 97.1 percent of whom voted. The people's congress then reconvened and, after listening to a report from the electoral commission, decided whether or not the election was valid. Finally, the people's congress nominated and voted on the township head.[85]

Having successfully elected township heads in Shiping county, in July and August 2004 the prefecture then moved on to implement the public recommendation and public election model for township party secretaries in neighboring Luxi county. The county adopted a method known as the "two recommendations" (*liangtui*): The party committee organized a meeting of all party members in each township to recommend candidates, and nonparty people were allowed to recommend candidates by way of a petition signed by at least thirty people. The township electoral commission reviewed the credentials, and a joint meeting of party and nonparty people then voted for the formal candidates after hearing all the candidates present their views.[86] The final decision was made by a meeting of all party members.

[83] Ibid., p. 68; and Zhou Ping, "Yunnansheng Honghezhou daguimo de xiang-zhen zhixuan yanjiu."

[84] Tan Zhongying and Zeng Xinyuan, "Xianji Fanweinei zhixuan xiangzhen-zhang yinchu de sikao," pp. 67–68.

[85] Ibid., p. 68.

[86] Xiao Lihui, "Xiangzhen dangwei lingdao banzi xuanju fangshi gaige yanjiu."

Finally, in 2006, Honghe Hani and Yi prefecture, with the exception of Luxi county (which had just elected its party committees), used the public recommendation and direct election system to select new party committees in all of its townships. This change-of-term election affected two cities, ten counties, and 126 township party committees. It was China's first large-scale election of a new party leadership at the township level and the first time a minority nationality autonomous prefecture carried out such an experiment.[87] As in Luxi county, the election used the "two recommendations" system. In Kaiyuan city, for example, 734 party members (out of 886) participated in nominating twenty-six candidates for party secretary, thirty-five candidates for deputy party secretary, and 111 candidates for party committee. Formal candidates were selected by a joint party–mass meeting. According to local regulations, the number of non-party people participating at this meeting could not be less than 20 percent; in Yangjie township of Kaiyuan city, ninety-five party representatives and twenty-two nonparty people were members of the joint committee. Finally, the two candidates for party secretary went to each village to give speeches and answer questions. The election itself took place at a meeting of all party members; a number of nonparty representatives to the township people's congress as well as CPPCC members and representatives of the masses were invited to supervise (but not participate in) the election.[88]

By 2004 the enthusiasm for inner-party democracy – at least for the variety that included all party members and representatives of the "masses" – was already dying out, but Luo Chongmin gave new life to the idea and created excitement throughout the prefecture. Once again, an impoverished area was leading China in exploring democratic options, opening up new questions about the relationship between economic development and political change. However, it turned out that, as in so many other

---

[87] Zhou Meiyan, "Dangnei minzhu yu renmin minzhu jiehe de youyi changshi," p. 4.
[88] Ibid., p. 5.

places in China, these experiments primarily reflected the force of the personality of the leader, in this case Luo Chongmin.[89] After Luo was transferred out of Honghe in 2007, the reforms he had initiated died. Luo went on to become head of the provincial Education Department and he continued to promote a variety of reforms, but no longer exploring paths of democratic change. Without him Honghe prefecture lost its interest in electing cadres.

Xuzhou

Reform in Xuzhou started in late 2003 when the party committee decided to experiment by selecting the head of Pei county, in northern Jiangsu on the border with Shandong province, through the public recommendation, public selection system. This was no instance of bottom-up democracy; on the contrary, it was overseen closely by the Organization Department of the Jiangsu provincial party committee. In September 2003 the provincial Organization Department decided on a plan for undertaking this election. Shortly thereafter, the Xuzhou party committee set up a Leadership Small Group for Public Recommendation and Public Selection (Gongtui gongxuan gongzuo lingdao xiaozu), which was led by the Xuzhou city party secretary, a deputy party secretary, and the head of the local Organization Bureau.[90]

In October the Xuzhou party committee convened a mobilization meeting to publicize the nomination process. Over the following two days, cadres who fit the criteria could register their names at the office of the leadership small group. Candidates had to be a full or deputy bureau chief (*juzhang* or *fujuzhang*) in a city-level organ; if they were at the deputy level, they also had to have served for at least two years and to have had at least one year of experience working in a township. Alternatively, they could be head or deputy head of an enterprise managed by the

---

[89] This is not to say that many local cadres did not support Luo; they did (though there were also dissenting voices). But without the number-one leader promoting reform, the momentum could not be sustained.

[90] Wang Yongbing, *Dangnei minzhu de zhidu chuangxin yu lujing xuanze*, p. 91.

city. They were also required to be college graduates and under the age of forty-five. Altogether there were eighty-eight people in the city who fit these criteria, of whom seventy registered as candidates.[91]

In the morning of October 24, the 754 people who made up the party committees in the various districts and counties under Xuzhou or who were heads or deputy heads of departments, companies, and service units under the city convened for the first round of "democratic recommendation." The top twelve vote-getters moved on to the second round. Only the twenty-nine people who were at the deputy city cadre level or above participated in nominating candidates in the second round. The qualifications of each candidate were read out loud, and the group elected six people out of this group by secret ballot.

The six remaining candidates then went to Pei county where, after spending four days investigating conditions, they each wrote a report. The reports were then evaluated by a committee from the provincial Organization Department.[92]

Finally, on November 9 the six candidates gathered to give speeches and respond to questions. They were allocated forty minutes to speak, and twenty minutes to respond to questions. An evaluation group and "public opinion evaluation" (*minyi ceyan*) group judged their speeches and responses. The participants on the public opinion evaluation group, who were appointed by the Leadership Small Group for Public Recommendation and Public Election did what the name of the group suggests: they graded the talks.[93]

The composition of the "public opinion evaluation group" suggests that there was no danger of this election producing results that would in any way challenge the status quo. The group consisted of fourteen people from the Pei township leadership group and its local people's congress, two people from its procuratorate, its four party secretaries, four people from its

---

[91] Ibid., p. 92.
[92] Ibid.
[93] Ibid.

comprehensive departments, and three each from the people's congress, the CPPCC, and party representatives, making a total of thirty-three members. Aside from Pei county, there were four people from each of the three other counties and county-level cities (including the party secretary, the county head, the head of the Organization Bureau, and one person from a comprehensive department), and three people from each of Xuzhou's three districts (including the party secretary, district head or deputy head, and the head of the Organization Bureau), making a total of twenty-one members. Finally, there were fifty-five people from organs directly under the city (including twenty-five from the city party committee and government departments, ten representatives to the city party congress, and ten from the CPPCC), making a total of 109 members of the group. After listening to the talks and responses, members of the group rated the candidates on a scale from 1 to 6.[94]

The evaluations of the candidates' research reports, speeches and responses, and the public opinion evaluations were weighed 3:3:4, and the highest three candidates entered the final round. Two deputy secretaries of the Xuzhou municipal government and a deputy party secretary of Pei county were the top three candidates. Each was then evaluated by the provincial Organization Department. On the basis of this evaluation, the Xuzhou party standing committee recommended two people to the party committee. Finally, on November 23, the party committee of Xuzhou municipality selected one of these final two candidates (one of the two deputy government secretaries who had made the final cut) to be the head of Pei county.[95]

Some Conclusions

Almost all instances of inner-party democracy for which we have documentation occurred in impoverished areas far from the urban areas; Xindu, in the suburbs of Chengdu, is an exception.

94 Ibid., p. 93.
95 Ibid., p. 94.

The interests of local cadres frequently brought them into direct conflict with local residents. Friends and relatives often pressured local cadres to put them on the payrolls; after all, jobs in such areas were scarce. There was an inevitable tendency for local governments to expand, which meant that they ran up debts and pressed the local population for more taxes. With the 1994 tax reform, these pressures increased. As cadres pressed harder to raise funds, residents resisted, sending petitions to higher levels and sometimes resorting to violence.

Political reform was one way to try to calm popular anger in a local area; more important, it was a way in which the local party secretary could show political accomplishment (*zhengji*) to his superiors in an area where it was fairly clear that one could not show political accomplishments through economic development – there simply were no resources or geographic conditions to develop the local economy significantly. And it was apparent that the Sichuan provincial Organization Department encouraged such efforts; as a poor province with few prospects for economic development, it needed to show its political accomplishments to Beijing.

Political reform was also driven by strong and often open-minded leaders: Zhang Jinming in Suining and Ya'an, Li Zhongbin in Xindu and Bazhong, Liu Qianxiang in Pingchang, and Luo Chongmin in Honghe. It is impossible to know what combination of idealism and political ambition was at work in their minds, but all were talented leaders who were willing to take risks. As inner-party democracy developed, there was a tendency for one leader to try to outdo what another leader had done somewhere else; after all, one could hardly establish political merit or a national reputation by simply replicating what someone else had already done. Perhaps, too, these leaders, working with other open-minded local cadres, promoted reform in a democratic direction by allowing all party members in a particular township to vote for their local leadership (the *gongtui zhixuan* model) and even by allowing representatives to the people's congresses to participate (though, of course, these representatives would have all been well vetted).

Competition between areas, the interests of local areas, and perhaps the open-mindedness of the party secretary seemed to push inner-party democracy in a more democratic direction, at least for a while. This logic, however, never really had a chance to take hold. Every election, no matter how democratic it appeared, was closely supervised by a leadership small group whose job it was to ensure that local leaders did not "lose control" (*shikong*); the risk that these political entrepreneurs took was that in the course of trying to establish political merit, things would get out of hand and local social order would deteriorate, leading to the end of their careers.

Perhaps more important, higher levels of the party organization could not afford for local officials to become too oriented toward the constituencies they served. Although everyone understood that local officials responding only to the desires of their superiors were the source of personalism and abuse of power at local levels, the party system instinctively viewed local political leaders who were genuinely responsible to their constituencies as an even greater organizational threat. So while there was a desire to use political reform to curb principal–agent problems, there was an even stronger impulse to pull back from the sorts of reform that would make lower-level governments more responsive to local needs than they were to party needs. Another way to put this is that electoral systems inherently constrain the authority that higher levels can exercise – they draw lines between higher and lower levels and demarcate the powers of each – and this was something the party organization would not let happen. It therefore chose to blur the lines and retain its own authority.

Thus, during the 2003–2005 period the enthusiasm for certain types of inner-party democracy waned. In particular, the party came to see direct recommendations and direct elections of township heads as divisive, in the same way that village elections had led some village heads to challenge the authority of village party secretaries. As a result, the CCP began to encourage a more modest approach to inner-party democracy, in particular by selecting party secretaries by the public recommendation, public selection method. This was a process that could be tightly controlled, as the Xuzhou election discussed above suggests.

The public recommendation, public selection model, however, took the democracy out of inner-party democracy. What this model allows for is slightly greater competition among local cadres who want to advance their careers; it represents simply a different path by which cadres can rise within the party. The party itself often underscores this fact by frequently transferring newly elected cadres to other positions. They clearly are not local politicians elected to serve a constituency, and the elections in which they take part are so tightly controlled that they do not seem to inhibit the same sort of corruption that became so prevalent when higher-level cadres simply appointed people to office. Indeed, the buying and selling of offices seems to have continued unabated.[96]

Ironically, one factor that may have contributed to this pulling back from the more democratic implications of inner-party democracy in the direction of a more authoritarian model is the abolition of the agricultural tax and miscellaneous fees in 2006. Whereas the 1994 tax reform stimulated experiments with inner-party democracy, the abolition of the agricultural tax was replaced by central and provincial subsidies. Between 1994 and 2006 Beijing had become quite wealthy and could afford to increase its aid to poor and impoverished counties – many of the same places that had pushed the boundaries of semi-competitive elections. Just as cadres in Maliu township largely abandoned their eight-step work method in favor of looking to the county for financial support, in Sichuan and elsewhere central subsidies removed the pressures to seek compromise with local society. As such pressures were reduced, inner-party democracy became an instrument for strengthening party control rather than a bridge to greater democracy, however defined.

---

[96] John P. Burns and Wang Xiaoqi, "Civil Service Reform in China," pp. 58–78.

4

Wenzhou

Social Capital without Civil Society

Inner-party democracy was one response to growing social tensions and abuses of power. It was pioneered in Sichuan but spread to other provinces, although mostly to the poorer parts of those provinces where local leaders lacked resources to spur economic development. The developed areas along the east coast presented different challenges. More than any other province, Zhejiang developed around the private economy, minimizing the role of the state. Moreover, it was not long before entrepreneurs began forming business associations. This pattern of development suggests that Zhejiang could pioneer a turn toward civil society. Students of civil society have generally looked to various nongovernmental organizations (NGOs) to support their hope that democratizing trends are emerging in China.[1] The emergence of NGOs is certainly an important story in contemporary China, but it is not clear precisely how they are expected to promote democratization: through the cultivation of civic values? Through resistance to the authoritarian state? Through the delegitimization of the state? Through the creation of a public sphere outside the control of the state, which would, in turn, impose constraints on the state and turn it, however incrementally,

---

[1] Jonathan Schwartz and Shawn Shieh (Eds.), *State and Society Responses to Social Welfare Needs in China.*

toward the rule of law and acceptance of citizen participation in political affairs?[2] Furthermore, most students of NGOs do not focus on business associations, perhaps because such associations are thought to be too close to the state; "real" NGOs are presumed to be more independent of, and perhaps hostile to, the state.

However, business associations seem to be likely vehicles for building institutionalized state–society relations in China. Entrepreneurs have an interest in a predictable environment, and curbing the arbitrary actions of local state officials would generally benefit the private sector. In addition, from the state's point of view, entrepreneurs are a benevolent social force, providing the sort of growth that the state is encouraging. Despite debates about admitting entrepreneurs into the party – something that was done surreptitiously at first and then openly under Jiang Zemin's "Three Represents" policy – local political elites and entrepreneurs have accommodated one another quite well.[3] Thus, if there is one social force the state is likely to feel relaxed about, it is the entrepreneurs.

Therefore, Zhejiang might be the logical place to look for indicators that emerging social forces are creating institutions, constraining arbitrary government actions, and building a civil society. Within Zhejiang, it was the southeastern city of Wenzhou that pushed against Communist orthodoxy faster and harder than anywhere else. Private entrepreneurs emerged rapidly in the aftermath of the Cultural Revolution (in fact, as described below, they did not even wait for the Cultural Revolution to end), creating the so-called Wenzhou model. Furthermore, business associations grew up faster and became more active in Wenzhou than elsewhere, and at least some of these associations seemed more independent of the state than those elsewhere.[4] Nevertheless, all this social capital has not created a civil society, whether understood as a network of associations bringing about better and

---

[2] Michael W. Foley and Bob Edwards, "The Paradox of Civil Society."
[3] Bruce Dickson, *Red Capitalists*; and Bruce Dickson, *Wealth into Power.*
[4] Kenneth W. Foster, "Embedded within State Agencies."

more responsive governance or as a force independent of and perhaps hostile to the state.

Wenzhou's willingness to push the boundaries seems rooted in a unique combination of factors, starting with Wenzhou's physical isolation. Lying in the southeast corner of Zhejiang, Wenzhou, isolated by the rugged mountains from Hangzhou, the provincial capital, originally was largely settled by migrants from northern Fujian; indeed, some 80 percent of Wenzhou-ese can trace their ancestry to Fujian.[5] The physical isolation of Wenzhou and the intermingling of people from different localities over time led to a unique dialect. Although every locality in China seems to have its own dialect, that in Wenzhou is said to be the most difficult for outsiders to learn; people working in Wenzhou for a decade or more confess that they are able to understand very little of the local language. Furthermore, Wenzhou dialect is spoken within a rather small geographic area; farther south, it is mutually unintelligible with the local dialects spoken in northern Fujian, just as it is mutually unintelligible with the dialect spoken in Taizhou to the north. Certainly the uniqueness of Wenzhou dialect infuses a strong sense of identity into the local population.

The sense of a unique identity and, more important, social capital were reinforced by overlapping family and religious networks. Traditionally, the Wenzhou-ese frequently settled in single-surname villages, so clan organizations were extremely important. Although these organizations were severely suppressed in post-1949 China, Wenzhou remained rural, and settlement patterns continued to reinforce the importance of family. After 1978, clan temples were rebuilt and family genealogies were resurrected and expanded. Similarly, religion had always been an important part of Wenzhou life. Prior to 1949 there were some 2,000 places of worship in Wenzhou, some 4,500 monks and nuns, and 115,000 Christians. Although religion, like clans, was suppressed after 1949, it revived quickly after the start of the

---

5 Yu Jianxing, Jiang Hua, and Zhou Jun, *Zai canyu zhong chengzhang de Zhong-guo gongmin shehui*, p. 48. This has been translated into English as Jianxing Yu, Jun Zhou, and Hua Jiang, *A Path for Chinese Civil Society*.

reform period, and today there are some 4,000 places of worship and 700,000 registered Christians.[6] There are many more unregistered Christians.

The other notable feature of Wenzhou is its high population in comparison to its arable land. By the early nineteenth century, Wenzhou had a population of about 1.9 million and a population density four to five times greater than China's average. Each person, on average, had only 1.1 mu of land, far below the 3 mu that can sustain a minimum livelihood for a family of five. Such population pressures meant that the population had to engage in industry and commerce. Already by the Southern Song dynasty, Wenzhou, with its developed commerce, had the reputation of being a "little Hangzhou." By the Qing dynasty, Wenzhou was well known for it herbal medicine, soy factories, delicacies from south China (*nan huo*), and silk. On the eve of the Communist revolution, one-quarter of Wenzhou's population was either full-time merchants or handicraft workers.[7]

As Wenzhou's commerce developed in late imperial and especially Republican China, business associations also developed. In particular, after the 1876 Chefoo Convention opened Wenzhou to trade, commerce developed rapidly. A chamber of commerce was first established in 1906, and the number of trade associations eventually peaked at 103. Although the Nationalist government tried to impose a corporatist structure on the trade associations, they continued to try to distance themselves from government.[8]

Even though mercantile activities were suppressed after 1949, they could not be completely wiped out without starving the population. After 1962 many places in Wenzhou allowed people to go out in search of a livelihood; in some places half the labor force

[6] Ibid., p. 49.
[7] Ibid., pp. 52–53.
[8] Chen Anjin and Xu Mingjun, "Jindai Wenzhou shanghui xingqi tanxi," pp. 68–73; Hu Zhusheng, *Wenzhou jindaishi*, pp. 219–230; and Yu Jianxing, Jiang Hua, and Zhou Jun, *Zai canyu zhong chengzhang de Zhongguo gongmin shehui*, pp. 35–41.

MAP 4. Zhejiang province, indicating locations of Wenzhou, Taizhou, and the capital, Hangzhou

left to seek their fortunes elsewhere. There were even "underground construction teams" and "underground transportation teams." In the late 1960s, as Cultural Revolution activists were "cutting off the tail of capitalism," commercial activities were continuing in Wenzhou. For example, in Liaoshi township of Yueqing county, the Liushi General Electronics Factory was established in 1969 with thirty-two workshops in different households. By 1979, the factory had an output value of 100 million yuan.[9] Nevertheless, there was little state investment in Wenzhou because of its distance from the provincial capital and because it

---

[9] Ibid., p. 54.

was considered a front-line area in any potential conflict in the Taiwan Straits.[10]

Emergence of the "Wenzhou Model"

Post-1949 China was not kind to Wenzhou. Wenzhou's population continued to increase, but its acreage did not. By 1978, per capita arable land was less than half a mu – not enough to sustain life. Agricultural production grew slowly, averaging about 5.5 percent per year, less than the provincial average. In 1977, per capita rural incomes averaged only 55 yuan. Wenzhou's finances were also in disarray; in 1976, debts reached 4.09 million yuan. Industrial output value was a modest 260 million yuan; 70 percent of the factories had suspended production; and 60 percent of wages were not being paid.[11] As in other areas of China, factions had battled one another, killing over 1,000 people in the course of the Cultural Revolution.[12]

Nevertheless, the social capital built up through family ties and religious practices, as well as Wenzhou's history of entrepreneurial traditions, well situated the city to take advantage of the new era that was inaugurated with the reform and opening up. The Household Responsibility System (HRS) spread quickly in Wenzhou, and agricultural production leaped ahead. Furthermore, Wenzhou did not stop at household contracting: "specialized households" and "key households" soon began to appear, and by late 1982 some 16 percent of rural households were undertaking specialized production, such as raising fish or poultry or engaging in handicraft production and transportation. With the contracting of land, efficiency increased rapidly, and soon 1.5 million Wenzhou-ese left the city to search for

---

[10] It should also be noted that Wenzhou was also isolated from Hangzhou. In the late 1970s, it took some 27 hours to travel from the provincial capital of Hangzhou to Wenzhou, so most travelers between these cities went first to Shanghai and then to Wenzhou via a land–water route.

[11] Hong Zhenning (Ed.), *Wenzhou gaige kaifang 30 nian*, p. 8.

[12] Ibid., p. 8.

livelihoods elsewhere. By October 1980, grassroots financial networks were beginning to grow.[13]

Nevertheless, "capitalism" still remained a sensitive issue in China, and in August 1982 there was a campaign to "strike hard at economic criminals." In Yueqing county, eight entrepreneurs, who came to be known as the "eight big kings" (*ba da wang*), were labeled economic criminals and thrown in prison, leading to a decline in industrial production in Yueqing. Indeed, Wenzhou's gross domestic product (GDP), which had grown by 20 percent in 1980, dropped to a 5 percent growth rate in 1981 and to under 10 percent in 1982. It was only after Beijing issued "Document No. 1" in 1984, which strongly affirmed the HRS, that Yueqing's entrepreneurs were released from prison and the local economy again began to boom, reaching a growth rate of about 25 percent.[14]

With the relaxation on entrepreneurial activities during this period, nonstate economic activities quickly overshadowed state-owned production. In 1980, state-owned commercial sales were 38 percent, collective sales 59 percent, and individual entrepreneurs only 2.2 percent of total sales. By the end of 1985, commercial retail sales reached 1.9 billion yuan, of which state stores accounted for 28 percent, collectives 45 percent, and individual entrepreneurs 28 percent.[15]

As the Wenzhou economy prospered and as the Wenzhou pattern of family-owned workshops and businesses began to take off, people started to speak about the "Wenzhou model," a term first used in Shanghai's *Liberation Daily* in January 1985.[16] There were already some 135,000 family enterprises in Wenzhou, employing over 330,000 people.[17] The Wenzhou model was

---

[13] Ibid., pp. 8–9.

[14] Ibid., p. 10.

[15] Ibid., p. 11.

[16] Zhu Kangdui, "Gaige kaifang yilai Wenzhou jingji fazhan de huigu yu zhan-wang," p. 24. However, Hong Zhenning says the term was not first used until May 12 of that year. See Hong Zhenning (Ed.), *Wenzhou gaige kaifang 30 nian*, p. 15.

[17] Ibid., p. 15.

contrasted with the "Sunan model" of southern Jiangsu province, which focused on the collective economy organized around township and village enterprises, and the "Guangzhou model," which was organized around a strong government bringing in foreign investment for processing work.[18] Debates over these different approaches to economic development became quite heated during the 1980s, with reformers coming out in defense of Wenzhou's practices. In 1985, Ma Hong, the head of the State Council's Development Research Center, published an article entitled "Investigation of Yueqing County's 10,000 Yuan Households," and in 1986 the famous sociologist Fei Xiaotong published an account of his trip to Wenzhou in the popular journal *Outlook Weekly*. Also in 1986 Dong Fureng, Zhao Renwei, and other economists from the Chinese Academy of Social Sciences (CASS) supported the Wenzhou model in the prestigious journal *Economic Research*.[19]

Such support did not prevent Wenzhou from coming under harsh criticism. During the campaign against "bourgeois liberalization" in 1987, following general secretary Hu Yaobang's ouster in January of that year, there was renewed criticism of Wenzhou's "capitalism." Following the Tiananmen crackdown in 1989, Wenzhou once again came under severe pressure with one investigation group after another inspecting the area.[20] This pressure had a real effect: Local economic growth fell to zero in 1989 and to a mere 2 percent in 1990.[21]

Deng Xiaoping's 1992 "Southern Journey" to Shenzhen, which gave new life to reform, also reenergized Wenzhou's private economy. In 1992 local GDP grew some 30 percent and in 1993 topped 40 percent.[22]

---

[18] On the Wenzhou model, see Kristen Parris, "Local Initiative and National Reform," pp. 242–263, and "The Rise of Private Business Interests," pp. 262–282.

[19] Hong Zhenning (Ed.), *Wenzhou gaige kaifang 30 nian*, p. 16.

[20] Zhu Kangdui, "Gaige kaifang yilai Wenzhou jingji fazhan de huigu yu zhanwang," pp. 23–24.

[21] Ibid., p. 23.

[22] Ibid.

The Growth of Business Associations

Industrial associations grew in Wenzhou along with the economy. The first association to appear was the Packaging Technical Association, which was founded in 1982. This was attached to the local Economic and Trade Office (Jingmao wei) and was very much a bureaucratic appendage supervising the packaging industry. This was followed by the Pottery Industry Association, which similarly was an administratively top-heavy organization.

In 1987 a famous incident occurred that accelerated the development of business associations. Wenzhou had already developed a reputation for churning out consumer goods, but it also had a well-deserved reputation for poor quality and counterfeit products. This practice undercut not only brands produced elsewhere in China but also those procured in Wenzhou. It made all goods produced in Wenzhou suspect and hence threatened the economic development of the city. By the mid-1980s, Wenzhou-made shoes were well known for their shoddy quality; thus in 1987 the government of Lucheng district, the area of Wenzhou where the shoe industry was concentrated, took the extreme action of burning 5,000 pairs of Wenzhou-made shoes in Hangzhou to demonstrate its determination to stamp out shoddy wares. Following this demonstration of government displeasure, the Lucheng district government organized the Shoe Industry Rectification Office (Luchengqu xieye zhengdun bangongshi) that then organized the Lucheng District Shoe Industry Association (Luchengqu xieye xiehui), which all shoe manufacturers were required to join. This government-organized trade association, under the district Economic and Trade Office, worked with leading shoe manufacturers to establish industry standards, as embodied in the Management Regulations on the Rectification of Quality of the Lucheng District Shoe Industry and the Provisional Regulations on After-Sales Services of the Shoe Industry. Enforcement of the new regulations was an important function of the association, and manufacturers that did not comply were shut down. Such efforts were successful in raising quality control, and soon Wenzhou-made shoes were once again selling well.[23]

Other associations soon followed suit. In November 1988, the Food Industry Association and the Department Store and Weaving Commercial Guild were established as autonomous nongovernmental associations. Shortly thereafter, the Urban Trust Cooperative Association, the Pawn Shop Association, the Association of Foreign-Invested Enterprises, and the Nonstate Enterprise Guild were set up in succession.

These emerging business associations gained support when the Zhejiang provincial Office of Economic Structural Reform (Tigaiwei) and the provincial Federation of Industry and Commerce (Gongshanglian) issued the "Provisional Methods [Governing] Economic Trade Associations in Zhejiang" in June 1989 and designated Wenzhou as an experimental area.[24] Shortly thereafter, despite the highly conservative atmosphere following the Tiananmen crackdown, the city people's congress transmitted the "Report on Views on the Experimental Establishment of Trade Associations and the Strengthening of Trade Governance."[25]

In 1990 the Wenzhou Federation of Industry and Commerce (FIC) hung up a sign reading the "Wenzhou General Chamber of Commerce." This was not separate from the FIC but rather represented an additional function of the FIC; it was, as the Chinese say, "two signs with one group [of officials]" (*liangkuai paizi, yitao banzi*). Most of the business associations that were established in the 1980s, at either the city or the district levels, were affiliated with the Economic and Trade Office at that level. Such associations were more bureaucratic – their heads (often retired officials) were appointed by the Economic and Trade Office and were regarded as instruments through which government policy

---

[23] Chen Shengyong, Wang Jinjun, and Ma Bin, *Zuzhihua, zizhu zhili yu minzhu*, p. 38. This chapter draws on and develops Joseph Fewsmith, "Chambers of Commerce in Wenzhou."

[24] Hong Zhenning (Ed.), *Wenzhou gaige kaifang 30 nian*, p. 275.

[25] Ibid., p. 275.

could be more effectively implemented. Businesses could influence government, at least to some extent, through these associations, but the businesses that exerted the most influence were the large ones that hardly needed associations to affect government policy, that is, those that could usually rely on personal connections. The General Chamber of Commerce tried to change this bureaucratic flavor by urging the creation of more autonomous associations.

Initially, the General Chamber of Commerce had a difficult time persuading trades to set up chambers of commerce. Businesses were reluctant to associate with the government, fearing bureaucratic control. Businesses also had diverse interests: Big businesses usually had personal channels to party and government leaders, whereas small businesses worried that the benefits of joining chambers of commerce would not be worth the costs. Moreover, the General Chamber of Commerce was a United Front organization, which meant that it was less able to affect government policy. Although trade associations (*hangye xiehui*) affiliated with the Economic and Trade Office were more bureaucratic and less reflective of industry needs, they did provide some direct channels to officials who could affect policy. But the General Chamber of Commerce had some advantages as well: Chambers of commerce were more inclusive and more open-minded right from the beginning. If they did not provide the same channels as the Economic and Trade Office, they nevertheless did offer some channels. Having the position of "director" or "board of directors" of some chamber of commerce on one's name card carried social prestige and provided legitimacy when meeting government officials (in other words, a meeting would seem to be less of a private conversation and more of an official function). Most important, the FIC, as part of its United Front function, had the authority to recommend successful business-persons to join local, provincial, or even national people's congresses as well as the Chinese People's Political Consultative Conference (CPPCC). Such appointments affirmed social prominence and conferred political legitimacy, in addition to providing legitimate fora for rubbing elbows with the political elite. As one FIC

FIGURE 4. Wenzhou General Chamber of Commerce

official pointed out, many chamber of commerce heads viewed their position as giving them a political status and access to resources monopolized by the government.[26] In one instance, an association was able to acquire from the local government 50 mu of land to be used by a company organized by the director and four other board members of the association.[27] This example illustrates how associations can distort public policy rather than improve governance.

With Deng Xiaoping's "Southern Journey" in 1992, the atmosphere in Wenzhou, and the nation at large, changed dramatically. The political debates over whether private businesses were capitalist or socialist ended (at least on the surface), and the number of private enterprises grew rapidly. Many "collective" enterprises took off their "red hats" (collective enterprises had

---

[26] Jiang Hua and Zhang Jianmin, "Minjian shanghui de daibiaoxing ji qi yingxiang yinsu fenxi," p. 83.

[27] Ibid., p. 81.

been an accepted part of the socialist economy, so many private companies sought out collective enterprises under which they could register in exchange for a management fee – something known as putting on a red hat) and registered openly as private enterprises. And many new enterprises opened as well. In this atmosphere, because the advantages of business organizations, whether trade associations or chambers of commerce, were obvious, many more rapidly emerged in succession. In 1993 the Wenzhou city government issued the "Response Agreeing to Strengthening Management of the Lucheng District Lighter Industry," which marked renewed government support for industrial associations.[28] The following year, the Wenzhou City Eyeglass Chamber of Commerce, the Wenzhou Fashion Industry Chamber of Commerce, and the Wenzhou Lighting Chamber of Commerce were established. In 1997, the State Economic and Trade Commission selected Shanghai, Guangzhou, Xiamen, and Wenzhou as experimental sites for trade associations and chambers of commerce. Wenzhou established a Leadership Small Group for Experimental Work with Trade Associations (Hangye xiehui shidian gongzuo lingdao xiaozu) and encouraged the formation of new trade associations and chambers of commerce.[29]

By August 2002 there were 104 such nongovernmental business associations at the city level. In addition, there were 321 associations at the county, county-level municipality, and district levels, with 42,624 members covering most of Wenzhou's industrial enterprises.[30] By 2011, there were 148 business associations at the city level.[31] Not only has the number of associations grown rapidly, but the number of enterprises participating in a given association has grown as well. For instance, the Wenzhou Fashion Industry Chamber of Commerce, founded in 1994,

---

[28] Hong Zhenning (Ed.), *Wenzhou gaige kaifang 30 nian*, p. 275.
[29] Ibid., pp. 275–276.
[30] Ibid., p. 228.
[31] Author's interviews.

originally had only ten members. In 1998, it had 156 members and by 2000 it had 287 members. In the first half of 2003, its membership suddenly jumped to 1,025 enterprises. This jump was due to efforts to reach out to manufacturers of women's and children's clothing that had been established as branches (*fenhui*) of the chambers. As membership expanded, the number of leaders grew. When founded, the Wenzhou Fashion Industry Chamber of Commerce had one chairman, two vice chairmen, and seven board members; by 2003, there was one chairman, twenty-two vice chairmen, forty-five members of the standing committee of the board of directors, and 121 board members. In 2011, the number of board members was expanded to 172.[32] Obviously, as the group expanded there was an effort to include more voices in the leadership.[33]

Organization and Structure

As noted earlier, chambers of commerce in Wenzhou were originally nurtured by the FIC, which is also known as the Wenzhou General Chamber of Commerce and is subordinate to the party's United Front Work Bureau. But at least some of Wenzhou's chambers of commerce – including the Wenzhou Lighting Chamber of Commerce and the Wenzhou Fashion Industry Chamber of Commerce – were initiated by the enterprises themselves. In this sense, they grew up "outside the system" (*tizhiwai*), though they quickly developed good relations with the FIC and the General Chamber of Commerce.[34] The roles of the FIC and its alter ego, the General Chamber of Commerce, however, became muddled in February 2002 when the Ministry of Civil Affairs promulgated the "Notice Reconfirming the Management Units for Social Groups" (*Guanyu chongxin queren shehui tuanti yewu guanli danwei de tongzhi*). This regulation allowed twenty-two

---

[32] Author's interviews.
[33] Hong Zhenning (Ed.), *Wenzhou gaige kaifang 30 nian*, p. 286.
[34] Yu Hui, "Hangye xiehui ji qi zai Zhongguo zhuanxingqi de fazhan."

different departments, but not the FIC, to supervise chambers of commerce or trade associations.[35] Apparently, this rule was adopted because the FIC is defined as a "societal" (*minjian*) organization (even though its employees are state cadres) and therefore it is not qualified to supervise societal organizations. The regulation caused considerable confusion in Wenzhou, and local authorities decided that newly organized industry associations would be supervised by the city Economic and Trade Office and other departments, but that those chambers of commerce that were already under the supervision of the FIC could remain there (in fact, the number gradually increased, and by 2011 there were thirty-seven chambers of commerce under the General Chamber of Commerce).[36] This led to the odd situation in which the FIC supervises numerous "chambers of commerce"; the Economic and Trade Office supervises more than forty "trade associations"; and other departments supervise other trade associations.[37] Such a violation of the corporatist intent of China's NGO laws reflects the competing interests of various government entities at the local level.[38]

The formal structure governing business associations is corporatist; the regulations promulgated by the Ministry of Civil Affairs are explicit that there should be only one association per industry in a given location. Associations are part of a hierarchical structure, with lower-level units at least formally subordinate to higher-level units and capped by peak associations. Moreover, associations must be registered with the government (technically, associations must be sponsored by an official organization before they can register with the Ministry of Civil Affairs at that level). The government can either accept

---

[35] Chen Shengyong, Wang Jinjun, and Ma Bin, *Zuzhihua, zizhu zhili yu minzhu*, p. 301. The regulations can be found at http://www.cso.org.cn/cso/article/list .asp?id=956, accessed February 5, 2012.

[36] Author's interview.

[37] Chen Shengyong, Wang Jinjun, and Ma Bin, *Zuzhihua, zizhu zhili yu minzhu*, chart on p. 196.

[38] Jiang Hua and Zhang Jianmin, "Minjian shanghui de daibiaoxing ji qi yingxiang yinsu fenxi," p. 84.

or deny registration, thus effectively licensing the establishment of NGOs.[39]

Nevertheless, Wenzhou's business associations escape easy categorization as corporatist organizations. Not only are there numerous government offices in Wenzhou that supervise business associations, but not all businesses are required to join the associations. Indeed, one of the problems of Wenzhou's business associations is the lack of participation. In a survey of sixty-eight business associations, more than half had a participation rate of less than 30 percent, and fewer than one-quarter had a participation rate of 70 percent or more.[40] On average, only about 20 percent of a given trade is represented in a business association. This biased representation derives from several factors. First, efforts to initiate a new association require the support of the leading enterprises in a given industry and those enterprises tend to serve the interests of big business. So the smaller enterprises understandably are reluctant to join. Second, because Wenzhou's business associations generally do not receive government subsidies, they rely on membership dues – and such dues weigh heavily on the small, family-owned workshops that make up so much of Wenzhou industry. The rate of participation is also affected by the role of the government. For instance, when the Lucheng District Shoe Association was first established in 1988, all 1,800 shoe manufacturers were required to join. As the government withdrew and membership became voluntary, the rate of participation fell. By the end of 2008, only about 400 of the 1,500 shoe manufacturers then in business continued to participate in the association.[41]

Despite the limited membership in the business associations, the rules that the associations make, generally in cooperation with the government, apply to all the enterprises in a given industry. For instance, the Hardware Industry Association and the

---

[39] "Zhonggong zhongyang bangongting, Guowuyuan bangongting guanyu jinyibu jiaqiang minjian zuzhi guanli gongzhuo de tongzhi."

[40] Jiang Hua and Zhang Jianmin, "Minjian shanghui de daibiaoxing ji qi yingxiang yinsu fenxi," p. 81.

[41] Ibid., p. 83.

Wenzhou Tobacco Implements Trade Association have established a patent-protection section. Any hardware or cigarette lighter enterprise that has designed a product can register its design with the association. Then if another enterprise copies the design, the first enterprise can register a complaint with the association. If the association upholds the complaint, it will forbid the second enterprise from continuing production, whether or not it is in fact a member of the association. Decisions can be enforced without coercion, both because association decisions are viewed as carrying government backing and because social relations are such an important part of doing business in Wenzhou that an enterprise that defies the association will not be able to remain in business.[42]

Wenzhou business associations also evade the vertical lines that usually separate associations in a corporatist system. Just as not all businesses are required to join its sector's association, some businesses join more than one association. Indeed, more than one-quarter of Wenzhou's enterprises participate in more than one trade association; nearly 14 percent participate in three trade associations, and 17 percent participate in more than three trade associations.[43] In addition, the Wenzhou-ese have redefined "sector" to allow multiple business associations. For instance, the shoe/leather industry has been subdivided into at least the following associations: the Wenzhou Leather Chamber of Commerce, the Wenzhou Shoe Material Association, the Wenzhou Shoe Chemical Association, and the Wenzhou Shoe Heel Chamber of Commerce. This trend is a very deliberate (and successful) method of avoiding the "one industry, one association" rule.[44]

Wenzhou business associations also evade the "one jurisdiction" rule, though they do so more quietly. For instance, associations in at least five other provinces have crossed provincial lines

[42] Author's interviews.
[43] Chen Shengyong, Wang Jinjun, and Ma Bin, *Zuzhihua, zizhu zhili yu minzhu*, p. 206.
[44] Author's interviews.

and established chambers of commerce in Wenzhou. Moreover, some chambers of commerce in districts outside Wenzhou have established branch associations in Wenzhou.[45]

Geographic Reach

One of the most interesting aspects of Wenzhou's trade associations is that they not only have promoted the interests of industries in Wenzhou but have also established associations outside Wenzhou to promote Wenzhou businesses throughout the country. Since 1995, over 130 chambers of commerce have been established by merchants from Wenzhou in other parts of China. There is even an office in the Wenzhou government that helps Wenzhou entrepreneurs establish such chambers in other parts of the country. One would think that registration of these chambers would be difficult, but it is the Wenzhou office that acts as the "supervising department" (*guanli bumen*), allowing them to register with the local Civil Affairs Bureau.

Of course, the reason other cities have been willing, and even eager, to allow Wenzhou merchants to organize locally is that they also bring investment. Sometimes these groups are able to apply pressure on Wenzhou by comparing its government unfavorably to other urban administrations. For instance, the head of the Wenzhou chamber of commerce in Shenyang, Liaoning province, told a conference in Wenzhou that in 2003 "people from Wenzhou invested over 6 billion yuan in Shenyang and this year [2004] the figure will reach 10 billion. Why? The government there plays the role of the nursemaid. Every day somebody specially goes to the enterprises to ask what they can do. So the CEOs can concentrate all their energies on building their businesses. In comparison, the services provided by the Wenzhou government have a way to go."[46]

---

[45] Author's interviews.
[46] Chen Shengyong, Wang Jinjun, and Ma Bin, *Zuzhihua, zizhu zhili yu minzhu*, p. 241.

The extension of Wenzhou chambers of commerce to so many cities in China is significant precisely because it "institutionalizes" informal governance. There are no laws that govern the establishment of such a horizontal network of chambers of commerce; indeed, its establishment seems to contradict the Ministry of Civil Affair's regulations. But by forging a special relationship between Wenzhou businesses and city governments around China, the Wenzhou-ese seem to be able to prevent other cities from doing the same and, most important, to obstruct the formulation of laws that would govern all cities and associations equally. The evolution of such informal institutions appeals to the interests of both the governing authorities and private business without constraining future actions by the local state. Since these associations are established at the sufferance of the local authorities, local chambers of commerce are always in the position of supplicants. Promulgating laws, depending on how they are read, will potentially give these chambers of commerce a more solid basis in law, but will also open the door to more competition from other places.[47]

Wenzhou chambers of commerce not only have influenced governments throughout China but also have defended the interests of otherwise scattered producers against foreign actions. The most famous instance of this occurred in 2002–2003 when the Wenzhou Tobacco Implements Trade Association, in cooperation with the Chinese government, defended the interests of manufacturers of lighters against the European Union. The Wenzhou Tobacco Implements Trade Association had been founded in 1991, and in 1993 the government gave it certain specific responsibilities, including investigating new enterprises applying for registration, providing technical advice on draft laws that affect trade interests, and collecting information on the tobacco trade.[48] A decade later, it had become a well-established trade association in one of Wenzhou's most important industries.

[47] Ibid.
[48] Huang Shaoqing and Li Zhengquan, "Qiye zizhi zuzhi de liliang."

The incident began in late 2001 when the trade association heard that the EU Commission on Standardization was drawing up regulations requiring lighters that cost under 2 euros to have safety mechanisms to protect children from accidents (these regulations would come to be known as the Child Resistance Act). The vast majority of lighters fitting this description were made in Wenzhou – the 500 or so Wenzhou industries that produce such lighters turn out some 600 million lighters per year, or 70 percent of global production and 80 percent of the European market,[49] so this EU action represented a major threat to the industry. This was the sort of trade requirement (or sanction) that Wenzhou manufacturers, almost all of which were small, family-operated operations, never could have fought on their own. But the Wenzhou Tobacco Implements Trade Association decided to resist EU actions by collecting relevant materials, raising funds, and hiring a lawyer.[50]

From the perspective of Wenzhou manufacturers, their reusable cigarette lighters encased in metal were fundamentally different from the plastic, disposable lighters that would also be affected by the regulation. Moreover, all the safety material the EU provided to the Wenzhou manufacturers related to only one case, thus demonstrating the overwhelming safety of lighters made in Wenzhou. It seemed apparent to Wenzhou manufacturers that the EU was using safety standards to erect trade barriers, and thus was not acting in accordance with World Trade Organization rules. [51]

The Wenzhou Tobacco Implements Trade Association responded strongly, through a specially organized committee, demanding substantial support from the government, and raising funds. Although there were some 500 manufacturers of lighters in the city, the financial burden – some two million yuan – was borne by the sixteen largest enterprises.[52] In March 2003,

[49] Ibid.
[50] Chen Shengyong, Wang Jinjun, and Ma Bin, *Zuzhihua, zizhu zhili yu minzhu,* pp. 49–51.
[51] Ibid., p. 49.
[52] Huang Shaoqing and Li Zhengquan, "Qiye zizhi zuzhi de liliang."

representatives from the Wenzhou Tobacco Implements Trade Association traveled to Europe with specialists from the Ministry of Foreign Trade and Economic Cooperation (MOFTEC, later renamed the Ministry of Commerce) and the lawyer they had employed. After seventeen days of negotiations with various parties, the EU indicated that it would revise the regulations, making the trade association an overnight sensation.[53]

This dispute had hardly gotten under way when the European Association of Lighter Producers accused China of dumping lighters on the European market. In response, in July 2003 the Wenzhou Tobacco Implements Trade Association took the lead in convening a meeting with its counterparts in Guangzhou and Ningbo. Again the associations decided to fight the charges by combining their resources to raise funds to hire an international lawyer. Faced with the Chinese reaction – and dissension within its own ranks – the EU quickly dropped its action. An association of private enterprises – albeit with government support – had managed to defend the interests of an industry composed of countless small producers who never could have defended themselves on their own.[54]

Relations between the Chambers of Commerce and Government

In general, the FIC has worked with the largest manufacturers in establishing associations. For instance, in the case of the Wenzhou Fashion Industry Chamber of Commerce, which has become perhaps the largest and most successful of the various industry associations in Wenzhou, there were only ten enterprises involved during its early stages. The lead was taken by Liu Songfu, head of Golden Triangle Enterprise (Jin sanjiao gongchang). Although the FIC supported the establishment of the association, it provided no funds; all costs of running the

[53] Ibid., and Chen Shengyong, Wang Jinjun, and Ma Bin, *Zuzhihua, zizhu zhili yu minzhu*, pp. 50–51.
[54] Ibid.

association during its first years – some 100,000 yuan – were borne by Liu and several other leaders.[55]

As with other industrial associations, the Wenzhou Fashion Industry Chamber of Commerce maintained a close association with political leaders. The deputy head of the FIC, Wu Ziqin, chaired the first congress of the chamber of commerce, and a number of political leaders were named either honorary board members or senior advisers. In addition, the support of the FIC, which was the sponsoring unit (*guakao danwei*) of the new chamber of commerce, was necessary for the chamber to register, to secure office space, and to encourage other enterprises to join.[56] The FIC authority also provided backing for the chamber's efforts to enhance quality control.

Over time, however, relations between the trade associations and government became somewhat more formalized, at least on the surface. For instance, the Wenzhou Fashion Industry Chamber of Commerce amended its charter in 2003 to specify that government officials should not be named as advisers. A reorganized Advisory Commission was composed of five prestigious entrepreneurs who had previously served as vice chairmen of the chamber.[57] This change was not an assertion of chamber independence from government supervision as much as a reflection of the growing trust the government had in this NGO to run its own affairs – without running afoul of government concerns. In Wenzhou 77 percent of the associations report that they freely elect their chairs in accordance with their own operating rules.[58] Moreover, the internal organization of the trade associations – the number of directors, the number of committees, and whether or not to organize training and consulting activities to raise funds – seems to be free of government interference. This move to separate government and business associations in terms of office holding (but not in terms of party organization; see below)

---

[55] Ibid., p. 285.
[56] Ibid., p. 293.
[57] Ibid., p. 294.
[58] Yu Jianxing, Huang Honghua, and Fang Liming, *Zai zhengfu yu qiye zhi jian*, p. 286.

anticipated national trends. In 2007 the State Council issued "Some Views on Accelerating the Reform and Development of Industry Associations and Chambers of Commerce," urging the separation of government and associations and prompting local governments to comply.[59]

Elections for leadership roles in at least some chambers are becoming more competitive. The Wenzhou Fashion Industry Chamber of Commerce was the first to introduce *cha'e* elections (in which the number of candidates exceed the number of positions), and others have now emulated this practice. Some have borrowed the practice of "sea elections" (*haixuan*) from the village elections, allowing the association head to be freely nominated by the members. In 2000, Liu Songfu, who had taken the lead in setting up the Wenzhou Fashion Industry Chamber of Commerce, was defeated by Chen Min, the leader of a new generation of entrepreneurs who have expanded both the scope and membership of chamber activities.[60]

Most chambers of commerce have a regulation that the chairs should serve a maximum of two terms, but some chairs are reluctant to give up their positions. That is what happened in the case of the Wenzhou Fashion Industry Chamber of Commerce, but ultimately Liu was defeated in his efforts to retain his position. In other instances, the chair will use his influence over the board of directors to revise the charter to allow multiple terms. In one instance, an association chair served five terms and only then revised the charter! Association elections are generally conducted by a show of hands, which makes challenging the chair more difficult.[61] The Wenzhou Fashion Industry Chamber of Commerce, however, conducts elections by secret ballot, perhaps explaining Liu's failure to retain his position.

The Fashion Industry Chamber of Commerce has been a model business association in many ways – it is more inclusive

---

[59] *Guanyu jiakuai tuijin hangye xiehui shanghui gaige he fazhan de ruogan yijian*, http://politics.people.com.cn/GB/1026/5825218.html#.
[60] Author's interviews.
[61] Jiang Hua and Zhang Jianmin, "Minjian shanghui de dabiaoxing ji qi yingxiang yinsu fenxi," p. 83.

and more democratic than most associations – reflecting the importance and diversity of the industry as well as its internal structure. Unlike most business associations, and in apparent violation of the governing regulations, the Wenzhou Fashion Industry Chamber of Commerce is one of two associations in Wenzhou that actually serve as "peak" associations (the other is the Wenzhou Electroplating Association). Under the Wenzhou Fashion Industry Chamber of Commerce there are six subordinate chambers, including the knitware, export ware, women's fashion, and sock branch chambers (*fenhui*) as well as six regionally based associations covering Wenzhou's administrative districts. This structure has attracted the participation of 1,800 of the 2,500 enterprises engaged in fashion in Wenzhou (including most of the manufacturers).[62] Such a rate of participation is well above the norm and suggests the uniqueness of this association.

Nevertheless, in an environment characterized by "strong state, weak society" (*qiang guojia, ruo shehui*), the hand of the state remains strong. Thus, nearly half – 48 percent – of all association secretaries, who are responsible for the day-to-day functioning of the associations, come from government departments,[63] and, as we will see below, the party has begun to establish party branches in the chambers of commerce and trade associations.

It is apparent that Wenzhou's chambers of commerce have a degree of influence over government policy, at least when policy proposals meet common goals. For instance, the regulations governing the shoe industry, mentioned above, represented a collaborative effort between government and industry representatives, even though they were drawn up at the behest of the government. Similarly, the "Tenth Five-Year Development Plan of the Wenzhou Industry Fashion Industry" was worked out by the Wenzhou Fashion Industry Chamber of Commerce in coordination with the Wenzhou Economic Commission. During sessions of the local people's congress and the local CPPCC, Wenzhou's

[62] Ibid., p. 86.
[63] Ibid.

chambers of commerce recommended that 141 entrepreneurs join the two bodies, and they raised fifty-four proposals. The FIC also organized members of the CPPCC to draft a proposal to create an industrial park.[64] It is apparent that the trade associations have given Wenzhou entrepreneurs a voice that they would not have had individually. Nevertheless, studies indicate that the influence of the trade associations still remains limited.[65]

Although government officials have withdrawn, at least to some extent, from participation in the trade associations, entrepreneurs are increasingly participating in politics, particularly the people's congresses and the CPPCCs at various levels. By 2003, a total of 421 members of sixty-four chambers of commerce were representatives to the people's congresses or the CPPCCs, including three representatives to the National People's Congress and thirteen representatives to the provincial people's congress.[66]

Social Capital, Not Civil Society: The Efficiency Revolution

In 2003, responding to higher-level calls to increase the openness and effectiveness of local government, Wenzhou launched an "efficiency revolution" (*xiaoneng geming*).[67] The aim of this movement was to make the management of local affairs more transparent through publicizing procedures and emphasizing accountability by making those responsible for decisions sign their names. It also focused approval procedures at one "window" that was supposed to respond to requests within a limited time period. An "efficiency revolution supervision center" was set up to handle complaints; by the beginning of 2004, it had

---

[64] Yu Jianxing, Huang Honghua, and Fang Liming, *Zai zhengfu yu qiye zhi jian*, p. 80.
[65] Chen Shengyong, Wang Jinjun, and Ma Bin, *Zuzhihua, zizhu zhili yu minzhu*, p. 263.
[66] Ibid., pp. 229–230.
[67] Yu Jianxing, Jiang Hua, and Zhou Jun, *Zai canyu zhong chengzhang de Zhongguo gongmin shehui*, p. 117.

already received and referred for administrative action 441 complaints, and 575 people had received demerits, of whom ninety were given administrative warnings.[68] Although at first blush this campaign appears as if the government was responding to societal demands for better governance, in fact it was inaugurated by the party secretary to establish his political accomplishments (*zhengji*).[69] No wonder Yu Jianxing and his colleagues conclude that even though the efficiency revolution was promoted vigorously, it had limited results.[70]

Despite winning an award from the China Center for Government Innovation in 2006,[71] the results were disappointing. For instance, government departments report a high degree of satisfaction with responses to proposals raised by representatives to the city's people's congress – often running between 80 and 90 percent. But a closer look reveals that the people's congress raised precisely the same proposal year after year, indicating that the representatives were not at all satisfied by the response to the original proposal.[72] Similarly, when interviewing business leaders in Wenzhou, Yu Jianxing and his colleagues asked them to grade the performance of the government. One replied "40 percent." He deducted points both for the government not doing much to support economic development and for interfering inappropriately in business operations. Another business leader was even harsher, giving the Wenzhou government a score of only 20 points. He criticized the government for its poor efficiency, the complexity of personal relationships, the privatization of public goods, low investment in education, and the old-fashioned thinking of government officials.[73] Government officials did not disagree. In a survey of forty-nine Wenzhou officials, only one thought the efficiency revolution had achieved obvious results;

[68] Ibid., pp. 118–119.
[69] Author's interview.
[70] Ibid., p. 136.
[71] "Disanjie 'Zhongguo difang chuangxin jiang' woshi 'xiaoneng geming' ruwei."
[72] Ibid., p. 131.
[73] Ibid., p. 131.

the majority (39) answered that "there were results, but they are not obvious," whereas nine simply responded that there had been no results.[74]

Similarly, the effectiveness of reforming the approval system has been limited. Efforts to limit the approvals that bureaucrats write personally (*pishi*) are important both because individual approvals prevent transparency and because they are often connected to corruption. The Wenzhou government has repeatedly stressed the importance of reforming this system, but in the same survey of forty-nine government officials, Yu Jianxing and his colleagues found that only 2 (4 percent) declared the results of this reform to be "very good," whereas 17 (35 percent) found it "comparatively good," 20 (41 percent) said it was "okay," and 4 (8 percent) concluded that it was "not good."[75]

The purpose of some of these governance reforms has been to give a greater role to the chambers of commerce and to industry associations. Regulations specify sixteen functions that these business associations are supposed to perform, but association leaders say that there are some functions that they do not want to take on or that they cannot fulfill even if they wanted to. Other functions have been given to the business associations in name only. When asked, "Do you believe that chambers of commerce and industry associations are truly viewed by the government as important?" 78 percent of the association leaders responded, "Only a minority of the chambers of commerce and industry associations are taken seriously."[76] In contrast, only 16 percent of the association leaders believed that government provides effective services.[77]

Wenzhou has had great success with its economic development and has become a model for the development of the private economy. But taking that model to another level – one that begins to demand responsiveness and accountability from the

---

[74] Ibid., p. 132.
[75] Ibid., p. 133. Three others declared they did not know, and the remaining three did not respond.
[76] Ibid., p. 135.
[77] Ibid., p. 135.

government – is proving difficult to achieve. As Yu Jianxing, Jiang Hua, and Zhou Jun put it, Wenzhou's marketization and privatization will not necessarily lead to improvements in governance.[78]

Party Branches and Private Enterprise

The Wenzhou Model revolves around the development of private enterprise. The development of business associations and their extension to other cities in China and throughout the world seem to be logical extensions of this bottom-up model of development. One can say the same thing about the rapid growth of religion in Wenzhou. Sometimes these developments are depicted as reflecting the weakness of the local state. It is certainly true that the local state lacks the state-owned and collective enterprises that would allow it to pursue a more statist model of growth, like that of its counterparts in southern Jiangsu, but the Wenzhou government has never been weak. Building the local economy was part of its job, and the economic growth reflected well on local cadres. But maintaining political control was also important to local government, not to mention to higher levels of government that worried that the growth of the private sector might weaken the role of the party. One can imagine local authorities developing different instruments of social control; after all, since 1995 the central party has been emphasizing rule of law. But rather than increasing the role of law or other instruments of social control, the local party organization in Wenzhou set out to fill in the "blank spaces" that had been created by the development of private enterprise.

In August 1987, the Zhenzhong Engineering and Machinery Factory in Rui'an city established a party branch (*zhibu*). This was the first party branch established in a nonstate enterprise in Wenzhou and, indeed, in all of Zhejiang.[79] With the nonstate economy booming in the wake of Deng Xiaoping's 1992

---

[78] Ibid., p. 133.
[79] Liao Yiru, "Wenzhou feigongyouzhi qiye dangjian gongzuo fazhan baogao," p. 204.

"Southern Journey," the Wenzhou party committee began emphasizing the importance of party building. It soon passed two resolutions – "Provisional Views on Strengthening Party Building Work in Rural Stock Enterprises" (*Guanyu jiaqiang nongcun gufen hezuo qiye dangjian gongzuo de shixing yijian*) and "Views on Strengthening Party Building in New Economic Organizations" (*Guanyu jiaqiang xin de jingji zuzhi dang de jianshe de yijian*) – to guide this work.[80] After the report of the 1997 Fifteenth Party Congress declared that nonstate enterprises were an integral component of the socialist market economy, party organizations at all levels were encouraged to accelerate party building. In Wenzhou, the goal was to cultivate party members in enterprises with fifty or more employees and to establish a party branches in enterprises with 100 or more employees. By the end of 2004, party branches had been established in 2,460 nonstate enterprises,[81] and by the end of 2009 there were 32,000 party members participating in 4,227 party organizations in nonstate enterprises.[82]

The literature on relations between the party and private enterprise in China has consistently maintained that relations are close and goals are compatible.[83] It is certainly true that China's entrepreneurs are not pushing for democratic reform, but it does not mean that they welcome party organizations into their enterprises. As one article puts it, "Some enterprise owners without high political consciousness or whose enterprises are of middling size believe that developing party organizations will not be of much help in developing their businesses."[84] Entrepreneurs are concerned that party activities will expend time and resources and will affect normal enterprise operations.[85] In other enterprises, individual party members are reluctant to reveal their

---

[80] Ibid.
[81] Ibid., p. 205.
[82] Chen Yaohui, "'Fei gong' dang zuzhi shuji."
[83] Bruce Dickson, *Red Capitalists*; Bruce Dickson, *Wealth into Power*; and Margaret M. Pearson, *China's New Business Elite.*
[84] Chen Jiaxi, "Siying qiye dangjian de kunnan yu fangxiang."
[85] Zhu Quanyong, "'Liang xin' zuzhi dang zuzhi zuoyong fahui."

status, fearing that it will have an adverse effect on their careers.[86] Even the party cadres sent to private enterprises are not exactly sure what they were supposed to do, other than to recruit new party members. Beginning in 2005 the Wenzhou party committee began to emphasize raising quality. Party building was made part of the responsibilities of the party secretary; it was also one of the goals of grassroots party leaders, and every year the grassroots party secretary had to sign a contract with the secretary at the next highest level specifying the goals for the year. Moreover, corresponding party-building offices were set up at each level. At the city level, a specialized office was set up in the Social Work Committee to take overall responsibility for party building. Similarly, a specialized office was set up in the Social Work Committee at the county (district) level, and a system of joint meetings was established to coordinate this party-building work with the heads of the economic work departments. Finally, at the township (street committee) level, an "Office for Party Building in Non-State Enterprises" was established. Each grassroots unit had to write a report on the progress of its work every month, hold a meeting to discuss the results every quarter, and undergo an inspection every six months and an evaluation every year.[87]

Of course, some entrepreneurs embrace having a party secretary form a party branch or party group in their enterprise. CEO of Zhengtai Group, Nan Cunhui, invited Wu Yan to serve as party secretary, becoming the first large-scale private enterprise to invite a party secretary into the workplace. Wu Yan had just retired from his position as office head of the Wenzhou Transportation Bureau and thus had many years of experience working in leadership circles of city government. He and Nan Cunhui apparently became very close, and Wu seems to have served Nan well. Nan Cunhui's enthusiasm to invite a party secretary into his enterprise was rewarded not only with the honor of being named an "outstanding youth" and a representative

---

[86] Chen Jiaxi, "Siying qiye dangjian de kunnan yu fangxiang."
[87] Liao Yiru, "Wenzhou feigongyouzhi qiye dangjian gongzuo fazhan baogao," pp. 207–208.

to the National People's Congress in Beijing but also by being invited to speak on numerous occasions.[88]

This phenomenon of inviting retired senior cadres to serve as enterprise party secretaries is widespread. The party secretaries of Shenli Group, Delixi, Senma, Hairuo, and Huafeng are all retired party officials.[89] In Wenzhou as a whole, more than 20 percent of enterprise party secretaries originally came from party work in government or service organizations. In private enterprises in Yueqing city 106 of the 480 party secretaries have backgrounds in government party work.[90] These party secretaries are normally given administrative positions, such as sitting on the board of directors, to justify their sizable salaries.

Enterprises reach out to retired cadres in the hopes that they will use their personal networks to help solve problems for the enterprise, all the while in the hopes of displaying political correctness. This is an arrangement that corrodes whatever tendency there might be for local government to take on a more regulatory role.

Although the party has had some success in establishing party organizations in private enterprises, it has been less successful in establishing party organizations in trade associations and other social organizations, including nonprofits. In 1999, the General Office of the Chinese Communist Party (CCP) promulgated a joint circular with the State Council on stepping up management of NGOs (*minjian zuzhi*).[91] Wenzhou selected its Fashion Industry Chamber of Commerce as a trial site for establishing a party organization. Over the course of the next two months, ninety-eight other party organizations were established in trade associations. As this rapid development suggests, these party organizations were rudimentary. Of the ninety-nine organizations, there was only one party committee and one general party branch; the

[88]   Chen Yaohui, "'Fei gong' dang zuzhi shuji."
[89]   Ibid.; and Ren Yinghong and Wang Jian, "Goujian feigong qiye dangjian pingjia tixi de yiju yu yuanze."
[90]   Chen Yaohui, "'Fei gong' dang zuzhi shuji."
[91]   "Zhonggong zhongyang bangongting, Guowuyuan bangongting guanyu jinyibu jiaqiang minjian zuzhi guanli gongzuo de tongzhi."

other ninety-seven were regular party branches. [92] In 2002 Zhejiang party secretary Zhang Dejiang went to Wenzhou to urge yet more rapid development of party organizations, and by the end of the year nearly 80 percent of the social organizations in Wenzhou had party organizations of some sort.[93]

Despite these efforts, the party organizations exist more in name than in reality.[94] A random survey of forty-two social organizations shows that only twenty of them had established party organizations, that most of their party organizations were provisional, and that the party organizations met rarely (twelve of the twenty party organizations reported no activities). In the trade associations, the party secretary was usually the group's secretary (*mishuzhang*) and spent most of his time involved in association functions rather than party activities.[95]

The fact that there have been limited efforts to develop party organizations in trade associations does not mean that party control is not strong. It merely means that party control tends to be exercised outside the organization rather than within. As suggested by the example of Nan Cunhui, head of the Zhengtai Group, successful entrepreneurs go out of their way to cultivate good relations with the party, and their associations are unlikely to do anything that the entrepreneurs who lead them do not want them to do. Moreover, most of the office managers of the trade associations are retired former officials, thereby facilitating the associations' expression of their interests, but also indicating that the associations understand very clearly the limits set by the party and government.

Conclusion

More than any other place in China, Wenzhou exemplifies the power of private enterprise and entrepreneurship to generate

---

[92] Guan Tinglian, "Wenzhou hangyexing shetuan dangjian gongzuo yanjiu," p. 212.

[93] Ibid., p. 213.

[94] Ibid., p. 217.

[95] Ibid., p. 218.

wealth. Based on the social capital accumulated in family ties, religion, and other relations, the Wenzhou-ese have developed family-based enterprises locally and throughout the country and the world. Networks provide information about investment opportunities, product possibilities, and business contacts. As these networks spread out from Wenzhou, they created easily the most extensive web of horizontal associational ties in China, a country with a decided governmental preference for vertical ties. The Wenzhou model stands in dramatic contrast to the planned economy that dominated China well into the reform era as well as in contrast to the nexus of the large state-owned and frequently well-connected enterprises that have emerged in recent years. If there is any place that had a chance of building a capitalist economy, complete with business associations pressing industry interests and, hopefully, a legal system that would become increasingly politically neutral, it is Wenzhou. Wenzhou's entrepreneurs not only outgrew the plan, they also seemed likely to outgrow Tang Tsou's "zone of indifference" and to forge new institutional arrangements by creating defined boundaries between state and society.[96]

However, this did not occur. If there is any group of NGOs that should be trusted by the CCP, it is the business associations. Whether one thinks of business associations as creating in Wenzhou a mature civil society, including better governance nurtured by thick networks of associations,[97] or merely as "alternative civilities"[98] that might prepare both society and state for a democratic transition, Wenzhou's business associations have fallen short. As Jiang Hua and Zhang Jianmin state, the vast majority of Wenzhou's business associations were created in a top-down manner and they suffer from administrative dominance, low rates of participation, and inadequate services.[99] The establishment of

---

[96] On the "zone of indifference," see Tang Tsou, "Introduction," p. xxiv.
[97] Robert Putnam, with Robert Leonardi and Raffaella Y. Nanetti, *Making Democracy Work*.
[98] Robert P. Weller, *Alternate Civilities*.
[99] Jiang Hua and Zhang Jianmin, "Minjian shanghui de daibiaoxing ji qi yingxiang yinsu fenxi," p. 78.

party branches in many private enterprises and business associations underscores the continuing efforts of the party-state to blur the lines between state and society that we have observed in other parts of China. Wenzhou's private economy may have outgrown the plan, but it has not outgrown the party-state. The establishment of party branches in private enterprises and trade associations also highlights both the party's determination to prevent the emergence of truly independent sectors and, perhaps ironically, the ability of private enterprises to distort public policy in ways that are favorable to them. Rather than moving toward a regulatory state, the CCP confers benefits on favored enterprises, possibly undermining their long-term competitiveness and certainly corrupting the CCP. The party-state remains dominant, and public policy is fragmented and distorted.

5

Consultative Authoritarianism

The Wenling Model

The municipality of Taizhou sits on Zhejiang's east coast, about two hours by bus north of Wenzhou. Taizhou is a prefectural-level city, a status below the provincial level but above the county level. Because of the particularities of China's administrative structure, Wenling, a county-level city, falls under Taizhou's jurisdiction. With a population of approximately 1.16 million people (as of 2006), Wenling is a large city in its own right, and one of China's most densely populated; indeed, it used to be independent of Taizhou, merging with the larger city only in 1994. Wenling is made up of eleven townships and five neighborhood associations. Its rural population is 971,000, whereas its urban population is 186,000 (though observation suggests that the number of those actually making a living from agriculture and fishing is considerably less than these figures would suggest, based on household registration).[1]

As part of the southern Zhejiang area, Wenling has much in common with Wenzhou to its south. Like Wenzhou, it was in a front-line area likely to be engulfed in any confrontation across the Taiwan Straits, and thus was deprived of central state

---

[1] Wu Xingzhi, "Gongmin canyu, xieshang minzhu yu xiangcun gonggong zhixu de chonggou." This chapter draws on Joseph Fewsmith, "Exercising the Power of the Purse?" and "Participatory Budgeting: Development and Limitations."

investment. Also like Wenzhou, Wenling has a long commercial tradition and a lively religious life, including a very visible Christian presence. It is not clear that religion plays a role in any of the experiments described below, though some argue that the religious influence embodies an egalitarian ethos.[2] It is also a city with high mobility. Of its 1.16 million residents, some 200,000 live away from the city on a long-term basis. Another 500,000 residents have migrated from elsewhere, attracted by the factories and other economic opportunities in the city. In 2006, the urban population of Wenling earned an average of 12,651 yuan per year, whereas the rural population made 6,229 yuan per year, making Wenling one of the wealthiest county-level units in China.[3]

The Wenling economy developed rapidly during the reform era as private enterprises (*minying qiye*) took off. Rather than the small, household-based enterprises of Wenzhou, Wenling's economic growth was spearheaded by large factories, particularly in the shoe and wool-sweater industries. These enterprises developed the "joint-stock cooperative system" (*gufen hezuo zhi*), which gave them a veneer of socialism (due to the use of the term "cooperative"), but they were really private partnerships.

Economic growth brought new interests into being and generated new conflicts, between factory owners and workers, among different industrial interests, and between private entrepreneurs and the local state. Village elections were marred by corruption and violence; indeed, these conflicts apparently worsened over time, sometimes escalating into large-scale mass incidents.[4] Perhaps most of all, economic growth bred a distance between government and society. Alienated local residents tended to distance themselves from government, and with the development of the private economy they generally needed (and expected) little from government (except, of course, at the higher reaches of enterprise

---

[2] Author's interviews.
[3] Wu Xingzhi, "Gongmin canyu," p. 48; and Yu Sunda, "Minzhu zhili shi zui guangfan de minzhu shijian," pp. 56–57.
[4] Wu Xingzhi, "Gongmin canyu," p. 50.

activity where entrepreneurial and government interests mingled freely and closely).[5]

In 1996 the Wenling Chinese Communist Party (CCP) Propaganda Bureau was directed by the Taizhou Propaganda Bureau to carry out another campaign, this time on "education on the modernization of agriculture and villages." The local party secretary, Jin Xiaoyun from Songmen, a town along the east coast, met with a leader of the Wenling Propaganda Bureau because he was worried that few people would show up at scheduled meeting. He was looking to do something different, both to increase attendance and perhaps to burnish his credentials (*zhengji*). Out of these discussions came the idea of inviting local residents to take the stage and express their opinions.

As a result, rather than face a sparsely attended, sullen meeting, Songmen leaders found over 150 people gathered for the meeting. Contrary to usual practice, there was a direct exchange of views between the "masses" and the cadres. People asked about important issues such as the investment environment and the development plan as well as about less critical issues including conflicts among neighbors. Leaders solved what issues they could on the spot and tried to explain the others.[6] Immediately after this first meeting, the Wenling Propaganda Bureau sent someone to Songmen to "squat" for some time and study the issue. The conclusions of this investigation must have been persuasive because only a month and a half later, the Wenling leadership began promoting this system in other townships.[7] These meetings took different forms and different names; Linchuan town opened a "service desk for the convenience of the people," whereas other places held "discussions of people's feelings," "grassroots democratic forums," "rural democracy days," and so forth.[8]

Not everyone welcomed these innovations. In particular, the Wenling Organization Bureau resented the Propaganda Bureau

[5] Ibid.
[6] Ibid., p. 51.
[7] Hu Zhen et al., "Jiceng minzhu jianshe de yizhong haoxingshi," p. 158.
[8] Wu Xingzhi, "Gongmin canyu," p. 52.

for taking the lead in this innovation and it criticized the Songmen party secretary. It should be noted that every other instance of political reform in China has been led either by the party secretary or by the Organization Bureau, usually the two working together, so the displeasure of the Organization Bureau is perhaps understandable. In any event, its criticism of the party secretary put the future of the reform in doubt. In addition, some early meetings were said to have resembled Cultural Revolution–style "struggle sessions" as people expressed long-pent-up resentments. Local cadres not only felt uncomfortable during such proceedings, they also saw them as an additional chore that was likely to be useless. However, Songmen party secretary Jin Xiaoyun felt differently. He took a group of leading cadres to Zhejiang University in Hangzhou, where they spent an entire day listening to professors lecture about the advantages of grassroots democracy. In the evening, the cadres spent hours discussing the advantages and disadvantages of democratic consultation, and by 2 A.M. when their meeting came to a close, the Songmen leadership was convinced that it should go forward.[9] By August 2000 the leadership adopted the name "democratic consultations" (*minzhu kentanhui*) to describe this new innovation. In September 2004, Wenling issued specific regulations to govern implementation of such democratic consultations.[10]

Village and Township Democratic Consultations

Democratic consultations operate somewhat differently at the village and at the township levels. At the village level, in 1998 peasant representative congresses (*nongmin daibiao dahui*) began to appear. Each production team (*xiaozu*) selected one or more representatives, depending on its size, and members of the village party committee and the village committee (the government side of village administration) became de facto members. In 1999, this

[9] Wang Junbo, "'Caogen minzhu,'" p. 190.
[10] "Zhonggong Wenling shiwei guanyu 'minzhu kentan' de ruogan guiding (shixing)," pp. 220–226.

system took on the name of a "village assembly" (*cunmin yishi-hui*). Such a system, regarded as an extension of the democratic consultation system,[11] has now spread throughout Wenling; of the villages under Songmen town, most convene an average of two assembly meetings per month.

Many of these meetings focus on topics of public finance, one of the most contentious issues in rural China. In one village under Ruoheng town, the meeting took on a much greater importance after the elected village head squandered over 1 million yuan of public funds in gambling, provoking a strong reaction among the peasants. Previously, they had trusted someone whom they had freely elected to manage finances honestly, but after this incident they no longer trusted anyone and insisted that matters of public finance should be handled openly by the village assembly. In addition to public finance, there are many other issues that directly affect the interests of villagers in an area like Ruoheng township: Urbanization brings up issues of land requisitions, paving roads, environmental preservation, and so forth, in all of which the village assemblies are involved.[12]

At the township level, democratic consultation is really a system of open hearings on public policy. When the democratic consultation system first began, discussions flowed from topic to topic, making resolution of any one particular issue difficult. After a while, however, it was decided that each democratic consultation should focus on a single issue. The topic for discussion is usually decided by the township party committee or the government, though there are provisions that allow the public to petition the authorities to hold a meeting on a particular topic. The topic, time, and place of the meeting are posted. Although everyone in the township is permitted to attend, no one (other than the leadership) is obligated to participate. These democratic consultation meetings are generally held once a quarter.

At least some democratic consultation meetings do have an impact on public policy and implementation at the township

---

[11]   Xiao Qing, "Wenling cunyihui," pp. 179–180.
[12]   Wang Junbo, "Qiaoran bianhua de 'xiangcun zhengzhi,'" p. 193.

level. For instance, a democratic consultation meeting held in Wenqiao town in July 2002 discussed the leadership's plan to merge two school districts. The leadership believed that the merger would save funds and strengthen the academic level of the surviving school. But such a merger would negatively affect the residents living in the district of the school that was being closed because it would increase either transportation costs or living expenses for those who had to reside in dormitories. Feelings ran very high. In the end, the leadership decided not to merge the two schools right away, but rather to allow parents to choose to which school they would send their children. Before long, the students who were enrolled in the weaker school began transferring to the better school, and the merger was effected without any public outcry.[13]

Similarly, a meeting was held in Songmen town in January 2004 to discuss the creation of a specialized market for products used in the fishing industry. Scattered vendors of these products were often crowded on the streets, causing traffic problems. Residents were asked to discuss whether a market should be established to accommodate them and, if so, where it should be built and who should provide investment. The several hundred people attending this meeting made a decision incorporating the public's preferences for the market's location and the way in which investments would be handled.[14]

Relations with the Local People's Congresses

As the democratic consultation system evolved over the years, from its origins in political work to an expansion of democratic participation and involvement in decision making, it became evident that efforts would be required to bring it within the formal structure of the governing apparatus. After all, the democratic consultation system was informal and "outside the system"

---

[13] Xie Qingkui, "Jiceng minzhu zhengzhi jianshe de tuozhan."
[14] Guo Yukuan, "Difang zhenggai chuangxin," pp. 169–170; see the minutes of this meeting on pp. 252–262.

(*tizhiwai*); without a formal place in the government system, it could easily be challenged or even abolished.

The people's congress system at the township level normally does not have a standing committee; instead, it simply maintains a chair and one or two vice chairs. In Zhejiang, however, there is a "presidium" (*zhuxituan*), made up of the chair, vice chair, and other government leaders, that is responsible for work between sessions of the people's congress (which normally meets only once a year). Moreover, the presidium is invested with responsibility to audit the budget approved by the people's congress and to make suggestions to the local government on important issues. Thus the people's congresses in Zhejiang have a sort of "semi-standing committee."[15]

As early as 2000 the document of the Wenling party committee that adopted the term "democratic consultation meeting" talked in terms of the meetings following the "Regulations Governing the Organization of the Presidiums of Township People's Congresses" (*Xiangzhen renmin daibiao dahui zhuxituan zuzhi tiaoli*) and coordinating relations between the people's congresses and the democratic consultation meetings. Beginning in 2003 the Wenling people's congress began promoting the integration of democratic consultation meetings and local people's congresses. Wenqiao town passed regulations stating that if there were important issues for the government to discuss with the people's congress when it was not in session, the congress should convene a democratic consultation meeting of congress representatives to decide how to proceed.[16] The following year, Songmen town held a meeting to discuss the relocation of the various fishmeal plants in an industrial district to reduce the pollution that was offending residents. This, too, was a contentious issue because it meant creating a district (hence, requisitioning land) and imposing costs on small producers to relocate their plants. In this case, after reaching a resolution, the town leadership asked

[15] He Junzhi, "Jihui jiegou yu liandong celüe."
[16] Jiang Huachun, "Minzhu kentan yu jiceng renda gongzuo jiehe de tansuo he shijian."

the local people's congress to ratify the decision, which it did, thus integrating for the first time the results of a democratic consultation meeting and the actions of the local people's congress.[17]

These democratic consultation meetings were considered a significant advance in the way local government operated, and in 2004 the China Center for Government Innovation awarded Wenling one of its ten prizes.[18]

Breakthrough in Financial Supervision

The lack of transparency in finance has been one of the primary sources of corruption and popular discontent, at both the village and township levels. Yet cadres have still resisted making financial affairs more transparent. This situation began to change in Wenling in 2004 and 2005. In late 2004, He Baogang, then a professor at the University of Tasmania, organized at Zhejiang University in Hangzhou a conference on deliberative democracy. Jiang Zhaohua, who had organized a series of democratic consultation meetings when he was party secretary of Wenqiao town, was persuaded that democratic polling would be a logical, and more scientific, way of extending his work and combining public participation and decision making. As new party secretary of Zeguo, Wenling's largest and most prosperous township, Jiang was eager to experiment with new forms of public participation. The method that He Baogang and Jiang Zhaohua promoted was based on techniques developed by James Fishkin, professor of political science at Stanford University.[19] Based on random sampling, 275 people were selected to discuss and rank the public construction projects then under consideration in Zeguo. What was startling to local officials was that the rank order by the random sample of the importance of various public works projects was quite different from that of the local officials. In April 2005

---

[17] Wang Junbo, "Qiaoran bianhua de 'xiangcun zhengzhi.'"
[18] Zhang Fang, "Wenling shi Xinhe zhen gonggong yusuan gaige de guocheng he zuofa," p. 15.
[19] James S. Fishkin, *When the People Speak.*

the local people's congress endorsed the new rankings that had been publicly selected. This process did not change the budget in Zeguo, nor did it even reveal the entire budget, but it did allow the public to become involved in deliberations over how to spend the capital construction budget.[20]

At nearly the same time, Li Fan, head of China and the World Institute, a private NGO in Beijing, took a different approach. In discussions with the new party secretary in Xinhe town and with the Wenling Propaganda Bureau, Li Fan focused on budgetary reforms. As a result, in July 2005 when the town's people's congress opened its session, town leaders listened to reports by the participants in the democratic consultation meetings, who were not members of the local people's congress, after they had reviewed the budget. This process, of course, required allowing the participants access to at least some of the budget, which normally was highly secret. In the afternoon, the township leaders presented the "Draft Report on the Financial Budget for 2005." Although this report was quite vague, the people's congress representatives were given a more detailed explanation of the budget figures. For the next two hours, the representatives raised questions about the budget. Those who were auditing the proceedings were supposed to pass their questions on to the people's congress representatives, but in the excitement of the meeting, many expressed their views directly. Finally, a resolution was presented to establish a financial affairs committee in the people's congress to oversee implementation of the town budget. This is the perhaps the first such financial affairs committee established in a people's congress at the towns level in China.

After the session ended at 5 P.M., members of this committee gathered with township leaders to further discuss the budget. By the time the people's congress reconvened the next morning, the town leaders had prepared a more detailed explanation of town expenditures and had made numerous adjustments to the budget in accordance with the demands of the people's congress representatives. For instance, the town had originally budgeted 700,000 yuan to replace aging vehicles, but

---

[20] He Baogang and Stig Thøgersen, "Giving the People a Voice?" pp. 675–692.

this line item was reduced to 500,000 yuan. Similarly, an extra 200,000 yuan was allocated to improve the running water system. This breakthrough in financial supervision opened the town budget to an unprecedented degree, taking the Xinhe experiment well beyond the "deliberative democracy" unfolding in Zeguo. This was the first time a town people's congress exercised such supervisory responsibility over a local budget. The process also furthered efforts to bring the democratic consultation system into the people's congress system. The establishment of a financial affairs committee within the people's congress contributed to making local finance more transparent. Wenling leaders vowed to expand this system in 2006.[21]

What led these two towns to initiate such innovations? Although both towns faced social tensions that the reforms helped to address, one cannot conclude that societal interests or conflicts pressured the leaders of the two towns to expand participation and to adopt more "democratic" procedures. On the contrary, in both cases the decision to reform was made by the local party secretary in a top-down fashion. Although both party secretaries were capable and open-minded, they each, perhaps, had different motivations. Jiang Zhaohua in Zeguo, who was originally a Zeguo native, was secure in his position, and the reforms he implemented were somewhat more limited. In contrast, the party secretary in Xinhe, Jin Liangming, was newly appointed. He was from Wenling, but not from Xinhe, and he faced a local township head from Xinhe who had served there for a long time. But Jin was appointed to serve concurrently as head of the local people's congress, so budgetary reform that strengthened the role of the people's congress actually served his interest in securing greater control over the local budget.[22] In neither case did budgetary reform erode the authority of the

---

[21] Zhang Fang, "Wenling shi Xinhe zhen dishisijie renmin daibiao dahui diwuci huiyi zhengfu yusuan minzhu kentan shilu"; and Cao Heli, "Xinhe zhen yusuan shencha gaige mengya."

[22] In Wenling, party secretaries sometimes serve concurrently as head of the local people's congress, but often they do not. Having a separate head of the local people's congress opens up an extra position to reward local officials, and is thus an attractive option for city leaders.

FIGURE 5. Discussing the budget in Wenling

party secretary, and in the case of Xinhe, it may have actually bolstered his authority.[23] The question is whether, once initiated, the budgetary reforms then constrained the behavior of the party or government, a question to which we will return below.

Deepening the Reforms

Perhaps uniquely among all of China's local reforms, the innovations in Wenling evolved and deepened year by year. In Zeguo, the pool of potential participants was expanded in the second year of experimentation with the new forms of public participation by using the electoral list rather than the household registration list, meaning that women had a much better chance of being selected. In fact, at the 2006 meeting, 42 percent of the participants were women. Moreover, the participants were given more detailed information about the proposed construction projects, and they were taken to the sites and encouraged to

---

[23] These conclusions are based on interviews with scholars and officials.

speak to experts. In 2008, Zeguo's experiment began to follow the Xinhe model more closely, as the town government provided a forty-eight-page budget detailing all proposed expenditures. Participants for the consultative phase were still chosen at random, following the Fishkin model. Indeed, this budget was so detailed that in certain cases it exceeded the participants' comprehension abilities. Nevertheless, several suggestions that were made at the democratic consultation meeting, such as increasing support for impoverished rural elders and for basic construction in poor villages, were subsequently adopted by the people's congress.[24] In 2009, for the first time, ten migrant workers were randomly chosen to take part in a separate discussion group. Although this number was not proportional to their overall population, it was the first time views of "nonresidents" were taken into consideration.[25] In 2010 there was a shift in focus to address issues of fairness.[26]

Xinhe town also deepened its reforms. Academic experts were invited to the March 2006 meeting to conduct a training session for the people's congress representatives. The academics stressed that the government's money was, after all, the public's money, and the public should participate in deciding how it is spent. That afternoon, a democratic consultation meeting convened. Participants were divided into three groups: agriculture, industry, and social development. Some eighty participants were given a detailed explanation of the budget (an improvement over the previous summer, when representatives to the people's congress received only a crude outline of the budget). More important, the congress deliberated and passed the "Xinhe Town Financial Budget Democratic Consultation Implementing Procedures (Draft)" to provide a legal foundation for such meetings.[27]

---

[24] Lang Youxing, "Xieshang jizhi hui dailai Zhongguo difang zhili hefaxing de tisheng yu gonggu ma?" p. 85.

[25] He and Thøgersen, "Giving the People a Voice?"

[26] Lang Youxing, "Xieshang jizhi hui dailai Zhongguo difang zhili hefaxing de tisheng yu gonggu ma?" p. 86.

[27] Zhang Fang, "Wenling shi Xinhe zhen dishisijie renmin daibiao dahui diwuci huiyi zhengfu yusuan minzhu kentan shilu."

A democratic consultation meeting was held thereafter. Town deputy head Xie Liming gave reports on implementation of the 2005 budget and plans for the 2006 budget, including a detailed explanation. Then the heads of the three groups who had earlier discussed the budget presented their reports. This was followed by open discussion of the issues. The representatives raised their hands, waited for a microphone to be passed to them, and then asked their questions – sometimes passionately – and the town head or a deputy would respond. For instance, when Chen Yuanfang expressed concern that the income from the leasing of land, as listed on the budget, would not materialize, town head Guo Hailing responded that on the basis of government studies, a fair number of people were willing to sell their land and therefore there would indeed be some income. Others raised questions about the fees for running water, road construction, and educational expenses, all of which still are contentious issues.[28]

Following the democratic consultation meeting, the people's congress presidium and representatives of the government convened a joint meeting to address the issues raised. During this vigorous discussion, government specialists, who were familiar with the budget, dominated and generally were able to persuade their colleagues. For instance, when some thought that the amount budgeted for agricultural training was insufficient, party secretary and people's congress head Jin Liangmin explained that the amount allocated would provide for as much training as that in the previous year and Xinhe's allocation for agricultural training was significantly higher than that in the surrounding towns.[29]

Finally, on the morning of March 9, the revised budget was reported back to the congress, which then divided into five groups for discussions. The representatives were entitled to raise proposals for revisions if they could secure the support of five or more people and as long as additions in one place were balanced by reductions elsewhere. In contrast to the July meeting when the representatives remained silent, this time there was significant

[28] Ibid.
[29] Ibid.

discussion, contributing to the drafting of eight resolutions. Two of the resolutions were adopted by the people's congress; the remaining six, reflecting some unfamiliarity with the process, did not call for specific amounts, as required by the regulations, and were simply exhortatory, encouraging the government to pay attention to this or that construction project. The full congress then passed the revised budget.[30]

Toward Institutionalization?

The greatest challenge to the Xinhe experiment occurred when the local party secretary, Jin Liangmin, was transferred out of the township. This was not a rebuke to his efforts; on the contrary, he had a reputation for being quite capable. The new secretary, in contrast, did not have the same enthusiasm for the participatory budget process that had been adopted during the previous three years. Rather than pin his hopes on greater control over the budget, he relied on his connections with the city government to secure investments for the town.[31] So in January 2007 the local people's congress met and passed the town budget, apparently in a single day and without significant discussion. The Wenling Propaganda Bureau, which had been promoting the Xinhe reform, was not even aware of the meeting until it was over. What occurred is not unusual in the history of reform in China, as efforts chronicled elsewhere in this volume attest. Reforms are often promoted, or at least supported, by local officials for personal reasons, which can span the range of human motivations from idealism to trying to distinguish oneself from one's peers in an effort to get a leg up in the competition for promotion. Whatever the reason (and in Xinhe's case the party secretary did seem to be motivated out of open-mindedness and a practical desire to control the budgetary process), when the official in question is transferred during the normal course of events, the reform tends to wither. Reforms are highly personalistic, and

[30] Ibid.
[31] Author's interview.

institutionalization is without question the most difficult part of the reform process.

The end of Xinhe's participatory budgeting process, however, provoked a local outcry. Officials who had promoted the experiment tried to rally support. Scholars who had participated in it attempted to generate ideas to revive it, and media outlets that had reported extensively on earlier reforms expressed disappointment. Even the former party secretary of Chongqing municipality, Huang Zhendong, who had supported the reforms in Maliu township and was then a member of the Standing Committee of the National People's Congress, visited Wenling and called for a revival of the Xinhe experiment.[32] Without a doubt, the most important source of backing for the process was Wenling city, particularly its people's congress, where Zhang Xueming held the position of chair.

Zhang's position in Wenling was unique. Born in 1959, Zhang served in both Zeguo and Xinhe towns, and was later deputy party secretary of Wenling and concurrent head of its powerful politics and law committee.[33] While serving in the latter position, the biggest case of organized crime in Zhejiang since 1949 was exposed. Over sixty people, including then mayor Zhou Jianguo, Public Security head Yang Weizhong, and Financial Department head Hong Lieming, were arrested and sentenced to long prison terms.[34] Although many leaders had been implicated in the scandal, Zhang emerged unscathed and with his reputation enhanced. His background and prestige made him a formidable head of the

---

[32] Huang led a delegation to Wenling on December 4, 2006, to discuss democratic consultation. See http://hasztsg.com/auto/db/detail.html?db=10101& rid=563163&agfi=0&cls=0&uni=False&cid=0&md=16&pd=6&mdd= 16&pdd=6&count=10&reds=%BB%C6%C1%BC%C6%BD,   accessed February 4, 2012. Local observers say that he expressed support for the Xinhe model, though this support must have been given in rather general terms since the people's congress meeting that bypassed democratic consultation had not yet taken place.

[33] On Zhang's background, see http://wldaily.zjol.com.cn/images/2007–01/29/ 11700527316401361548985784797.pdf, accessed November 24, 2011.

[34] Dong Hua, "Lijian chuqiao chu'e wujin"; and Qiu Shui and Song Anming, "Shei chongdangle hei'e shili."

city people's congress. His support for continuing the experiment in Xinhe was certainly critical in persuading the new party secretary to restore the participatory budgeting.

But doing this had its own complications. According to Chinese law, once the people's congress has met and approved the local budget, it cannot be reconvened to reconsider the budget. But it can be convened to consider amendments to the budget, so that is what happened. The local party secretary, seeing the degree of support for Xinhe's reform, reversed his position, and on April 4, 2007, a second session of the fifteenth people's congress was held. At that session, Zhang Xueming praised the reform Xinhe had pioneered and vowed to extend the reform throughout all the towns of the city as well as to the city itself.[35]

The meeting took place over two days (in contrast to the one-day meeting that had approved the budget). The discussions were apparently lively, frequently focusing on the budget itself, which was not on the agenda, rather than on the amendments to the budget. Finally, a resolution adjusting the budget was passed.[36]

In 2007 the issue was not so much formulating the budget as it was building support for the reform. The Xinhe town reform survived in part because it had become a model that was widely discussed throughout the country. Leaders in Wenling city took pride in its status as a pioneer and supported the reform ever-more vigorously.

Debate

The course of reform in Xinhe took yet another turn in the following year. Up until that point, the questions raised by the representatives to the people's congress were civil, even if sometimes sharp, and town officials had replied with as much detail and persuasiveness as they could muster. The meeting that opened on February 24, 2008, however, proved much more contentious. At the democratic consultation portion of the session,

---

[35] Yang Ziyun, "Xinhe yusuan minzhu jianjin gaige," p. 228.
[36] Ibid.

representatives from Tangxia district asked that the amount of funds to be invested in Tangxia Middle School be increased. That afternoon, deputy township head Lou Jianrong replied that the amount that the representatives had requested be invested – one million yuan – was too large for a resolution to readjust the budget, so the township would have to handle it through a separate measure.[37]

Hearing that their request was not going to be made into a resolution, the representatives from Tangxia district indignantly left the meeting hall. Outside the building, one representative shouted, "3.5 million yuan is allocated for the construction of a park, so why is no money used to support the education of our children?" Town officials attempted to talk to the heads of the Tangxia delegation, explaining the intention to merge Tangxia Middle School with the city school, and to move Tangxia Elementary School into the current middle-school building. Whatever funds needed for maintenance of Tangxia Middle School would be allocated. But this explanation was not conveyed clearly by the leaders of the Tangxia delegation to its members, with the result that they still felt that their resolution had been denied.[38]

The Tangxia district delegation nevertheless was persuaded to return to the meeting hall. However, due to the unhappiness of the members, the atmosphere at the meeting became "lively." One representative declared, "Which is more urgent – nurturing our children or maintaining the old city district? The government should increase funding for education and not allocate funds to construct the urban district."[39]

All of a sudden a real debate was emerging between representatives who had differing interests, but the 2006 resolution to hold a joint meeting with people's congress representatives and participants in the democratic consultation meeting had no provisions for debate. The previous procedure had been for representatives to raise questions and for town officials to respond. Now,

---

[37] Chen Peichan, "Yangguang caizheng," pp. 242–243.
[38] Ibid.
[39] Ibid., p. 244.

representatives were arguing with one another over priorities. Li Fan and Chen Yimin of the Wenling Propaganda Bureau quickly conferred with the town leaders, who then decided to allow for debate. More precisely, they decided that after various resolutions on adjusting the budget were drafted, they would convene the people's congress and permit debate. As Zhou Meiyan, a researcher with the Shanghai people's congress, commented, this was the first time in the history of China's people's congresses that there had been debate between representatives.[40]

Everyone quickly realized that a debate would allow representatives a chance to try to persuade one another, to build coalitions, and to compromise. Such possibilities, however, were not taken advantage of. In the end, two new resolutions, one calling for increased funding to maintain the old city district and one to rebuild a road, went down in defeat (the resolution on Tangxia Middle School was not presented). This was the first time resolutions were defeated, reflecting, to a certain extent, the emergence of interest advocacy – but without the necessary logrolling to achieve consensus. The final budget was passed by a show of hands rather than by a formal vote because township officials were worried that the budget might not be passed – and no local congress had ever failed to pass the budget. Rather than confront a "constitutional" crisis, the leadership deviated from democratic norms and called for a show of hands, which pressured the representatives to vote in favor of the budget.

By 2009 the situation in Xinhe had returned to normal. The party secretary still was not enthusiastic about the process and would not consider ways to deepen the reform, but neither did he work to stifle the meetings. The "democratic consultation" session was held in the afternoon of the first day of the 2009 meeting. A total of fourteen representatives raised questions. One asked what would happen if the government were not able to sell the land at the estimated price (about half of the income in Xinhe township comes from the sale of land). Another argued that

---

[40] Zhou Meiyan, "Xinhe renda yusuan shenji de shijian yu sikao," pp. 312–313.

expenditures for the disabled should be increased from 370,000 yuan to 500,000 yuan. Another complained about the high costs of hooking up to running water, and still another commented on the need to spend more money to maintain historical sites so as to boost tourism.[41]

After listening to these comments for two hours, the presidium retreated to a conference room to debate how the budget should be revised. Perhaps somewhat strangely, this discussion was presided over by the town party secretary, not the chair of the people's congress. The next morning, after listening to the government's proposed resolutions for revising the budget, the representatives broke up by district (there are seven districts in Xinhe town). The discussions at these district conferences were quite vigorous, focusing largely on issues of public safety and the environment. Sure enough, when the plenary session reconvened, a resolution to increase the public safety budget from 1.48 million yuan to 1.68 million yuan was tabled, as was a second resolution to increase the "daily sanitation" budget from 600,000 yuan to 1 million yuan. The extra funds were to come out of the preparatory funds.[42]

Unlike the previous year when the resolutions raised by representatives had focused on the interests of their particular districts, these resolutions affected the welfare of all the people in the town, so there was very little discussion. Accordingly, the presidium called a vote and the representatives marked their ballots and put them into the ballot box at the front of the hall. The first resolution carried with 68 votes in favor, 14 against, and 6 abstentions; the second resolution carried with 73 in favor, 9 against, and 6 abstentions.[43]

During the now seven years that this experiment in participatory democracy has been carried out, it appears that the regulations became more precise, the procedures were followed more carefully, and the representatives grew more skilled in

---

[41] Author's interviews with participants.
[42] Meeting records.
[43] Ibid.

expressing their interests and in drafting resolutions that were likely to appeal to the majority of the representatives.

Extension of "Deliberative Democracy"

The evolution of deliberative democracy (more accurately called "consultative authoritarianism"), or participatory budgeting, in Zeguo and Xinhe towns suggests a gradual deepening of the system. As Lang Youxing notes, the general trajectory of the reforms has been from improving cadre–mass relations through democratic consultation to providing input on decision making and to a type of hearing system in which public policies are aired.[44] Just as the nature of the meetings has evolved, the system of democratic consultation and participatory budgeting has spread to more townships, upward to the city government, and into new areas. In 2008, participatory budgeting was expanded to six of Wenling's eleven towns. The willingness of a town to adopt participatory budgeting depends on a number of factors, including relations among the various actors, the state of finance in the various towns, and the perceived degree of local contention. There is also a general reluctance for one area to copy another area. If the desire to demonstrate political accomplishment is one motivation for initiating reform, copying gets little credit in terms of the cadre evaluation system. However, in this case, once there were clear signals from the city level, specifically the city people's congress, towns were much more willing to adopt this system. But as they adopted it, they endeavored to outdo one another. So once it became clear that they were expected to adopt some form of participatory budgeting, there was a degree of competition to demonstrate enthusiasm and creativity.

For instance, Ruoheng town began to distribute budget information to the people's congress representatives one month before the congress convened. This provided adequate time for the representatives to absorb the information and to discuss the issues

---

44 Lang Youxing, "Xieshang jizhi hui dailai Zhongguo difang zhili hefaxing de tisheng yu gonggu ma?" p. 80.

with friends and neighbors. Similarly, Wenqiao town adopted an innovation whereby a preliminary budget was presented to the representatives at a democratic consultation meeting before the budget was finalized and presented to the people's congress. Wenqiao even discussed a "gender budget" at one such forum. The local women's association invited about fifty women to an afternoon democratic consultation meeting to discuss how parts of the budget, particularly those parts related to education, would affect women. Though one might assume that women, who clearly play a secondary role in China's political system, might have remained quiet at such a meeting, in fact their rate of participation and the sharpness of their views compared favorably with those of the representatives of industry who had met in the morning.[45]

Beginning in 2008, participatory budgeting was adopted in the Transportation Bureau (Jiaotongju) of Wenling city. In this case, the government prepared a draft budget, which was subsequently reviewed by the standing committee of the people's congress. Thereafter, over eighty people, including people's congress representatives, leaders from different townships and neighborhood associations, relevant experts, retired cadres, and common people, participated in a democratic consultation meeting. After extensive discussions, the people's congress standing committee finalized the budget and passed it on to the congress for approval. Six months later, another democratic consultation meeting was held to assess how well the budget was being followed. These events were all covered by local television and newspapers, and relevant documents were posted on the Web site of the people's congress.[46]

The following year, the experiment to make Wenling's budget more transparent was pushed even further, with the participation of eight bureaus that accounted for almost half of the budget. The push for greater openness was led by the Irrigation Bureau, which was headed by Jin Liangming, the former party secretary

---

[45] Based on author's observation, March 17, 2010.
[46] Zhang Xueming, "Cong 'zhengfu yusuan' dao gonggong yusuan," p. 57.

of Xinhe town. In February, Jin invited representatives from the people's congress, the Finance Bureau, and the townships and neighborhood associations to examine the budget and to make suggestions. In July, when the people's congress finally met, the budgets of all eight bureaus were posted on-line.[47]

Effectiveness

There seems to be little doubt that the budgetary reforms in Wenling, whether they have followed the Zeguo model or the Xinhe model (since 2008 Zeguo, in fact, has basically followed the Xinhe model), have brought an unprecedented openness to budgetary affairs at the local level. Moreover, they have infused a degree of life into an organ – the township people's congress – that is normally lifeless and even useless. But one still has to question the limitations of this model.

One obvious limitation is the composition of the township people's congress. About one-third of congress representatives are township or village cadres and about two-thirds of all representatives are party members. Other representatives are successful entrepreneurs or retired cadres (with more than a little overlap between these groups). Even if one includes the "democratic consultation" phase, the degree of representativeness is disappointing. About 230 people participate in this phase, or roughly double the 110 members of the local people's congress (using the figures from Xinhe). About 45 percent of all participants are party members; many are village cadres of one sort or another; and many others are entrepreneurs. In other words, participants in both the democratic consultation phase and the party congress deliberations are very much part of the socioeconomic elite; they are not in any sense an oppositional, or even potentially oppositional, political force. Although some face competitive elections, most are selected as representatives by the party. Perhaps it is best to view them as part of an expanded local elite, willing to protect

47 Jiang Yun, Zhang Min, and Wu Minli, "Yangguang yusuan pobing zhi ju."

local (elite) interests but not willing to challenge the prevailing order.[48]

The main weakness in the Xinhe model is in its implementation. Ideally, the people's congress would meet toward the end of the calendar year to pass the budget for the following year. As it now stands, the congress meets in the spring (sometimes even later), after a significant part of the year has already passed. Also ideally, the congress should meet quarterly so that it can supervise implementation, but even in Xinhe, it has been able to meet only twice a year. Xinhe has tried to compensate for this deficiency by establishing a Finance and Economics Committee. The committee was expanded in 2006 from five to eight people in an effort to allow it to play a more important role, but it still has been a disappointment. The primary reason that this committee cannot play a more important role in supervising implementation of the budget and in participating in the drafting of the budget for the next year is that its members generally come from the presidium of the people's congress, and the presidium is too close to the township government to be truly independent. Most significant, no township in Wenling has yet to convene a year-end meeting to review how the budget was actually implemented. Thus supervision over expenditures remains weak. Indeed, the budgets made public and approved by the people's congresses are probably not the entire budgets. Township governments retain pockets of money that can be used at their discretion for matters that come up over the course of the year. The relationship between government and business at the local level is such that businesses will fund certain events at the government's request.[49]

Aside from these structural issues, there are also issues about the effectiveness of the Wenling/Xinhe model in restraining local expenditures. Interviews with local officials suggest that the openness of this budgetary reform does indeed bring pressures on officials to limit their spending. For instance, there is some evidence

[48] Author's interviews.
[49] Author's interviews.

that this process has restrained the indebtedness of Xinhe township. In 2004 Xinhe had a deficit of 55 million yuan, but by 2006 the deficit was reduced to 43 million yuan. Efforts to restrain indebtedness explain the expansion of budgetary openness to the city level.[50] However, evaluating this and other trends is difficult in the absence of data from other townships. Is the spending in Xinhe township more restrained or better directed than that in other townships?

Moreover, it is surprisingly difficult to compare various line items in the budget. For instance, under the "government operations budget," the 2005 budget specified that there were 102 employees, of whom seventy-five were retirees, and three people had "left their posts" (*tuizhi renyuan*), costing a total of 6.5 million yuan. However, "wages and welfare" costs in the 2009 budget, amounting to 7.78 million yuan, including twenty-eight contractors (*zipin renyuan*), but the budget did not specify the number of other employees. In other years, the cost of contractors was listed separately, sometimes specifying the number and sometimes not. So it is extremely difficult to answer such basic questions as whether or not the cost of township employees is increasing and, if so, whether this is due to more employees or to higher wages.[51]

The 2005 budget allocated 1.2 million yuan for a "Social Security and Housing Fund," but that item was reduced 40 percent to only 500,000 yuan in the 2006 budget and it disappeared altogether in subsequent budgets. Were these funds no longer needed? Were these expenses folded into other line items? There is no record of representatives having complained about these expenditures and there is no explanation for their disappearance. To take another example, "Communist Party Activities" are listed in the 2009 budget as costing 1.3 million yuan (why party activities are a line item in a government budget is a different matter!). There is also a separate line item for "Activities

---

[50] Author's interview.
[51] Data on Xinhe's budget can be found in Li Fan (Ed.), *Wenling shiyan yu Zhongguo difang zhengfu gonggong yusuan gaige*.

of Mass Organizations" for 410,000 yuan. In the 2008 budget, however, there is one line item for "Party Building and Discipline Inspection" that amounts to 500,000 yuan, and a separate item of 1 million yuan for the costs for the "Federation of Labor, Communist Youth League, and Women's Association Committees." Are these items comparable? Should we assume that total expenditures on party activities fell from 1.51 million yuan in 2008 to 1.3 million yuan in 2009? Probably, but it is difficult to know for sure.[52]

Sustainability

Whatever shortcomings the Wenling model has, it nevertheless has been sustained over a long period (eight years as of 2012), and its procedures have been improved and expanded into new locations and areas of governance. Although other areas have adopted various measures to open their budgets, none has yet been as successful as Wenling. How can we explain this success, and what does it bode for the future?

When looking at Wenling, it is difficult to ignore the number of people who were willing to take the initiative, whether Songmen party secretary Jin Xiaoyun and Propaganda Bureau cadre Chen Yimin in 1999, or Jiang Zhaohua and Jin Liangming in Zeguo and Xinhe towns in 2005, or people's congress head Zhang Xueming throughout the decade. There are many reasons why local cadres favor reform, whether from a desire to distinguish themselves, from idealism, or due to some combination of both. Zhang Xueming possessed an unusual combination of characteristics. As noted above, he had held important positions in Wenling city (deputy party secretary and head of the politics and law committee), had established a reputation for integrity, and, as head of the people's congress, had no hope of further advancement (since age and career trajectory meant he could not serve as secretary of the Wenling party

[52] Ibid.

committee). He could thus give play to his ideals with little risk to his future. And the role of the people's congresses in Zhejiang, at least on paper, allowed him (as well as Jin Liangming) to be innovative. If the party secretaries in Wenling had opposed these efforts, the reforms would have failed, but the need to restore Wenling's reputation in the wake of the corruption scandal and the desire to deal more successfully with burgeoning social contradictions led the party secretaries to back the efforts by Zhang Xueming and others.

The roles of the media and outside experts were also critical. From the beginning the media played a role in developing the Wenling "brand," while academic experts provided advice and introduced the Wenling experience to others. By now, Wenling has become the subject of numerous academic studies and master's and doctoral theses. Its growing reputation was an important factor in overcoming the reluctance of Xinhe's new party secretary to carry out the reform. And Wenling leaders are very conscious of their reputation and seek to preserve it.

Even now, however, the continuity of the Wenling reform depends less on its support from social forces in Wenling than it does on appealing to higher-level leaders. From the beginning, Wenling's reforms had to win the support not only of local leaders but also of those in Taizhou, to which Wenling is subordinate. It was a major victory for local reformers when Premier Wen Jiabao endorsed Wenling's deliberative wage-setting policy in November 2007.[53] More recently, Zhejiang party secretary Zhao Hongzhu has suggested that reforms similar to those in Wenling can be popularized throughout the province.[54] The importance of these higher-level endorsements points to the still very strong authoritarian and hierarchical system in which the reforms are taking place. Democratic consultation and participatory budgeting may absorb societal views and ameliorate conflict, but the impetus behind continued reforms remains the appeal to

---

[53] Yang Lin, "Wenling: Minzhu kentan zhi hua."
[54] Author's interviews.

higher-level authorities. Thus, He Baogang, who has promoted "deliberative democracy," has also, and more appropriately, used the term "deliberative authoritarianism."[55]

Given the support higher levels have shown for Wenling, one might think that promotion of democratic consultation and participatory budgeting would have been incorporated into the cadre evaluation system, but this is not the case. Some cadres who have supported these reforms have been promoted, most obviously Jiang Zhaohua, who became a deputy party secretary of Wenling city. However, this can largely be attributed to the importance of Zeguo, the largest town in Wenling, and to the fact that Zeguo secretaries are generally promoted. But Jin Liangming's transfer from Xinhe to the Irrigation Bureau did not constitute a promotion. And local observers do not believe that the aloofness of Xinhe's party secretary to participatory budgeting will affect his chances of promotion. The party system, including the Organization Bureau, remains distinct from the people's congress system and the promotion of Wenling's reforms. The Organization Bureau has never fully embraced Wenling's reforms, as the absence of town elections (of either the public recommendation, public selection [*gongtui gongxuan*] or public recommendation and direct election [*gongtui zhixuan*] type) suggests. Personnel decisions are made by the party system, particularly the Organization Bureau, not by the people's congress system or the Propaganda Bureau.

Although the Wenling model has been touted as a way of enhancing the legitimacy of local government by increasing the political participation of local citizens and enhancing interactions between the local state and citizens, it is more accurate to say that the system strengthens intra-elite legitimacy, not only by expanding participation of the political elite (well beyond the very small group that normally dominates local government), but also by including in the deliberations the economic and societal elite. To the extent that the system can restrain the arbitrary use of power, expand the participation of the local elite, and subject

---

[55] He and Thøgersen, "Giving the People a Voice?"

spending to some control, it is a system that serves the purposes of both higher- and local-level elites. These features do not make it democratic, nor do they suggest a trend in that direction. On the contrary, to the extent that the system enhances intra-elite legitimacy, it still reinforces authoritarian, if less abusive, power.

Conclusion

The Chinese Communist Party (CCP) has understood the need for some sort of political reform since the 1980s. Deng Xiaoping gave his well-known speech, "Reform of the Party and State Leadership System," in August 1980, and thereafter, in the early 1980s the party began regularizing party affairs, including inner-party life and retirement. The topic of political reform was hotly debated in 1986, and the *People's Daily* reprinted the text of Deng's 1980 speech on July 1, 1987, in anticipation of the Thirteenth Party Congress that would be convened that fall.[1] At the congress, Zhao Ziyang outlined the first effort to systematically separate the party from the government apparatus and to create a civil service.[2] In those years, however, the party's focus on political reform centered on increasing economic efficiency, even though liberal intellectuals spoke hopefully of democracy.

The violent suppression of protesters around Tiananmen Square and elsewhere in 1989 led to a reversal of efforts to separate the party from the state; any party groups that had been removed from government bureaucracies were quickly reintroduced. Nevertheless, the topic of political reform never

[1] Deng Xiaoping, "Dang he guojia lingdao zhidu de gaige."
[2] Zhao Ziyang, "Yanzhe you Zhongguo tese de shehuizhuyi daolu qianjin."

disappeared entirely, and the collapse of the Soviet Union in 1991 forced the CCP to think about the issue systematically.[3] One result of these deliberations was the enactment of regulations on the selection and appointment of cadres, issued on a trial basis in 1995. These regulations were drawn up under the auspices of Zeng Qinghong, a close protégé of Jiang Zemin, who at the time headed the Central Organization Department. The regulations were based on an understanding that the very closely held power to appoint cadres – as laid out in Chapter 1 of this volume – had led to the personalization of power and corruption. The basic solution, as encompassed in these regulations, was a proposal to involve more people in the selection process, in other words to promote "inner-party democracy." It is very clear that the Central Organization Department supported such an expansion of inner-party democracy and that Sichuan province responded to this appeal.

Although the notion of inner-party democracy goes back decades, what gave it new life was not only the palpable example of the collapse of the Soviet Union but also the increasing number of mass incidents taking place throughout the country in the early and mid-1990s. In late 1992 Jiang Zemin declared, "Problems in the rural areas have provoked the peasants' discontent and anger,"[4] and shortly thereafter, as if to prove the general secretary's point, peasants in Renshou county, Sichuan, rioted, in January and then again in June 1993, on a scale that shocked leaders in Beijing. Wan Li, head of the National People's Congress (NPC), who had done as much as anyone to promote the rural reforms in the late 1970s and early 1980s, said that when asked what they needed, the peasants of Renshou responded, "We need nothing but Chen Sheng and Wu Guang," the legendary leaders of the peasant revolt that brought down the Qin dynasty in 209 BCE.[5]

---

[3] David Shambaugh, *China's Communist Party*, pp. 41–86.
[4] Cited in Thomas P. Bernstein, "Farmer Discontent and Regime Responses," p. 213.
[5] Thomas P. Bernstein, "Farmer Discontent and Regime Responses," p. 213.

This admission suggests that new and different efforts were needed to monitor the behavior of local officials. The economic reforms of the 1980s were decentralizing, giving local cadres incentives, indeed demands, to develop the local economies, but they also provided opportunities for local cadres to pursue their own economic interests. Sometimes they prospered by starting legitimate businesses, but often they engaged in corruption of various sorts. As the economic interests of cadres clashed with the interests of local villagers, the temptation to use power to secure resources (such as land) and opportunities was often irresistible. This problem was exacerbated by the centralizing tax reform of 1994 and by the elimination of agricultural and miscellaneous fees in 2006. Higher-level authorities had no choice but to turn a blind eye to local cadres who squeezed local peasants for money; after all, it was the higher-level authorities who were insisting on economic development.

If the personalization of power was the source of the problem, then involving more people in the promotion of cadres was an obvious solution. Although there had been several local experiments with inner-party democracy in the early 1990s, it was really with the promulgation of the 1995 regulations on the selection and appointment of cadres that such experiments expanded, both in numbers and in boldness. Incentives varied according to position in the system. The drawing-up of the 1995 regulations reflected concerns of Jiang Zemin and Zeng Qinghong at the very highest levels. Implementation was left to the organization departments at the central and provincial levels. The Central Organization Department certainly had an interest in expanding inner-party democracy – both because its head Zeng Qinghong had promoted it and because as an organization it wanted to find better ways to monitor local officials. At the other end of the spectrum, local – township – cadres had an interest in these experiments, though their interests varied from person to person and place to place. People such as Zhang Jinming, who supervised the Buyun election, seem to have been motivated primarily by idealism, although the initial problem Zhang faced in Xinqiao and Baoshi was one of restoring government legitimacy after serious cases of corruption. Liu Qianxiang in Pingchang county hoped to deflect pressures from the many cadres who had been laid off following the reorganization and merger of towns and villages. No doubt Liu was also motivated to some extent to establish his political merit, although that hope was dashed after a clash with his superior. Candidates who run for various offices are more motivated to try to find a way to climb the bureaucratic ladder than they are to serve a particular constituency. Even if they desire to serve the local population, they are inevitably transferred to a new position – their loyalty is to the party organization, not to the locality.

In between the extremes of the highest levels of political power and the local cadres who face immediate problems of governance are large bureaucracies with little, if any, interest in expanding political participation. County party secretaries might promote someone who resolved a governance issue by expanding inner-party democracy, but they have no interest in being constrained by similar pressures. Indeed, county party secretaries face few constraints in their behavior, and devising mechanisms that might effectively monitor their behavior seems impossible within the bounds of the current system. No wonder that those who study corruption complain that it is becoming worse, despite, and sometimes because of, efforts to expand participation. Including more actors in promotion decisions means that there are now even more people whom supplicants for office need to please.

However, the real clash is between increasing participation in the process of deciding promotions – whether limited, as in the "public recommendation, public selection" (*gongtui gongxuan*) model, or more inclusive, as in the "public recommendation and direct election" (*gongtui zhixuan*) model – and the principle of "the party controls the cadres" (*dang guan ganbu*), which has long guaranteed the centralization of power. After all, there is a logic to the old system. Power is concentrated in the hands of a few people, and ultimately only in the person of the party secretary, because responsibility is also concentrated. Accountability in the system means being accountable to one's immediate superior to carry out those tasks assigned by that superior, and this means granting the subordinate the power he (or occasionally she) needs to get things done. That power includes the right to promote people. Asking cadres to act in a democratic way (a "democratic work style") is one thing; forcing them to do so by constraining their power and behavior through institutions is quite another. The Organization Departments, from the top on down the bureaucratic ladder, might want to solve governance issues, but they certainly do not want to see their own power eroded.

So one is confronted with a contradiction: the number of inner-party elections of one sort or another undoubtedly expanded over the years as they moved from Sichuan into Yunnan, Henan, Hubei, Jiangsu, and elsewhere, but their vigor declined. The high tide of inner-party democracy appears to have crested early in the twenty-first century. By the 2006 election cycle, inner-party democracy was becoming more formalistic, and for the 2011–2012 election cycle there are no signs of any new breakthroughs.

If inner-party democracy has been disappointing, so, too, have been civil society, at least if business associations are considered a part of civil society, and "deliberative democracy." The rise of private business has reshaped the political economy of many parts of China, but nowhere more so than in southeastern Zhejiang. The development of business associations and the establishment of Wenzhou chambers of commerce throughout China (and the outside world) draw on elements of Chinese tradition (which never established the sort of independence that burgher communities had in early modern Europe) and suggests that the sorts of institutions and horizontal links that might constrain the state and nurture the rule of law have yet to develop. Perhaps they will come eventually, but there is no evidence that the chambers of commerce or trade associations are pressuring governments for better policies, less corruption, a more neutral administration of policy, and so forth. On the contrary, evidence suggests that private interests are just as eager to "blur the lines" as is the CCP. Indeed, developing private relations and distorting public policy is much more profitable and less politically dangerous than is lobbying for a regulatory state guided by law, even though the latter is probably in China's best long-term interests.

Nowhere has a reform, however limited, lasted longer than that in Wenling, and there is some evidence that the budgetary openness and greater role of the local people's congress may be spreading, though it is still too early to be sure. It is also too early to say that Wenling's reforms have been institutionalized and form an effective constraint on government action. As Chapter 5 points out, the Wenling experiment came about and has been sustained by the convergence of a number of factors: the growth of a wealthy entrepreneurial elite, a leadership that was emerging from scandal, open-minded leaders, leaders maneuvering for greater control, and a head of the local people's congress – Zhang Xueming – whose support was bolstered by his prestige. Emerging as a model has been good for Wenling. Being a model has brought it fame, and as a result its cadres seem to have better chances of promotion. The Organization Bureau, which initially opposed the reform, has softened its opposition as it too has benefited (through its ability to provide promotions). But nothing is certain. A change of political leadership or a change in the political climate could well set back or even erase the progress that has been made so far.

The Wenling experiment has increased political participation to some extent by incorporating the wealthy entrepreneurs of the area. But there has been no move toward inner-party democracy or any other form of political reform. The Organization Bureau and political elite remain firmly in charge of personnel movements. Participatory budgeting is indeed a step forward, but it remains "consultative authoritarianism" with no clear path in the direction of democratic participation.

There are those who remain optimistic that experiments in inner-party democracy and "deliberative democracy" (*xieshang minzhu*, as it is usually called in China) will gradually promote a liberalization of the Chinese polity and some form of democracy. After all, China's economic reform progressed in an incremental fashion; why shouldn't its political reform? And economic growth under authoritarian rule eventually gave way to democracy in Korea and Taiwan; perhaps China will follow a similar trajectory.

The issue of the creation of institutions, however, is critical. Unless new institutions can emerge and effectively constrain the behavior of local cadres, as well as make the CCP follow rules and make the goods it distributes truly public, the path of incremental reform seems to be effectively blocked. If the emergence of social conflict on the one hand and new economic interests on the other creates pressures to draw the lines between state and society more clearly, the CCP has been very effective at blurring such lines (with the help of those societal interests that benefit from blurred lines).

It is, of course, possible that societal pressures and ideational changes will sooner or later bring about the collapse of the regime, as they have in so many other authoritarian systems. However, at such a time the absence of institutions will make the formation and consolidation of some sort of democratic regime even more difficult. So whether one thinks in terms of systemic evolution or more convulsive change, the issue of institutions is vital.

As the analysis in this volume suggests, China has pursued political reform with very limited results for more than a decade. During this time, mass incidents have grown in number, scale, and intensity (to the extent these things can be judged accurately). Does this matter? Can China continue to follow the path of fitful and mostly unsuccessful political reform and emerge, perhaps in another decade or so, as a more open and democratic (in whatever sense of the word) polity? Probably not. The only consistent concern running through the implementation of the various political reforms has been that they must not get out of control. This is one reason that they have mostly been implemented in smaller and more out-of-the-way places. As tensions rise in Chinese society, it will become increasingly difficult to pursue political reform precisely because the odds of experiments spinning out of control will increase.

Indeed, there are some indications that the Chinese government is beginning to pursue alternative strategies; if it is not completely abandoning political reform, then at least it is doing other things simultaneously. In late 2010, Hu Jintao convened a Politburo "collective study session" to discuss "the correct handling of contradictions among the new people in the new era." Hu went on to call for strengthening (*jiaqiang*) and innovating (*chuangxin*) "social management" (*shehui guanli*).[6]

The issue of social management was subsequently highlighted in the "Outline of the Twelfth Five-Year Plan for National Economic and Social Development," adopted by the Fourth Session of the Eleventh National People's Congress, which met in Beijing in March 2011. Unlike similar documents in the past, in this outline there is a special section on enhancing and innovating social management.[7] The document establishes a three-level understanding of social management, including building a more "service-oriented" government in order to "prevent and reduce" the number of social problems, strengthening "dynamic management" to "resolve the masses' legitimate and rational appeals," and strengthening the party-state's ability to manage the sudden outbreak of public incidents. It also calls for establishing a "social stability risk and evaluation mechanism" that will assess the social impact of construction projects, including land requisitions, before they are undertaken.[8]

This new emphasis on social management reflects increased high-level concerns over mass incidents, but also suggests that the party leadership believes that in the short run measures other than political reform are more likely to maintain social stability. These measures include an emphasis on "people-centered services," which appears to be a new formulation to replace the government's 2004 goal of building a "service-oriented government." "Social organizations" apparently are intended to be vested with new supervisory powers. As Zhou Yongkang, the Politburo member in charge of the Central Political and Legal

---

[6] "Hu Jintao zhuchi zhonggong zhongyang zhengzhiju di ershisanci jiti xuexi."
[7] See Zhang Guo and Chen Fengli, "Minsheng yu shehui guanli duli cheng 'pian.'"
[8] *Woguo guomin jingji yu shehui fazhan shi'er wu guihua gangyao.*

Leadership Commission, puts it, "We should continuously attach importance to developing, managing, and supervising" social organizations and "include them in party committees and the government-led social organizations' system."[9]

Although social services and "coordination" of social organizations are intended to be the mainstays of social management, media commentary makes clear that the strengthening of police work is also part of the agenda. This security work was intended to develop from China's experience of hosting the 2008 Olympics. Following the close of the games, Minister of Public Security Meng Jianzhu called for "turning the Olympic experience into a lasting mechanism." The following year, Zhou Yongkang echoed this, by saying, "We should apply the successful experience of security at the Beijing Olympics in developing a public order prevention and control system."[10]

The new emphasis on social management suggests that the CCP sees a need to address social issues through a combination of better services and stronger police work rather than through political reform. If the increased social tensions will make political reform more, rather than less, difficult to carry out, then the turn to social management, including the strengthening of public security, suggests that prospects for political reform are not bright. China pursued political reform since the mid-1990s as an important tool to better monitor the behavior of local cadres and to address social unrest, but these efforts appear to be petering out just as social tensions are increasing. In the future, looking back over the decade from the mid-1990s through the first few years of the current century, Chinese leaders may well wish that they had pursued political reform more vigorously when they had had the chance.

---

[9] Zhou Yongkang, "Jiaqiang he chuangxin shehui guanli jianli jianquan Zhongguo tese shehuizhuyi shehui guanli tixi."

[10] Zhou Yongkang, "Shenru guanche luoshi kexue fazhanguan cujin jingji pingwen jiaokuai fazhan baozhang shehui gongping zhengyi weihu shehui hexie wending."

Glossary

Cai Ronghui	蔡荣辉
Chen Yuanfang	陈元方
Chen Yun	陈云
Deng Xiaoping	邓小平
Guo Hailing	郭海灵
Guo Luoji	郭罗基
Hu Qiaomu	胡桥木
Hu Yaobang	胡耀邦
Hua Guofeng	华国锋
Huang Dengren	黄登仁
Huang Zhendong	黄镇东
Jiang Nanxiang	蒋南翔
Jiang Zemin	江泽民
Jiang Zhengcheng	姜正成
Jin Liangming	金良民
Jin Xiaoyun	金小云
Li Aihua	李爱华
Li Chuncheng	李春城
Li Fan	李凡
Li Hongbin	李洪彬
Li Yuanchao	李源潮

Li Zhongbin	李仲彬
Lou Jianrong	娄建荣
Lü Rizhou	吕日周
Luo Chongmin	罗崇敏
Mao Zedong	毛泽东
Nan Cunhui	南存辉
Qiu He	仇和
Tan Xiaoqiu	谭晓秋
Wu Yan	吴炎
Xie Liming	谢立明
Yu Jingzhong	俞敬忠
Zhang Chu	张楚
Zhang Jinming	张锦明
Zhang Xueming	长学明
Zhao Ziyang	赵紫阳
Zhou Meiyan	周梅燕
Zhou Xingyi	周兴义
Baoshi town	包石镇
Bazhong city	巴中市
Binhai county	滨海县
Chongqing city	重庆市
Honghe Hanni-Yi Autonomous prefecture	红河哈尼族彝族自治州
Huaiyin city	淮阴市
Kai county	开县
Kaiyuan city	开远市
Linchuan town	淋川镇
Luxi county	泸西县
Maliu township	麻柳乡
Nanbu county	南部县
Paihui village	徘徊村
Pei county	沛县
Renshou county	仁寿县
Rongjing county	荣经县
Ruoheng township	若横镇

Shiping county		石屏县
Shuyang county		沭阳县
Sihong county		泗洪县
Siyang county		泗阳县
Songmen town		松门镇
Suining city		遂宁市
Sunan		苏南
Suqian city		宿迁市
Suyu county		宿豫县
Taizhou city		台州市
Tangxia district		塘下片
Weng'an county		瓮安县
Wenling city		温岭市
Wenqiao town		温桥镇
Wu'an city		武安市
Xindu district		新都区
Xinhe town		新河镇
Xinqiao township		新桥乡
Xuzhou		徐州
Yandongzi village		岩洞子村
Yangjie township		羊街乡
Yuanping county		原平
Yucheng district		雨城区
Zeguo town		泽国镇
Zhuozi county		卓资县
ba da wang	八大王	eight big kings
babu gongzuofa	八步工作法	"Eight-Step Work Method"
baiyoulu	柏油路	oiled road
banshichu	办事处	offices
banzi	班子	leading group or squad
baofa	宝法	magic weapon
bianzhi	编制	authorized number

cha'e	差额	elections in which the number of candidates exceed the number of positions
changrenzhi	常任制	standing representative system
cun dangzhibu yu cun weiyuanhui lianxi huiyi	村党支部与村委员会联席会议	joint conference of the village party branch and the village committee
cuncai xiangguan	村财乡管	village accounts managed by township
cunmin yishihui	村民议事会	village assembly
cunzhang	村长	village head
dagongzi	打工仔	worker
dang guan ganbu	党管干部	party controlling the cadres
dangnei minzhu	党内民主	inner-party democracy
dangqun lianxi hui	党群联席会	joint party–mass meeting
Dangzheng lingdao ganbu xuanba renyong gongzuo	党政领导干部选拔任用工作暂行条例	"Interim Regulations on the Selection and Appointment of Leading Cadres of the Party and State"
daxue zhuanke	大学专科	vocational institute
fenhui	分会	branches
fenliu	分流	to be separated (from government organs)
fu keji	副科级	deputy office rank
fuchuji	副处级	deputy department level
fuchuzhang	副处长	deputy office head

ganbu guanshi bu guanqian	干部管事不管钱	"cadres manage affairs, not money"
ganbu kaohe zhidu	干部考核制度	cadre evaluation system
geming dang	革命党	revolutionary party
gexing guanyuan	个性官员	"officials with personality"
Gongshanglian	工商联	Federation of Industry and Commerce (FIC)
gongshi	公示	"public showing"
gongtui gongxuan	公推公选	"public recommendation, public selection"
gongtui gongxuan gongzuo lingdao xiaozu	公推公选工作 领导小组	leadership small group for public recommendation and public selection
gongtui zhixuan	公推直选	public recommendation and direct election
gongwei	工委	work committee
gongxuantuan	公选团	electoral group
guakao danwei	挂靠单位	sponsoring unit
guandao	官倒	official profiteering
guanli bumen	管理部门	supervising department
Guanyu chongxin queren shehui tuanti yewu guanli danwei de tongzhi	关于重新确认 社会团体业务 管理 单位的通知	"Notice Reconfirming the Management Units for Social Groups"
Guanyu dangnei zhengzhi shenghuo de ruogan zhunze	关于党内政治 生活的若干准则	"Guiding Principles on Political Life within the Party"

Guanyu jiakuai tuijin hanye xiehui shanghui gaige he fazhan de ruogan yijian	关于加快推进行业 协会商会改革和 发展的若干意见 展的若干意见	"Some Views on Accelerating the Reform and Development of Industry Associations and Chambers of Commerce"
Guanyu jiaqiang gongzuo nongcun gufen hezuo qiye dangjian de shixing yijian	关于加强农村股份 合作企业党建作的试行意见	"Provisional Views on Strengthening Party Building Work in Rural Stock Enterprises"
Guanyu jiaqiang xin de jingji zuzhi dang de jianshe de yijian	关于加强新的经济 组织党的建设 的意见	"Views on Strengthening Party Building in New Economic Organizations"
Guanyu tongyi Luchengqu jiaqiang dui dahuoji hangye guanli de pifu	关于同意鹿城区 对打火机行业加 强 管理的批复	"Response Agreeing to Strengthening Management of the Lucheng District Lighter Industry"
Guanyu xiugaidang de zhangcheng baogao	关于修改党 的章程的报告	"Report on the Revision of the Party Charter"
Guanyu zujian tongye gonghui jiaqiang hangye shidian yijian de baogao	关于组建同业 公 会加强行业试点 意见的报告	"Report on Views on the Experimental Establishmen of Trade Associations and the Strengthening of Trade Governance"
gufen hezuo zhi	股份合作制	joint-stock cooperative system

haitui	海推	"sea recommendation"
haixuan	海选	village "sea election"
hangye xiehui	行业协会	trade association
hangye xiehui shidian gongzuo lingdao xiaozu	行业协会试点 工作领导小组	leadership small group for experimental work with trade associations
Jiaodian fangtan	焦点访谈	"Focus Interview"
jiaotongju	交通局	transportation department
Jin sanjiao gongchang	金三角工厂	Golden Triangle Enterprise
Jingji yanjiu	经济研究	*Economic Research* (journal)
Jingmao wei	经贸委	Economic and Trade Office
jingshen weiji	精神危机	spiritual crisis
Jinling yaoye jituan	金陵药业集团	Jinling Pharmacy Group
ju	局	bureau
juzhang	局长	bureau chief
laodong jileigong	劳动积累工	unpaid labor
liangkuai paizi, yitao banzi	两块牌子, 一套班子	"two signs 'but [only]' one group of officials"
liangtui yixuan	两推一选	"two recommendations, one selection" system
licai xiaozu	理财小组	finance committee
luancun	乱村	"chaotic" village
Luchengqu xieye xiehui	鹿城区鞋业协会	Lucheng District Shoe Industry Association

Luchengqu xieye zhengdun bangongshi	鹿城区鞋业整顿办公室	Shoe Industry Rectification Office
maiguan maiguan	买官卖官	buying and selling of office
minjian	民间	societal
minjian zuzhi	民建组织	nongovernmental organization (NGO)
minyi ceyan	民意测验	public opinion evaluation
minying qiye	民营企业	private enterprise
minzhu ceping	民主测评	"democratic evaluation"
minzhu kentanhui	民主恳谈会	democratic consultation
mishuzhang	秘书长	secretary
nan huo	南货	delicacies from south China
nancun	难村	"difficult" village
naoshixiang	闹事乡	"troublemaker"
neiding	内定	internally designated (candidate)
nongcun kuaiji weituo daili zhi	农村会计委托代理制	"village accounting agency system"
nongmin daibiao dahui	农民代表大会	peasant representative congress
nongmin yiwugong	农民义务工	unpaid labor
paichusuo	派出所	police station
pishi	批示	approval
qiang guojia, ruo shehui	强国家, 弱社会	"strong state, weak society"
qingtui	清退	to be laid off
quanneng zhuyi	全能主义	"totalistic"
shehui ren	社会人	societal person
shikong	失控	to lose control

shuanghekou	双河口	two rivers junction
Shuanghekou	双河口大桥	Small Group for the
daqiao lingdao	领导小组	Construction of the
xiaozu		Two Rivers Junction
		Bridge
siqingli	四清理	"four cleanups"
tedian	特点	special characteristic
Tigaiwei	体改委	Office of Economic
		Structural Reform
tizhiwai	体制外	outside the system
tuizhi renyuan	退职人员	people who left their
		posts
wei renmin fuwu	为人民服务	to serve the people
weida chuangzao	伟大创造	great creation
wenhua weiji	文化危机	cultural crisis
Wenzhou	温州服装商会	Fashion Industry
fuzhuang		Chamber of
shanghui		Commerce
xiang	乡	township
Xiangzhen renmin	乡镇人民代	"Regulations
daibiao dahui	表大会主席	Governing the
zhuxituan zuzhi	团组织条例	Organization of the
tiaoli		Chair's Committees
		of Township
		People's Congress
xiaoneng geming	效能革命	efficiency revolution
xiaozu	小组	production team
xiefen shijian	泄愤事件	"anger-venting
		incidents"
Xindu qu Mulan	新都区木兰镇	"Implementing
zhen dangweishuji	党委书记的实	Methods for the
de shishi banfa	施办法	Public
		Recommendation
		and Direct Election
		of the Mulan
		Township Party
		Secretary"

xinyang weiji	信仰危机	belief crisis
Xuanqu lianxi huiyi	选区联席会议	Conference of Electoral Districts
xuantiaosheng	选调生	"selected student"
yibashou	一把手	number one leader
yifa zhiguo	依法治国	"governing the country through law"
yijiantiao	一肩条	"carrying both posts on one shoulder pole"
yipiao foujue	一票否决	single vote veto
yishi yyi	一事一议	village consultation
yizhi sanhua	一制三化	"one mechanism and three transformations"
you zhuan you hong	又专又红	"both red and expert"
Yushan gang	玉山	"Jade Mountain" gang
zengliang minzhu	增量民主	"incremental democracy"
Zhejiangsheng hangyexing jingjituan shixing banfa	浙江省行业性经济社团试行办法	"Provisional Methods [Governing] Economic Trade Associations in Zhejiang"
zhen	镇	town
zhengji	政绩	political accomplishment
zhibu	支部	party branch
zhidu	制度	system
zhiqing	知青	"sent-down youth"
zhizheng dang	执政党	ruling party

Zhongguo gongchandang difang zuzhi xuanju gongzuo tiaoli	中国共产党地方组织选举工作条例	"Regulations Governing CCP Organization of Local Elections"
Zhongguo gongchandang jiceng zuzhi xuanju gongzuo zanxing tiaoli	中国共产党基层组织选举工作暂行条例	"Provisional Regulations Governing Grassroots CCP Organizing Elections"
Zhongguo gongchandang nongcun jiceng zuzhi gongzuo tiaoli	中国共产党 农村基层组织 工作条例	CCP Regulations on the Organization of Grassroots Work in the Rural Areas
Zhongwu xueyuan	钟吾书院	Zhongwu Academy
zhuxituan	主席团	"presidium"
zipin renyuan	自聘人员	contractors

Bibliography

Bao Yonghui and Xu Shousong. *Zhengdao: Qiu He shinian* [Governing: Ten years of Qiu He]. Hangzhou: Zhejiang renmin chubanshe, 2009.

Bergsten, C. Fred, et al. *China: The Balance Sheet*. New York: Public Affairs, 2006.

Bernstein, Thomas P. "Farmer Discontent and Regime Responses." In Merle Goldman and Roderick MacFarquhar (Eds.), *The Paradox of China's Post-Mao Reforms*, pp. 197–219. Cambridge, Mass.: Harvard University Press, 1999.

Brook, Timothy, and B. Michael Frolic (Eds.). *Civil Society in China*. Armonk, N.Y.: M.E. Sharpe, 1997.

Burns, John P., and Wang Xiaoqi. "Civil Service Reform in China: Impacts on Civil Servants' Behaviour." *The China Quarterly*, no. 201 (March 2010): 58–78.

Cai Dingjian. "Women xuyao zenyang de gaigejia?" [What type of reformer do we need?]. *Xinwen zhoukan*, no. 5 (2004), available at http://www.51ar.net/magazine/html/109/109544.htm, accessed November 24, 2011.

Cao Heli. "Xinhe zhen yusuan shencha gaige mengya" [The birth of the budget inspection reform in Xinhe township]. *Caijing*, August 8, 2005, available at http://magazine.caijing.com.cn/2005-08-08/110064422.html, accessed November 24, 2011.

Chan, Vivian Pik-Kwan. "Beijing Indicates Recognition of Landmark Township Election." *South China Morning Post*, March 1, 1999, p. 9.

Chen Anjin and Xu Mingjun. "Jindai Wenzhou shanghui xingqi tanxi" [Analysis of the rise of chambers of commerce in modern Wenzhou]. *Zhejiang shehui kexue*, no. 4 (April 2010): 68–73, 127.

Chen, Fong-jing, and Jin Guantao. *From Youthful Manuscripts to River Elegy: The Chinese Popular Cultural Movement and Political Transformation, 1979–1989.* Hong Kong: Chinese University Press, 1997.

Chen Jian. "Zhuozhe gaige guanghuan de zhuanzhi he renzhi geng zhide jingti" [Be wary of autocratic and personal rule covering up the bright light of reform], available at http://www.world-china.org/newsdetail.asp?newsid=1283, accessed February 5, 2012.

Chen Jiaxi. "Siying qiye dangjian de kunnan yu fangxiang" [The difficulty and direction of establishing party organizations in private enterprises]. *Lilun tantao*, no. 1 (January 2009): 136–139.

Chen Peichan. "Yangguang caizheng: Wenling zai gudu zhong qianxing" [Sunshine finance: Wenling advancing alone]. In Li Fan (Ed.), *Wenling shiyan yu Zhongguo difang zhengfu gonggong yusuan gaige*, pp. 242–243.

Chen Shengyong, Wang Jinjun, and Ma Bin. *Zuzhihua, zizhu zhili yu minzhu* [Organized, self-governance, and democracy]. Beijing: Zhongguo shehui kexue chubanshe, 2004.

Chen Xiwen. "Dangqian de nongcun jingji fazhan xingshi yu renwu" [The developmental situation and tasks of the rural economy at present]. *Nongye jingji wenti*, no. 1 (January 2006): 7–11.

Chen Yaohui. "'Fei gong' dang zuzhi shuji" [Party secretaries in "non-state" (enterprises)]. *Wenzhouren*, no. 13 (May 10, 2010): 8–10.

Chen Yun. "Jianchi an bili yuanze tiaozheng guomin jingji" [Readjust the national economy in accordance with the principle of proportionality], March 21, 1979. In *Chen Yun wenxuan (yijiuwuliu-yijiubawu nian)*, pp. 226–231.

Chen Yun. "Tiba peiyang zhongqingnian ganbu shi dangwu zhi ji" [Promoting and cultivating young and middle-aged cadres is an urgent task], May 8, 1981. In *Chen Yun wenxuan (yijiuwuliu-yijiubawu nian)*, pp. 262–266.

Chen Yun wenxuan (yijiuwuliu-yijiubawu nian) [Selected works of Chen Yun (1956–1985)]. Beijing: Renmin chubanshe, 1986.

"Dangzheng lingdao ganbu xuanba renyong gongzuo zanxing tiaoli" [Interim regulations on the work of selecting and appointing leading cadres of the party and state], February 9, 1995. In Zhongyang jiwei fagui shi, zhongyang zuzhibu bangonting (Eds.), *Zhongguo gongchandang dangnei fagui xuanbian*, pp. 398–410.

Deng Xiaoping. "Dang he guojia lingdao zhidu de gaige" [On the reform of the party and state leadership system]. *Renmin ribao*, July 1, 1987. This speech was originally published in *Deng Xiaoping wenxuan (1975–1982)*, pp. 280–302. Beijing: Renmin chubanshe, 1983.

Deng Xiaoping. *Deng Xiaoping wenxuan (yijiuqiwu-yijiubaernian)* [Selected works of Deng Xiaoping (1975–1982)]. Beijing: Renmin chubanshe, 1983.

"'Dianxing quntixing shijian' de jinghao" [Alarm of a "typical mass incident"]. *Liaowang*, no. 36 (September 8, 2008): 28.

Dickson, Bruce J. "Conflict and Non-compliance in Chinese Politics: Party Rectification, 1983–87." *Pacific Affairs*, vol. 63, no. 2 (Summer 1990): 170–190.

Dickson, Bruce J. *Red Capitalists in China: The Party, Private Entrepreneurs, and Prospects for Political Change.* New York: Cambridge University Press, 2003.

Dickson, Bruce J. *Wealth into Power: The Communist Party's Embrace of China's Private Sector.* New York: Cambridge University Press, 2008.

Ding Buzhi. "Weng'an, 'bu an' de xiancheng" [Weng'an, an "unsafe" county seat]. *Nanfang zhoumo*, July 10, 2008, available at http://www.infzm.com/content/14365, accessed November 24, 2011.

"Direct Election of the Township Leader," available at http://www.innovations.harvard.edu/awards.html?id=6192, accessed January 14, 2012.

"Disanjie 'Zhongguo difang chuangxin jiang' woshi 'xiaoneng geming' ruwei." [Our city selected for "China local innovation award" for its "efficiency revolution"], available at http://old.yjdj.com/newscenter/Info.asp?NewsID=31320&BigClassID=11&BigClassName=&SmallClassID=79&SmallClassName=&SpecialID=0, accessed February 5, 2012.

Dong Hua. "Lijian chuqiao chu'e wujin: Wenling '3.23' zhuan'an da puguang" (Drawing the sharp sword from its sheath, removing evil completely: Wenling's "March 23" special case exposed). *Lüshi shijie*, no. 6 (2001): 9–12.

Edin, Maria. "State Capacity and Local Agent Control in China: CCP Management from a Township Perspective." *The China Quarterly*, no. 173 (March 2003): 35–52.

Ertman, Thomas. *Birth of the Leviathan: Building States and Regimes in Medieval and Early Modern Europe.* New York: Cambridge University Press, 1997.

Fang Ning. "Yong minzhu he fazhi de banfa chuli maodun" [Using democracy and rule of law to resolve contradictions]. *Renmin ribao*, October 21, 2010, p. 23.

Fewsmith, Joseph. "An 'Anger-Venting' Mass Incident Catches the Attention of China's Leadership." *China Leadership Monitor*, no. 26

(Spring 2008), available at http://www.hoover.org/publications/china-leadership-monitor/3557, accessed November 30, 2011.

Fewsmith, Joseph. "Bo Xilai and Reform: What Will Be the Impact of His Removal?" *China Leadership Monitor*, no. 38 (Summer 2012). Available at http://www.hoover.org/publications/china-leadership-monitor.

Fewsmith, Joseph. "Bo Xilai Takes on Organized Crime." *China Leadership Monitor*, no. 32 (May 10, 2010), available at http://www.hoover.org/publications/china-leadership-monitor/article/5353, accessed November 24, 2011.

Fewsmith, Joseph. "Chambers of Commerce in Wenzhou and the Potential Limits of 'Civil Society' in China." *China Leadership Monitor*, no. 16 (Fall 2005), available at http://www.hoover.org/publications/china-leadership-monitor/3487, accessed February 5, 2012.

Fewsmith, Joseph. *China since Tiananmen: From Deng Xiaoping to Hu Jintao*, 2nd ed. New York: Cambridge University Press, 2008.

Fewsmith, Joseph. "Exercising the Power of the Purse?" *China Leadership Monitor*, no. 19 (Fall 2006), available at http://www.hoover.org/publications/china-leadership-monitor/3508, accessed February 3, 2012.

Fewsmith, Joseph. "Institutional Innovation at the Grassroots Level: Two Case Studies." *China Leadership Monitor*, no. 18 (Spring 2006), available at http://www.hoover.org/publications/china-leadership-monitor/3501, accessed February 1, 2012.

Fewsmith, Joseph. "Notes on the First Session of the Eighth National People's Congress." *Journal of Contemporary China*, vol. 1, no. 3 (Summer 1993): 81–86.

Fewsmith, Joseph. "Participatory Budgeting: Development and Limitations." *China Leadership Monitor*, no. 29 (Summer 2009), available at http://www.hoover.org/publications/china-leadership-monitor/3578, accessed February 3, 2012.

Fewsmith, Joseph. "Political Creativity and Political Reform in China?" In Brantly Womack (Ed.), *China's Rise in Historical Perspective*, pp. 227–246.

Fewsmith, Joseph. "Promotion of Qiu He Raises Questions about Direction of Reform." *China Leadership Monitor*, no. 17 (Winter 2006), available at http://www.hoover.org/publications/china-leadership-monitor/3494.

Fishkin, James S. *When the People Speak: Deliberative Democracy*. Oxford: Oxford University Press, 2009.

Florini, Ann, Hairong Lai, and Yeling Tan. *China Experiments: From Local Innovation to National Reform*. Washington, D.C.: Brookings Institution Press, 2012.

Foley, Michael W., and Bob Edwards. "The Paradox of Civil Society." *Journal of Democracy*, vol. 7, no. 3 (July 1996): 38–52.

Foster, Kenneth W. "Embedded within State Agengies: Business Associations in Yantai." *The China Journal*, no. 47 (January 2002): 41–65.

Fu Guibao and Xu Chenglun. "Tuoshan chuzhi renmin neibu maodun yinfa de qunti shijianxing shijian" [Appropriately handle mass incidents arising from contradictions among the people]. *Gong'an yanjiu*, no. 11 (November 2006): 55–58.

Gandhi, Jennifer. *Political Institutions under Dictatorship*. New York: Cambridge University Press, 2008.

Gao Peiyong. "Jian quan fenpei jizhi diaocheng liyi geju" [Improve the allocation system to adjust the pattern of interests]. *Renmin ribao*, October 21, 2010, p. 23.

Gao Xinjun. "Difang zhengfu chuangxin yuanhe nan chixu" [Why are local government innovations difficult to sustain?]. *Zhongguo gaige*, May 17, 2008, available at http://news.xinhuanet.com/politics/2008–05/17/content_8195456.htm, accessed November 24, 2011.

Gao Xinjun. "Pingchangxian dangnei minzhu gaige zhi shang" [The death of Pingchang's reforms.] *Zhongguo xiangcun faxian*, no. 2 (2010): 107–109.

Gao Xinjun. "Weiji guanli he houxuanju zhili de chenggong fanli: Dui Chongqing Kaixian Maliuxiang 'babu gongzuofa' zhidu chuangxin de fenxi" [A successful example of crisis management and post-electoral governance: An analysis of the "eight-step work method" institutional innovation in Maliu township in Chongqing's Kai county], available at http://www.chinaelections.org/newsinfo.asp?newsid=98698, accessed November 24, 2011.

Goldman, Merle, and Roderick MacFarquhar (Eds.). *The Paradox of China's Post-Mao Reforms*. Cambridge, Mass.: Harvard University Press, 1999.

Guan Tinglian. "Wenzhou hangyexing shetuan dangjian gongzuo yanjiu" [Study of party building work in Wenzhou trade groups]. In Jin Hao and Wang Chunguang (Eds.), *2010 nian: Wenzhou jingji shehui xingshi fenxi yu yuce*, pp. 211–223.

"Guanyu dangnei zhengzhi shenghuo de ruogan zhunze" [Several principles on political life in the party]. In Zhongyang jiwei fagui shi, zhongyang zuzhibu bangonting (Eds.), *Zhongguo gongchandang dangnei fagui xuanbian*, pp. 40–55.

Guo, Peng. "Asymmetrical Information, Suboptimal Strategies, and Institutional Performance: The Paradox of the 1995 Regulations of China's Official Promotion System." Ph.D. dissertation, Boston University, 2004.

Guo Songmin. "Qiu He de 'huise didai zhili moshi'" [Qiu He's governance model for the gray area]. *Nanfang zhuomo*, February 5, 2004, available at http://hlj.rednet.cn/c/2004/02/09/520898.htm, accessed November 24, 2011.

Guo Yukuan. "Difang zhenggai chuangxin: Jujiao Zhejiang Wenling 'minzhu kentanhui'" [Innovation in local political reform: Looking at Wenling's "democratic consultation meetings" in Zhejiang]. In Mu Yifei (Ed.), *Minzhu kentan*, pp. 168–175.

Guowuyuan bangongting. "Guanyu jiakuai tuijin hangye xiehui shanghui gaige he fazhan de ruogan yijian" [Some views on accelerating the reform and development of industry associations and chambers of commerce], available at http://politics.people.com.cn/GB/1026/5825218.html#, accessed February 5, 2012.

Guowuyuan fazhan zhongxin ketizu. "Guowuyuan yanjiu jigou dui Zhongguo yiliao gaige de pingjia yu jianyi" [The evaluation and suggestions on China's health-care reform by a research organ of the State Council]. *Renmin wang*, August 4, 2005, available at http://politics.people.com.cn/GB/30178/3592637.html, accessed November 24, 2011.

Han Fuguo, *Minying jingji zhidu bianqian zhong de gongshanglian: zuzhi de shuangzhong daili* [The Federation of Commerce and Industry in the midst of the changes in the private economy: Organized dual agency]. Beijing: jingji kexue chuban she, 2006.

Harding, Harry. *Organizing China: The Problem of Bureaucracy, 1949–1976*. Stanford, Calif.: Stanford University Press, 1981.

He Baogang and Stig Thøgersen. "Giving the People a Voice? Experiments with Consultative Authoritarian Institutions in China." *Journal of Contemporary China*, vol. 19, no. 66: 675–692.

He Junzhi. "Jihui jiegou yu liandong celüe: Difang renda zai Wenling 'minzhu kentan' zhong de chengzhang" [Opportunity structure and associated strategy: The growth of the local people's congress out of Wenling's "democratic consultation"]. Paper presented at Xieshang canyü jizhi yü Zhongguo jiceng zhili guoji xueshu yantaohui [International Conference on Participatory Mechanisms and China's Grassroots Governance], Wenling, Zhejiang, July 6–7, 2010, available at http://www.wlrd.gov.cn/article/view/5184.htm, accessed November 28, 2011.

He Zengke. "Chuangxin tizhi cong yuantou shang yufang he zhili fubai" [Renew the system so as to prevent and control corruption at its source]. In He Zengke et al., *Zhongguo zhengzhi tizhi gaige yanjiu*, pp. 356–403.

He Zengke. "Nongcun zhili zhuanxing yu zhidu chuangxin – Hebei sheng Wu'an shi 'yizhi sanhua' jingyan de diaocha yu sikao"

[The transformation of governance and institutional innovation in villages – An investigation and reflections on the experience of 'one mechanism and three transformations' in Wu'an city, Hebei province]. In He Zhengke, Gao Xinjun, Yang Yuedong, and Lai Hairong (Eds.), *Jiceng minzhu he difang zhili chuangxin*, pp. 1–26.

He Zengke, Gao Xinjun, Yang Xuedong, and Lai Hairong (Eds.). *Jiceng minzhu he difang zhili chuangxin* [Grassroots democracy and innovations in local governance]. Beijing: Zhongyang bianyi chubanshe, 2004.

He Zengke et al. *Zhongguo zhengzhi tizhi gaige yanjiu* [Studies on China's political structural reform]. Beijing: Zhongyang bianyiju chubanshe, 2008.

Hong Zhenning (Ed.). *Wenzhou gaige kaifang 30 nian* [Thirty years of reform and opening in Wenzhou]. Hangzhou: Zhejiang renmin chubanshe, 2008.

Hu Jintao. "Gaoju Zhongguo tese shehuizhuyi weida qizhi duoqu qianmian jianshe xiaokang shehui xin shengli er fendou" [Hold high the great banner of socialism with Chinese characteristics and strive for new victories in building a moderately prosperous society in all respects], October 15, 2007. In Zhonggong zhongyang wenxian yanjiushi (Ed.), *Shiqida yilai zhongyao wenxian xuanbian*, 1.1–43.

"Hu Jintao zhuchi zhonggong zhongyang zhengzhiju di ershisanci jiti xuexi" [Hu Jintao chairs the twenty-third collective study of the CCP Politburo], *Xinhua wang*, September 29, 2010. Available at http://news.xinhuanet.com/politics/2010–09/29/c_13535934.htm, accessed January 20, 2012.

Hu Zhen et al. "Jiceng minzhu jianshe de yizhong haoxingshi" [A good form of building grassroots democracy], available at http://news.sina.com.cn/c/2004–12-07/10495146300.shtml, accessed November 28, 2011. In Mu Yifei (Ed.), *Minzhu kentan*, pp. 151–163.

Hu Zhusheng. *Wenzhou jindaishi* [Modern history of Wenzhou]. Shenyang: Liaoning renmin chubanshe, 2000.

Hu Zujun. "Guanyu gong'an jiguan yufang he chuzhi quntixing shijian de sikao" [Thoughts on preventing and handling mass incidents]. *Gong'an yanjiu*, no. 4 (April 2009): 14–18.

Huang Shaoqing and Li Zhengquan. "Qiye zizhi zuzhi de liliang: Wenzhou dahuoji yingde Oumeng fanqingxiao susong qishi" [The strength of enterprise self-governing organizations: Lessons gained from Wenzhou's lighters winning against the European Union anti-dumping suit], *Xin qingnian quanheng zazhi*, April 13, 2006, available at http://finance.sina.com.cn/review/observe/20060413/16052499197.shtml, accessed January 20, 2012.

Jiang Hua and Zhang Jianmin. "Minjian shanghui de daibiaoxing ji qi yingxiang yinsu fenxi" [Analyzing the factors influencing the representativeness of societal chambers of commerce]. *Gonggong guanli xuebao*, vol. 6, no. 4 (October 2009): 78–127.

Jiang Huachun. "Minzhu kentan yu jiceng renda gongzuo jiehe de tansuo he shijian" [Explorations and practice of integrating democratic consultation and the work of local people's congresses]. *Fazhi yü jiandu*, no. 14 (2006), available at http://www.wlrd.gov.cn/article/view/675.htm, accessed November 24, 2011.

Jiang Yun, Zhang Min, and Wu Minli. "Yangguang yusuan pobing zhi ju" [An ice-breaking move in budgetary openness]. *Zhejiang zai xian xinwen wangzhan*, November 12, 2009, available at http://zjnews.zjol.com.cn/05zjnews/system/2009/11/12/016015494.shtml, accessed November 24, 2011.

Jiang Zemin. "Accelerating the Reform, the Opening to the Outside World and the Drive for Modernization, so as to Achieve Greater Successes in Building Socialism with Chinese Characteristics." Report Delivered at the Fourteenth National Congress of the Communist Party of China on October 12, 1992, available at http://www.bjreview.com.cn/document/txt/2011–03/29/content_363504.htm, accessed January 28, 2012.

Jiang Zemin. "Hold High the Great Banner of Deng Xiaoping Theory for an All-Round Advancement of the Cause of Building Socialism with Chinese Characteristics to the Twenty-First Century." Report Delivered at the Fifteenth National Congress of the Communist Party of China on September 12, 1997, available at http://www.bjreview.com.cn/document/txt/2011–03/25/content_363499_5.htm, accessed November 24, 2011.

Jiang Zemin. "Quanmian jianshe xiaokang shehui, kaichuang Zhongguo tese shehuizhuyi shiye xin jumian" [Build a well-off society in an all-round way and create a new situation in building socialism with Chinese characteristics]. In Zhonggong zhongyang wenxian yanjiushi (Ed.), *Shiliuda yilai zhongyao wenxian xuanbian*, 1.1–44.

"Jiang Zemin zai qingzhu jiandang bashi zhounian dahuishang de jianghua" [Jiang Zemin's talk at the meeting celebrating the 80th anniversary of the founding of the party], available at http://www.people.com.cn/GB/shizheng/16/20010702/501591.html, accessed January 20, 2012.

Jin Hao and Wang Chunguang (Eds.). *2008 nian Wenzhou jingji shehui xingshi fenxi yu yuci* [Wenzhou's economic and social circumstances: Analysis and prediction, 2008]. Beijing: Shehui kexue wenxian chubanshe, 2008.

Jin Hao and Wang Chunguang (Eds.). *2009 nian Wenzhou jingji she-hui xingshi fenxi yu yuci* [Wenzhou's economic and social circumstances: Analysis and prediction, 2009]. Beijing: Shehui kexue wenxian chubanshe, 2009.

Jin Hao and Wang Chunguang (Eds.). *2010 nian: Wenzhou jingji she-hui xingshi fenxi yu yuce* [Wenzhou economic and social circumstances: Analysis and prediction, 2010]. Beijing: Shehui kexue wenxian chubanshe, 2010.

Jing Yuejin. *Dangdai Zhongguo nongcun "liangwei guanxi" de weiguan jiexi yu hongguan youshi* [Micro analysis and macro view of "relations between the two committees" in villages in contemporary China]. Beijing: Zhongyang wenxian chubanshe, 2004.

Jowitt, Kenneth. *New World Disorder: The Leninist Extinction.* Berkeley: University of California Press, 1992.

Lai Hairong. "Jingzhengxing xuanju zai Sichuansheng xiangzhen yi ji de fazhan" [The development of competitive elections at the township level in Sichuan province]. *Zhanlüe yu guanli*, no. 2 (2003): 57–70.

Lai Hairong. *Zhongguo nongcun zhengzhi tizhi gaige: Xiangzhen ban-jing zhengxing xuanju yanjiu* [China's rural political reform: A study of township semi-competitive elections]. Beijing: Zhongyang bianyi chubanshe, 2009.

Lang Youxing. "Xieshang jizhi hui dailai Zhongguo difang zhili hefax-ing de tisheng yu gonggu ma?" [Can the deliberative mechanism increase and consolidate the legitimacy of China's local governance?]. Paper presented at Xieshang canyü jizhi yu Zhongguo jiceng zhili guoji xueshu yantaohui [International Conference on Participatory Mechanisms and China's Grassroots Governance], Wenling, Zhejiang, July 6–7, 2010.

Lee, Hong Yung. *From Revolutionary Cadres to Party Technocrats in Socialist China.* Berkeley: University of California Press, 1991.

Li Bing et al. (Eds.). *Quxiao nongyeshui hou nongcun gongzuo jizhi biange yantao* [An exploration of the change in the village work mechanism since the abolition of the agricultural tax]. Chengdu: Sichuan Academy of Social Sciences and Meishan Municipal Government, 2006.

Li Changping. *Wo xiang zongli shuo shihua* [I spoke the truth to the premier]. Beijing: Guangming ribao chubanshe, 2002.

Li, Cheng (Ed.). *China's Changing Political Landscape: Prospects for Democracy.* Washington, D.C.: Brookings Institution Press, 2008.

Li, Cheng. *China's Leaders: The New Generation.* Lanham, Md.: Rowman & Littlefield, 2001.

Li Fan et al. *Chuangxin yu fazhan: Xiangzhenzhang xuanju zhidu gaige 2008* [Innovation and development: Reforming the township head election system in 2008]. Beijing: Dongfang chubanshe, 2000.

Li Fan (Ed.). *Wenling shiyan yu Zhongguo difang zhengfu gonggong yusuan gaige* [The Wenling experiment and China's local government: Reform of public budgets]. Beijing: Zhishi chanquan chubanshe, 2009.

Li Fan (Ed.). *Zhongguo jiceng minzhu fazhan baogao, 2004* [Grassroots democracy in China, 2004]. Beijing: Zhishi chanquan chubanshe, 2005.

Li Hongbin. "Maliuxiang dangwei tuixing 'babu gongzuofa' qingkuang jieshao" [Introduction to the circumstances surrounding Maliu township's introduction of the "eight-step work method"]. March 30, 2004. Unpublished.

Li Hongbin. "Zai shi lingdao lai Maliu diaoyan zuotanhui shangde huibao" [Report at the investigation seminar for municipal leaders coming to Maliu township], February 26, 2004. Unpublished.

Li Jiajie. "'Gongtui zhixuan' yu 'deng'e xuanju' bijiao'" [Comparing "public recommendation and direct elections" and "elections with the number of candidates equaling the number of positions"]. In Wang Changjiang (Ed.), *Dangnei minzhu zhidu chuangxin*, pp. 104–125.

Li, Lianjiang. "The Politics of Introducing Direct Township Elections in China." *The China Quarterly*, no. 171 (September 2002): 704–723.

Li, Lianjiang. "The Two Ballot System in Shanxi Province: Subjecting Village Party Secretaries to a Popular Vote." *The China Journal*, no. 42 (July 1999): 103–118.

Li, Lianjiang, and Kevin J. O'Brien. "The Struggle over Village Elections." In Merle Goldman and Roderick MacFarquhar (Eds.), *The Paradox of China's Post-Mao Reforms*, pp. 129–144.

Li Ling. "Sichuan dang dahui changrenzhi shidian diaoyan de sikao" [Thoughts on Sichuan's experiment with the standing representative system for party congresses], March 18, 2006, available at http://wendang.baidu.com/view/cba89e0c52ea551810a687bc.html, accessed November 24, 2011.

Li Rong. "Zhang Jinming: Zhongguo jiceng minzhu shijian de tanluzhe" [Zhang Jinming: Exploring the practice of local democracy in China]. *Xin xibu*, no. 9 (September 2009): 22–25.

Liao Yiru. "Wenzhou feigongyouzhi qiye dangjian gongzuo fazhan baogao" [Report on the development of party building work in Wenzhou's non public enterprises]. In Jin Hao and Wang Chunguang (Eds.), *2009 nian Wenzhou jingji shehui xingshi fenxi yu yuci*, pp. 203–217.

Lieb, Ethan J., and Baogang He (Eds.). *The Search for Deliberative Democracy in China*. New York: Palgrave Macmillan, 2006.

Lin Weiping. "Shehui xiefen shijian de jili yu gong'an zhifa weidu" [Mechanism of social anger-venting incidents and the magnitude of law enforcement by public security organs]. *Gong'an yanjiu*, no. 5 (May 2010): 16–23.

Liu Binglu. "Qiu He Suqian shinian zhilu" [Ten years of Qiu He and Suqian]. *Xin jingbao*, January 26, 2006, available http://news.xinhuanet.com/politics/2006–01/26/content_4101458.htm, accessed November 24, 2011.

Liu Qianxiang. "Nongcun shehui zouxiang minzhu zhili de lujing xuanze: Pingchangxian zhixuan xiangzhen dangwei lingdao banzi guangda jiceng minzhu de diaocha yu yanjiu" [The route to democratic governance in rural society: Investigation and research on grassroots democracy in the direct election for the party leading groups in Pingchang county]. In Wang Changjiang et al. (Eds.), *Dangnei minzhu zhidu chuangxin*, pp. 36–50.

Liu Qianxiang. "Sichuansheng Pingchangxian gongtui zhixuan xiangzhen dangwei lingdao banzi chenshu baogao" [Report on Public Recommendation and Direct Election for the township party leading groups in Pingchang county of Sichuan province]. In Wang Changjiang et al. (Eds.), *Dangnei minzhu zhidu chuangxin*, pp. 309–313.

Liu Zifu. *Xin qunti shijian guan – Guizhou Weng'an "6.28" shijian de qishi* [A new view on mass incidents – what the "June 28" incident in Guizhou's Weng'an tells us]. Beijing: Xinhua chubanshe, 2009.

Lu Biao. "Zhengyi Qiu He" (The controversial Qiu He). *Nanfang zhoumo*, February 12, 2004, available at www.chinaelections.org/printnews.asp?newsid=38184, accessed November 24, 2011.

Lu Tang and Du Bin. "'Shandong Qixia 57 ming cunguan jiti cizhi shijian' zhenxiang: Minxuan cunguan youzhi wuquan?" [The truth about the collective resignation of 57 village officials in Qixia village of Shandong: Do village officials elected by the people have office without power?]. *Beijing qingnian bao*, August 2, 2002, available at http://www.chinaelections.org/newsinfo.asp?newsid=62415, accessed November 24, 2011.

Lü, Xiaobo. *Cadres and Corruption: The Organizational Involution of the Chinese Communist Party*. Stanford, Calif.: Stanford University Press, 2000.

Lu, Yili. *Non-Governmental Organizations in China: The Rise of Dependent Autonomy*. London: Routledge, 2009.

Luo Changping. "Weng'an '6.28' shijian liubian" [Complete account of Weng'an's "June 28" incident]. *Caijing*, no. 14 (July 7, 2008), at http://www.caijing.com.cn/2008/wengan/, accessed December 1, 2011, and, http://news.qq.com/a/20080707/000976_1.htm, accessed November 24, 2011.

Luo Ke. "'Gaigepai guanyuan' de Zhongguo mingyun" [The Chinese fate of "reform-minded officials"]. *Fenghuang zhoukan*, no. 1 (2010), available at http://www.chinaelections.org/newsinfo.asp?newsid= 166968, accessed November 24, 2011.

Manion, Melanie. *Retirement of Revolutionaries in China: Public Policies, Social Norms, Private Interests.* Princeton, N.J.: Princeton University Press, 1993.

March, James G. (Ed.). *Handbook of Organizations.* Chicago: Rand McNally, 1965.

Miller, Alice. "The Bo Xilai Affair in Central Leadership Politics." *China Leadership Monitor*, no. 38 (Summer 2012). Available at http://www.hoover.org/publications/china-leadership-monitor.

Miller, Alice L. "Institutionalization and Changing Dynamics of Chinese Leadership Politics." In Cheng Li (Ed.), *China's Changing Political Landscape*, pp. 61–79.

Minzhengbu. "Guanyu chongxin queren shehui tuanti de zhuguan danwei de tongzhi" [Notice reconfirming the management units for social groups]. Available at http://www.cso.org.cn/cso/article/list .asp?id=956, accessed February 5, 2012.

Minzner, Carl F. "Riots and Cover-Ups: Counterproductive Control of Local Agents in China." *University of Pennsylvania Journal of International Law*, vol. 31, no. 1 (Fall 2009): 53–123.

Moe, Terry M. "Power and Political Institutions." In Ina Shapiro, Stephen Skowronek, and Daniel Galvin (Eds.), *Rethinking Political Institutions: The Art of State*, pp. 32–71.

Mu Yifei (Ed.). *Minzhu kentan: Wenlingren de chuangzao* [Democratic consultation: An invention of the people of Wenling]. Beijing: Zhongyang bianyiju, 2005.

Naughton, Barry J., and Dali L.Yang (Eds.). *Holding China Together: Diversity and National Integration in the Post-Deng Era.* New York: Cambridge University Press, 2004.

North, Douglass C. "Institutions." *Journal of Economic Perspectives*, vol. 5, no. 1 (Winter 1991): 97–112.

North, Douglass C. *Institutions, Institutional Change, and Economic Performance.* New York: Cambridge University Press, 1990.

O'Brien, Kevin J., and Lianjiang Li. *Rightful Resistance in Rural China.* New York: Cambridge University Press, 2006.

O'Donnell, Guillermo, and Philippe C. Schmitter. *Transitions from Authoritarian Rule: Tentative Conclusions about Uncertain Democracies.* Baltimore, Md.: Johns Hopkins University Press, 1986.

Oi, Jean C., and Zhao Shukai. "Fiscal Crisis in China's Townships: Causes and Consequences." In Elizabeth J. Perry and Merle Goldman (Eds.), *Grassroots Political Reform in Contemporary China*, pp. 75–96.

Parris, Kristen. "Local Initiative and National Reform: The Wenzhou Model of Development." *The China Quarterly*, no. 134 (June 1993): 242–263.

Parris, Kristen. "The Rise of Private Business Interests." In Merle Goldman and Roderick MacFarquhar (Eds.), *The Paradox of China's Post-Mao Reforms*, pp. 262–282.

Pearson, Margaret M. *China's New Business Elite: The Political Consequences of Economic Reform*. Berkeley: University of California Press, 1997.

Perry, Elizabeth J., and Merle Goldman (Eds.). *Grassroots Political Reform in Contemporary China*. Cambridge, Mass.: Harvard University Press, 2007.

Pierson, Paul. *Politics in Time: History, Institutions, and Social Analysis.* Princeton, N.J.: Princeton University Press, 2004.

Putnam, Robert, with Robert Leonardi and Raffaella Y. Nanetti. *Making Democracy Work: Civic Traditions in Modern Italy.* Princeton, N.J.: Princeton University Press, 1993.

"Qiu He: Yige zhengyi guanyuan de chengming qianhou" [Qiu He: Before and after this controversial official became famous]. *Xinshiji zhoukan*, November 21, 2006, available at news.sina.com.cn/c/2006–11-21/173211577927.shtml, accessed November 24, 2011.

Qiu Shui and Song Anming. "Shei chongdangle hei'e shili: Zhejiangsheng Wenlingshi bufen dangyuan ganbu zhuanru hei" [Who can resist evil forces: Some cadres from Wenling city, Zhejiang province, are caught up in organized crime]. *Dangyuan ganbu zi you*, no. 11 (2001): 50–51.

Read, Benjamin. *Roots of the State: Neighborhood Organization and Social Networks in Beijing and Taipei.* Stanford, Calif.: Stanford University Press, 2012.

Ren Yinghong and Wang Jian. "Goujian feigong qiye dangjian pingjia tixi de yiju yu yuanze" [The basis and principle for constructing an evaluation system for party construction in nonpublic enterprises]. *Zhonggong Fujian shengwei dangxiao xuebao*, no. 7 (July 10, 2007): 64–66.

Rong Jingben et al. *Cong yalixing tizhi xiang minzhu hezuo tizhi de zhuanbian: Xianxiang liangji zhengzhi tizhi gaige* [The transition from a pressured system to a democratic cooperative system: Political structural reform at the township and county levels]. Beijing: Zhongyang bianyi chubanshe, 1998.

Rosenblum, Nancy L. (Ed.). *Liberalism and the Moral Life*. Cambridge, Mass.: Harvard University Press, 1989.

Rowe, William, T. *Commerce and Society in a Chinese City*. Stanford, Calif.: Stanford University Press, 1984.

Ru Xin, Lu Xueyi, and Li Peilin (Eds.). *2004 nian: Zhongguo shehui xingshi fenxi yu yuce* [Chinese society: Analysis and forecast, 2004]. Beijing: Shehui kexue wenxian chubanshe, 2004.

Ru Xin, Lu Xueyi, and Li Peilin (Eds.). *2009 nian: Zhongguo shehui xingshi fenxi yu yuci* [Chinese society: Analysis and forecast, 2009]. Beijing: Shehui kexue wenxian chubanshe, 2008.

"Safety Chief Praises Media Watchdogs." *South China Morning Post*, March 28, 2002.

Saich, Tony, and Xuedong Yang. "Innovation in China's Local Governance: 'Open Recommendation and Selection.'" *Pacific Affairs*, vol. 76, no. 2 (Summer 2003): 185–208.

Schwartz, Jonathan, and Shawn Shieh (Eds.). *State and Society Responses to Social Welfare Needs in China: Serving the People*. London: Routledge, 2009.

Shambaugh, David. *China's Communist Party: Atrophy and Adaptation*. Berkeley: University of California Press, 2008.

Shapiro, Ina, Stephen Skowronek, and Daniel Galvin (Eds.). *Rethinking Political Institutions: The Art of the State*. New York: New York University Press, 2006.

Sheng Huaren. "Yifa zuohao xianxiang liangji renda huanjie xuanju gongzuo" [Do a good job in the change of term for people's congress elections at the town and township levels]. *Qiushi*, no. 16 (August 18, 2006): 37–42.

Sheng Ruowei. "Sichuan Ya'an shi dangdaihui changrenzhi shidian diaocha" [Investigation of the experiment with the standing representative system for party congresses in Sichuan's Ya'an city]. *Renmin ribao*, February 19, 2008, available at www.chinaelections.org/printnews.asp?newsid=122935, accessed November 24, 2011.

Shi Xin. "'Guanchang heshi' xianxiang saomiao" [A description of the phenomenon pf buying and selling of government positions]. *Minzhu yu fazhi*, no. 265 (April 21, 1998): 26–28.

Shirk, Susan (Ed.). *Changing Media, Changing China*. Oxford: Oxford University Press, 2011.

Shklar, Judith N. "The Liberalism of Fear." In Nancy Rosenblum (Ed.), *Liberalism and the Moral Life*, pp. 21–38.

Silberman, Bernard S. *Cages of Reason: The Rise of the Rational State in France, Japan, the United States, and Great Britain*. Chicago, Ill.: University of Chicago Press, 1993.

Slater, Dan. *Ordering Power: Contentious Politics and Authoritarian Leviathans in Southeast Asia.* New York: Cambridge University Press, 2010.

Sullivan, Lawrence R. "The Role of the Control Organs in the Chinese Communist Party, 1977–83." *Asian Survey*, vol. 24, no. 6 (June 1984): 597–617.

Sun Chunfang, "Renmin daxue wancheng 17 sheng nongcun tudi diaocha: Chao sicheng nongmin caoyu zhengdi, jin ercheng shu qiangzheng" (Chinese People's University completes survey of rural land in 17 provinces: Over 40 percent encountered land seizures; nearly 20 percent were coerced). *21 shiji jingji baodao* [21st Century Economic Herald], February 7, 2012, available at http:epaper.21cbh.com/html/2012–02/07/content_16922.htm?div=-1.

Sun Liping. "Shehui zhixu shi dangxia de yanjun tiaozhan" [Social order is a critical challenge at present]. *Jingji guancha bao*, February 25, 2011, available at http://opinion.hexun.com/2011-02-25/127571301.html, accessed November 24, 2011.

Tan Zhongying and Zeng Xinyuan. "Xianji fanweinei zhixuan xiangzhenzhang yinchu de sikao" [Thoughts brought on by direct elections for township heads within a county]. In Li Fan (Ed.), *Zhongguo jiceng minzhu fazhan baogao, 2004*, pp. 64–75.

Tanner, Murray Scot. "China Rethinks Unrest." *The Washington Quarterly*, vol. 27, no. 3 (Summer 2004): 137–156.

Thøgersen, Stig, Jorgen Elklit, and Dong Lisheng. "Consultative Elections of Chinese Township Leaders: The Case of an Experiment in Ya'an, Sichuan." *China Information*, vol. 22, no. 1 (March 2003): 67–89.

Tian Shubin, Li Ziliang, and Wang Yan. "Shiwan baixing xuan 'xiangguan'" [A hundred thousand commoners elect their "town official"]. *Banyue tan*, no. 21 (2004): 16–20.

Tsou, Tang. *The Cultural Revolution and Post-Mao Reforms: A Historical Perspective.* Chicago, Ill.: University of Chicago Press, 1986.

Tsou, Tang. "Introduction." In Tsou, *The Cultural Revolution and Post-Mao Reforms*, pp. xv–xliii.

Tsou, Tang. "Reflections on the Formation and Foundations of the Communist Party-State in China," In Tsou, *The Cultural Revolution and Post-Mao Reform*, pp. 259–334.

The Twelfth Five-Year Plan for National Economic and Social Development of the People's Republic of China. Beijing: Zhongyang bianyiju, 2011.

Wakeman, Frederic, Jr. "The Civil Society and Public Sphere Debate: Western Reflections on Chinese Political Culture." *Modern China*, vol. 19, no. 2 (April 1993): 108–138.

Wang Changjiang, Zhou Hongyun, and Wang Yongbing (Eds.). *Dangnei minzhu zhidu chuangxin: Yige jiceng dangwei banzi "gongtui zhixuan" de anli yanjiu* [Inner-party democracy as institutional innovation: Case study of a grassroots party committee's "public recommendation and direct election"]. Beijing: Zhongyang bianyi chubanshe, 2007.

Wang Junbo. "'Caogen minzhu': Zai zhiduhua de yangguangxia" ["Grassroots democracy": Under the light of institutionalization]. In Mu Yifei (Ed.), *Minzhu kentan*, pp. 189–192.

Wang Junbo. "Qiaoran bianhua de 'xiangcun zhengzhi'" [Quiet change in rural politics]. In Mu Yifei (Ed.), *Minzhu kentan*, pp. 193–196.

Wang, Sally. "Tension after Village Leader Dies in Custody." *South China Morning Post*, December 13, 2011, p. 6.

Wang Weibo. "Fengbao yanzhong de Weng'an guanyuan" [Weng'an officials in the eye of the storm]. *Zhongguo xinwen zhoukan*, no. 25 (2008), available at http://www.qikan.com.cn/Article/xwzk/xwzk200825/xwzk20082505.html, accessed November 24, 2011.

Wang, Xiangwei. "Official's Half-Billion Yuan Stash Just Drop in Bucket." *South China Morning Post*, June 14, 2010, p. 5.

Wang Xiaoqi. *China's Civil Service Reform*. Abington, Oxford: Taylor & Francis, 2012.

Wang Yongbing. *Dangnei minzhu de zhidu chuangxin yu lujing xuanze: Yige jiceng dangwei banzi "gongtui zhi xuan" de anli yanjiu* [The innovation of the inner-party democracy system: A case study of "public recommendation and public election" of a grassroots party committee]. Beijing: Zhongyang bianyi chubanshe, 2010.

"Wei shenma Zhongguo yigai bu hui chenggong? Anli: Jiangsu Suqian maiguangshi yigai diaoyan, kanbinggui wenti wei jiejue" [Why hasn't China's health-care reform been successful? Case study: Survey of the sell-off style of health reform in Jiangsu's Suqian; The problem of expensive health care has not been solved], available at http://www.daifumd.com/_daifumd/blog/html/199/article_39934.html, accessed November 24, 2011.

Weller, Robert P. *Alternative Civilities: Democracy and Culture in China and Taiwan*. Boulder, Colo.: Westview, 2001.

Weller, Robert P. (Ed.). *Civil Life, Globalization, and Political Change in Asia: Organizing between Family and State*. London: Routledge, 2005.

Wen Shengtang. "2003 nian de fanfubai douzheng" [The struggle against corruption in 2003]. In Ru Xin, Lu Xueyi, and Li Peilin (Eds.), *2004 nian: Zhongguo shehui xingshi fenxi yu yuce*, pp. 158–171.

White, Tyrene. "Village Elections: Democracy from the Bottom Up?" *Current History*, vol. 97, no. 620 (September 1998): 263–267.

Whiting, Susan H. "The Cadre Evaluation System at the Grass Roots: The Paradox of Party Rule." In Barry Naughton and Dali Yang (Eds.), *Holding China Together: Diversity and National Integrating in the Post-Deng Era*, pp. 101–119.

Whyte, Martin King. *Myth of the Social Volcano: Perceptions of Inequality and Distributive Injustice in Contemporary China*. Stanford, Calif.: Stanford University Press, 2010.

Winckler, Edwin A. "Institutionalization and Participation on Taiwan: From Hard to Soft Authoritarianism?" *The China Quarterly*, no. 99 (September 1984): 481–499.

Woguo guomin jingji yu shehui fazhan shi'er wu guihua gangyao [Outline of the 12th five-year plan for China's economic and social development], March 17, 2011, available at http://news.sina.com.cn/c/2011-03-17/055622129864.shtml, accessed January 20, 2012.

Womack, Brantly (Ed.). *China's Rise in Historical Perspective*. Lanham, Md.: Rowman & Littlefield, 2010.

Wong, Edward, and Michael Wines. "Provincial Officials Meet Leader of Protesters Who Took Over Chinese Village." *The New York Times*, December 21, 2011, p. 10.

Wu Qingcai. "Premier Wen Jiabao's Stories of Visiting the Countryside on Two Occasions." *Zhongguo xinwenshe*, March 11, 2004. In *BBC Summary of World Broadcasts*, March 14, 2004.

Wu Xiang. "Yangguan dao yu dumu qiao" [The broad road and the single plank road]. *Renmin ribao*, November 5, 1980, p. 2.

Wu Xingzhi. "Gongmin canyu, xieshang minzhu yu xiangcun gonggong zhixu de chonggou – Jiyu Zhejiang Wenling xieshangshi zhili moshi de yanjiu" [Citizen participation, deliberative democracy, and the deconstruction of rural public order – A case study of the deliberative governance model in Wenling, Zhejiang]. Ph.D. dissertation, Zhejiang University, 2008, available at http://www.docin.com/p-189017808.html, accessed November 28, 2011.

Xiang Guolan. "Tuijin dangnei minzhu de zhidu chuangxin – Ya'an dang daibiao dahui changrenzhi anli fenxi" [Promoting innovation in inner-party democracy – Analysis of the case of Ya'an's party congress permanent representative system], available at http://www.chinainnovations.org/Item/28573.aspx xiang guolan, accessed November 28, 2011. In Yu Keping (Ed.), *Zhongguo difang zhengfu chuangxin: Anli yanjiu baogao (2003–2004)*, pp. 175–198.

Xiao Lihui. "Xiangzhen dangwei lingdao banzi xuanju fangshi gaige yanjiu" [Study of the reform in the way township party leading groups are elected]. *Zhonggong zhongyang dangxiao xuebao*, April 28, 2009, available at www.chinaelections.org/printnews.asp?newsid=147578, accessed November 24, 2011.

Xiao Qing. "Wenling cunyihui: Nitu li tansheng Zhongguo xin xing-tai minzhu zhengzhi" [Wenling's village assemblies: A new form of democratic politics born in China's soil]. In Mu Yifei (Ed.), *Minzhu kentan*, pp. 176–181.

Xie Qingkui. "Jiceng minzhu zhengzhi jianshe de tuozhan" [The development of grassroots democratic politics]. In Mu Yifei (Ed.), *Minzhu kentan*, pp. 19–34.

Xu Xianglin. "Dang guan ganbu tizhi xia de jiceng minzhushi gaige" [Democratic-type reforms at the grassroots level under the "party controls the cadres" system]. *Zhejiang xuekan*, no. 1 (2004): 106–112.

Yang, Guobin. *The Power of the Internet in China: Citizen Activism Online*. New York: Columbia University Press, 2009.

Yang Lin. "Wenling: Minzhu kentan zhi hua" [Wenling: The blossoming of democratic consultation]. *Liaowang xinwen zhoukan*, October 26, 2009, available at http://www.ccpg.org.cn/Article/ShowArticle.asp?ArticleID=810, accessed November 24, 2011.

Yang Minghong. "Quxiao nongyeshuihou de Zhongguo xiangcun zhili jiegou" [The governance structure in Chinese villages and townships following the abolition of the agricultural tax]. In Li Bing et al. (Eds.), *Quxiao nongyeshui hou nongcun gongzuo jizhi biange yantao*, pp. 153–166.

Yang Ziyun. "Xinhe yusuan minzhu jianjin gaige" [The incremental reform of Xinhe's budgetary democracy]. *Zhongguo gaige*, no. 6 (2007): 17–21. Reprinted in Li Fan (Ed.), *Wenling shiyan yu Zhongguo difang zhengfu gonggong yusuan gaige*, pp. 225–234.

Ye Jianping, Feng Lei, Jiang Yan, Luo Yi Pu Luo Si Te Man, and Zhu Keliang, "2008 nian nongcun tudi shiyongquan diaocha yanjiu" [Survey of rural land-use right, 2008]. *Guanli shijie*, 2010, no. 1 (January).

Yi Hongwei. "Sichuan jiceng zhenggai ciqi bifu" [The ups and downs of Sichuan's local government reform]. *Nanfeng chuang*, no. 17 (August 11–24, 2010): 23–27.

Young, Graham. "Control and Style: Discipline Inspection Commissions since the 11th Congress." *The China Quarterly*, no. 97 (March 1984): 24–52

Yu Hui. "Hangye xiehui ji qi zai Zhongguo zhuanxingqi de fazhan" [Trade associations and their development during China's period of transition]. *Zhongguo jingji tizhi gaige yanjiu gonggong chengce yanjiu wang*, available at http://www.chinanpo.gov.cn/web/show Bulltetin.do?id=30041&dictionid=1831&catid=, accessed November 24, 2011.

Yu Jianrong. "Nongmin you zuzhi kangzheng jiqi zhengzhi fengxian – Hunan sheng H xian diaocha" [Organized struggles of peasants and their political risks – An investigation of county H in Hunan]. *Zhanlüe yu guanli*, no. 3 (2003): 1–16.

Yu, Jianxing, Jun Zhou, and Hua Jiang. *A Path for Chinese Civil Society: A Case Study on Industrial Associations in Wenzhou, China*. Lanham, Md.: Lexington Books, 2012.

Yu Jianxing, Huang Honghua, and Fang Liming. *Zai zhengfu yu qiye zhi jian: Yi Wenzhou shanghui wei yanjiu duixiang* [Between government and enterprise: Research based on Wenzhou's chambers of commerce]. Hangzhou: Zhejiang renmin chubanshe, 2004.

Yu Jianxing, Jiang Hua, and Zhou Jun. *Zai canyu zhong chengzhang de Zhongguo gongmin shehui: Jiyu Zhejiang Wenzhou shanghui de yanjiu* [China's civil society, maturing through participation: Studies based on chambers of commerce in Wenling, Zhejiang]. Hangzhou: Zhejiang daxue chubanshe, 2008.

Yu, Keping. *Democracy Is a Good Thing: Essays on Politics, Society, and Culture in Contemporary China*. Washington, D.C.: The Brookings Institution, 2009.

Yu Keping. *Zengliang minzhu yu shanzhi zhuanbian zhong de Zhongguo zhengzhi* [Incremental democracy and good governance]. Beijing: Shehui kexue wenxian chubanshe, 2003.

Yu Keping (Ed.). *Zhongguo difang zhengfu chuangxin: Anli yanjiu baogao (2003–2004)* [Innovation in China's local government: Reports on case studies, 2003–2004]. Beijing: Beijing daxue chubanshe, 2006.

Yu Sunda. "Minzhu zhili shi zui guangfan de minzhu shijian" [Democratic governance is the broadest democratic practice]. *Zhejiang shehui kexue*, no. 1 (2003): 30–33, available at http://www.chinaelections.org/NewsInfo.asp?NewsID=56091, accessed November 28, 2011. In Mu Yifei (Ed.), *Minzhu kentan*, pp. 56–65.

Zha Qingjiu. "Minzhu buneng chaoyue falü" [Democracy must not transcend the law]. *Fazhi ribao*, January 19, 1999, available at http://www.chinaelections.org/NewsInfo.asp?NewsID=74609 zha qingjiu, accessed November 28, 2011.

Zhai Guang. "Tuoshi maiguan maiguan jiaoyi" [Seeing through the trade of selling and buying offices]. *Zhongguo jiancha*, no. 6 (2002): 53–55.

Zhang Fang. "Wenling shi Xinhe zhen dishisijie renmin daibiao dahui diwuci huiyi zhengfu yusuan minzhu kentan shilu" [A record of the democratic consultation meeting on the government budget held by the fifth session of the fourteenth people's congress of Xinhe town, Wenling city). *Beijing yü fenxi*, no. 87 (August 1, 2005), available at http://www.world-china.org/newsdetail.asp?newsid=533, accessed November 28, 2011.

Zhang Fang. "Wenling shi Xinhe zhen gonggong yusuan gaige de guocheng he zuofa" [The process and methods of public budget reform in Xinhe town, Wenling city]. In Li Fan (Ed.) *Wenling shiyan yu Zhongguo defang zhengfu gonggong yusuan gaige.*

Zhang Guo and Chen Fengli. "Minsheng yu shehui guanli duli cheng 'pian'" [People's livelihood and social management become "separate chapters"]. *Beijing qingnian bao,* March 6, 2011.

Zhang Li. "Zuifu zhengyi de shiwei shuji" [The most controversial city party secretary]. *Nanfang zhoumo,* February 5, 2004, available at http://www.people.com.cn/GB/guandian/2333334.html, accessed November 24, 2011.

Zhang Xueming. "Cong 'zhengfu yusuan' dao gonggong yusuan" [From "government budget" to public budget]. Paper presented at Xieshang canyu jizhi yu Zhongguo jiceng zhili guoji xueshu yantaohui [International conference on participatory mechanisms and China's grassroots governance], Wenling, Zhejiang, July 6–7, 2010.

Zhang Yulu. "Qiu He: Zai falü yu zhengce zhi jian 'wudao'" [Qiu He: "Dancing" between law and policy]. *Banyue xuandu,* no. 7 (July 2007): 40–41, available at http://wuxizazhi.cnki.net/Article/BYXD200707026.html, accessed November 28, 2011.

Zhao Shukai. "Xiangcun zhili: Zuzhi he chongtu" [Rural governance: Organization and conflict]. *Zhanlüe yu guanli,* no. 6 (2003):1–8.

Zhao, Ziyang. *Prisoner of the State: The Secret Journal of Premier Zhao Ziyang,* trans. Bao Pu, Renee Chiang, and Adi Ignatius. New York: Simon & Schuster, 2009.

Zhao Ziyang. "Yanzhe you Zhongguo tese de shehuizhuyi daolu qianjin" [Advance along the path of socialism with Chinese characteristics]. *Renmin ribao,* November 4, 1987, p. 1.

Zheng, Yongnian. *Technological Empowerment: The Internet, State and Society in China.* Stanford, Calif.: Stanford University Press, 2008.

"Zhengyi renwu dangxuan fushengzhang, Qiu He shengqian ju tupo yiyi?" [Controversial figure Qiu He elected vice governor, what breakthrough meaning is there in Qiu He's promotion?]. *Renmin wang,* October 10, 2006, available at http://politics.people.com.cn/GB/30178/4092364.html, accessed November 24, 2011.

"Zhonggong Pingchang xianwei guanyu zai xiangzhen huanjie zhong kaizhan gongtui zhixuan dangwei lingdao banzi shidian de shishi yijian" [Views of the Pingchang county party committee on implementing the experiment of developing public recommendation and public election of party committee leading groups during the change of term]. In Wang Changjiang, Zhou Hongyun, and Wang Yongbing (Eds.), *Dangnei minzhu zhidu chuangxin,* pp. 303–308.

"Zhonggong Wenling shiwei guanyu 'minzhu kentan' de ruogan guiding (shixing)" [Some regulations governing "democratic consultations" by the CCP Wenling party committee (for trial implementation)], September 29, 2004, available at http://www.360doc.com/content/11/0425/00/4881689_112090989.shtml, accessed November 28, 2011. In Mu Yifei (Ed.), *Minzhu kentan*, pp. 220–226.

"Zhonggong zhongyang bangongting, Guowuyuan bangongting guanyu jinyibu jiaqiang minjian zuzhi guanli gongzuo de tongzhi" [Notice from the CCP General Office and the State Council General Office regarding the strengthening of management work over NGOs]. *Zhongbanfa* [1999] No. 34, November 1, 1999, available at http://law.lawtime.cn/d455288460382.html, accessed November 24, 2011.

"Zhonggong zhongyang guanyu nongye he nongcun gongzuo ruogan zhongda wenti de jueding" [CCP Central Committee decision on some serious problems in agricultural and rural work], October 14, 1989. In Zhonggong zhongyang wenxian yanjiushi (Ed.), *Shiwuda yilai zhongyao wenxian xuanbian*, 1.554–579.

Zhonggong zhongyang wenxian yanjiushi (Ed.). *Shiliuda yilai zhongyao wenxian xuanbian* [Selected important documents since the Sixteenth Party Congress]. Beijing: Zhongyang wenxian chubanshe, vol. 1, 2005.

Zhonggong zhongyang wenxian yanjiushi (Ed.). *Shiqida yilai zhongyao wenxian xuanbian* [Selected important documents since the Seventeenth Party Congress]. Beijing: Zhongyang wenxian chubanshe, vol. 1, 2009.

Zhonggong zhongyang wenxian yanjiushi (Ed.). *Shiwuda yilai zhongyao wenxian xuanbian* [Selected important documents since the Fifteenth Party Congress]. Beijing: Renmin chubanshe, vol. 1, 2000.

Zhonggong zhongyang zuzhibu dangjian yanjiusuo ketizu (Ed.). *Xinshiqi dangjian gongzuo redian nandian wenti diaocha baogao (4): Guanyu dangnei minzhu wenti yanjiu* [Report on contentious and difficult problems of party building in the new period (4): Research on problems in inner-party democracy]. Beijing: Zhongyang bianyi chubanshe, 2004.

Zhonggong zhongyang zuzhibu ketizu (Ed.). *Zhongguo diaocha baogao 2000–2001: Xin xingshi xia renmin neibu maodun yanjiu* [China investigation report 2000–2001: A study of contradictions among the people under the new conditions]. Beijing: Zhongyang bianyi chubanshe, 2001.

Zhongguo shehui kexueyuan, "shehui xingshi fenxi yu yuce" ketizu ["Social situation analysis group," China Academy of Social Sciences].

"Liwan kuanglan: Zhongguo shehui fazhan yingjie xin tiaozhan" [Making vigorous efforts to turn the tide]. In Ru Xin, Lu Xueyi, and Li Peilin (Eds.), *2009 nian Zhongguo shehui xingshi fenxi yu yuci*, pp. 1–14.

Zhongyang jiwei fagui shi, zhongyang zuzhibu bangonting (Eds.). *Zhongguo gongchandang dangnei fagui xuanbian 1978–1996* [A selection of internal regulations of the Chinese Communist Party 1978–1996]. Beijing: Falü chubanshe, 1996.

Zhou Hongyun. "Sichuansheng Pingchangxian xiangzhen gaige qingkuang jiqi sikao" [Town and township reform in Sichuan's Pingchang county and some considerations]. In Wang Changjiang, Zhou Hongyun, and Wang Yongbing (Eds.), *Dangnei minzhu zhidu chuangxin*, pp. 3–35.

Zhou Meiyan. "Dangnei minzhu yu renmin minzhu jiehe de youyi changshi" [A meaningful experiment combining inner-party democracy and people's democracy]. *Renda yanjiu*, no. 6 (2006): 4–11.

Zhou Meiyan. "Xinhe renda yusuan shenji de shijian yu sikao" [Budgetary auditing by Xinhe people's congress: Practice and reflections]. In Li Fan (Ed.), *Wenling shiyan yu Zhongguo difang zhengfu gonggong yusuan gaige*, pp. 312–313.

Zhou Ping. "Yunnansheng Honghezhou daguimo de xiangzhen zhixuan yanjiu" [Study of the large-scale township direct elections in Yunnan's Honghe prefecture]. *Xueshu tansuo*, no. 2 (2005): 65–71.

Zhou Qingzhi. *Zhongguo xianji xingzheng jiegou jiqi yunxing: Dui W xian de shehuixue kaocha* [The structure and operation of China's county-level administration: A sociological investigation of county W]. Guizhou: Guizhou renmin chubanshe, 2004.

Zhou Qiren. "Suqian 'maiguangshi yigai'" [Suqian's privatizing health reform]. *Guancha xing zhoukan*, July 21, 2006, available at www .newcenturynews.com/Article/Print.asp?ArticleID=24134, accessed November 24, 2011.

Zhou Yongkang. "Jiaqiang he chuangxin shehui guanli: Jianli jianquan Zhongguo tese shehuizhuyi shehui guanli tixi" [Strengthening and innovating social management by establishing and improving the socialist management system with Chinese characteristics]. *Qiushi*, no. 9 (May 1, 2011): 5–11, available at http://dangjian .ccnt.com.cn/xxyd.php?col=650&file=30149, accessed January 28, 2012.

Zhou Yongkang. "Shenru guanche luoshi kexue fazhanguan: Cujin jingji pingwen jiaokuai fazhan baozhang shehui gongping zhengyi weihu shehui hexie wending" [Implement the scientific development principle in a deep and thorough-going manner, promote stable and relatively rapid economic development, guarantee social fairness and righteousness, and maintain social harmony and stability]. *Qiushi*, no. 3 (February 1, 2009): 3–7.

Zhu Kangdui. "Gaige kaifang yilai Wenzhou jingji fazhan de huigu yu zhanwang" [A look back at the development of the Wenzhou economy since reform and opening and its prospects for the future]. In Jin Hao and Wang Chungang (Eds.), *2008 nian Wenzhou jingji shehui xingshi fenxi yu yuci*, pp. 22–28.

Zhu Quanyong. "'Liang xin' zuzhi dang zuzhi zuoyong fahui: Nanti ji duice" [The difficulty of bringing to bear the function of the party organization in the "two new" organizations and how to respond]. *Tansuo*, no. 1 (January 2009): 44–49.

Zhuang Guobo. *Lingdao ganbu zhengji pingjia de lilun yu shijian* [The theory and practice of evaluating the political achievements of leading cadres]. Beijing: Zhongguo jingji chubanshe, 2007.

Index

Qiu He, 52–60, 62–7, 97

Read, Benjamin, 11
Religion, 53, 110, 135, 143
Renshou county, 73, 171
Retirement system, 3
Rightful resistance, 25
Rong Jingben, 22
Rongjing county, 85
Rui'an city, 135
Ruoheng town, 161

Seventh Party Congress, 69
Shandong, 36, 52
Shanxi, 29, 35, 71
Sheng Huaren, 87
Shenyang, 125
Shiping county, 100
Shklar, Judith, 10, 16
Shuyang county, 52–6, 58, 65, 67, 97
Sichuan, vi, 11–13, 73, 76, 96, 108–9, 171
Sihong county, 52
Silberman, Bernard, 9
Siping county, 63
Siyang county, 52
Sixteenth Party Congress, 94, 98
Slater, Dan, 9
Social capital, 108–9
Social management, 177–8
Songmen town, 140, 145, 147–8, 166
Suining city, vi, 73, 75–6, 78, 82, 87–8, 96, 98, 105
Sunan model, 115
Suqian city, 52–3, 58–5, 67, 97

Taizhou, vi, 110, 112, 142, 144
Tan Xiaoqiu, 80, 83
Third Plenary Session of the Eleventh Central Committee, 1–2
Thirteenth Party Congress, 68, 70, 170
Three Represents, 109
Tiananmen, 4–5, 34, 71, 115, 117, 170
Tilly, Charles, 9

Trade associations, 111, 118, 120, 174
Tsou, Tang, 140
Two-ballot system 35, 40
"Two recommendations, one selection," 39

United Front, 118
Urban Trust Cooperative association, 117

Wan Li, 171
Wang Guangmei, 28
Wang Qi, 19
Wen Jiabao, 63, 167
Weng'an, 18–19, 26–7
incident at, 19, 21–3
Wenling, 14, 142–9, 151–2, 155, 157, 162–4, 166–8, 175
Wenqiao town, 147–8, 162
Wenzhou, vi, 108, 110–12, 114, 116–17, 119–22, 124–8, 132–43, 174
model, 14, 109, 113–14, 135, 140
Wenzhou General Chamber of Commerce, 117–8, 121
Wenzhou Federation of Industry and Commerce (FIC), 117–18, 121–2, 128–30
Wenzhou Leather Chamber of Commerce, 124
Wenzhou Shoe Chemical Association, 124
Wenzhou Shoe Heel Chamber of Commerce, 124
Wenzhou Shoe Material Association, 124
Wenzhou Tobacco Implements Trade Association, 124, 126–8
World Trade Organization, 127
Wu Guang, 171
Wu Yan, 137
Wu Ziqin, 129
Wu'an city, 36–8

Xie Limin, 154
Xindu district, 87–90, 96, 104